# MANAGING INFORMATION SYSTEMS

*An Integrated Approach*

# MANAGING INFORMATION SYSTEMS

## *An Integrated Approach*

by

Eugene J. Wittry

Rachel Subrin
Editor

Published by

Society of Manufacturing Engineers
Publications Development Department
Marketing Division
One SME Drive • P. O. Box 930
Dearborn, Michigan 48121

# Managing Information Systems: An Integrated Approach



First Edition
First Printing



Library of Congress Catalog Card Number: 87-62436
International Standard Book Number: 0-87263-296-2
Manufactured in the United States of America

This book is dedicated to Nancy, my wife and best friend. She encouraged the effort. She tolerated the frequent occasions when I spent more time with my word processor than I did with her. And, most important, she had an unswerving belief that the fellow who couldn't remember to bring home the milk really did know something worthwhile about his chosen profession.

# Contents

# Preface

One more book on the subject of managing data? What makes this one different, or of value?

This book is directed at the immediate, practical, day-to-day aspects of planning, developing, and operating information systems. It takes into account human motivations as well as technical aspects of information management.

I have spent 30 years in the information management business. During that time I have seen and participated in the development of many information systems, most of them computer related. Many of them have failed in some degree to fulfill their envisioned purposes. The reasons for the failures, some of them of my causing, were usually human biases.

Some examples of typical human biases are:

- The systems analyst who believes he knows what is good for the user.
- The manager who is convinced that his problem will go away if someone would just develop some sort of computer program.
- The employee who modifies his reports of business transactions in order to keep his boss from knowing too much about what he does.
- The boss who wants the operation of the business to change, but doesn't want to give up the performance measures with which he has become comfortable.

It became apparent that these human biases could be identified and analyzed in the expectation that future systems failures might be minimized. It also became apparent that Japanese industry was becoming very successful in developing systems to improve its effectiveness.

I have taught college courses part time for many years. The contact with young, probing minds is refreshing. During these years I have noticed that the typical computer science curriculum is highly technical with little emphasis on the practicalities of the workplace. For this and the above reasons, I developed a college level course on "Management Information Systems." I have taught it in the Industrial Engineering Department of Bradley University for six or seven years.

With the encouragement of Dr. Joe Emanuel of Bradley, I decided to put the course into book form so that it might obtain wider exposure. The result is this book. I hope the reader finds it beneficial.

Many of the ideas in the book are not original with me. Many of them came from work associates over the years. I have attempted to link these ideas into a consistent framework. After all, imitation is the sincerest form of flattery. I will not try to thank all of the idea sources by name, for fear of overlooking someone. Each should recognize his or her own idea.

I hope you enjoy the book and find it to be beneficial.

# 1

# *Introduction*

## Objective

The objective of this text is to provide the reader with practical insights into information systems principles, the application of information systems to business functions, management responsibilities for developing and operating information systems, and limitations in human ability to adapt to changes required by information systems.

There has been much emphasis in recent years on revamping business practices in the United States. Most members of management are involved in rethinking business systems. Management needs a better understanding of the elements of good business systems. This is true whether or not the systems are mechanized. Any student who anticipates a management career will require reasonable competency in information system concepts.

## Description

The text addresses several major topics:

- Principles of information systems and the application of the computer to assist in solving business problems
- Disciplines required to ensure successful development and operation of information systems, mechanized or manual
- Responsibilities of line management and computer systems staff relative to the development of information systems
- Case studies of information systems in a manufacturing environment
- Application of information systems principles to CIM (computer integrated manufacturing).

The text alternates chapters on the theory of information systems principles with chapters discussing the application of these principles to case studies. The case studies are based upon the experiences of large equipment manufacturers. Thirty years ago, large vehicles such as trucks, tractors, and farm machinery were produced on assembly lines and stored as finished stock product. The stock units were then modified to customer order by the addition of options. These options were usually external additions to the product. They were installed in a customizing area of the factory.

Today, the marketplace has evolved to the point where most products are completed on the assembly line to customer order. This is a change from "build-to-stock" practices to "build-to-order" practices. It has placed a significant strain on the systems by which major equipment manufacturers operate their facilities. It also provides a wide variety of excellent material for case studies in a text such as this.

Each chapter contains exercises to help the reader/student reinforce the theory and the experience represented in the text. It is recommended that each exercise be completed when encountered, before progressing with the reading. The answers to some of the exercises are embedded in the text following the exercises. The answers to the rest of the exercises are included in Appendix A. The author's experience in teaching this material in the classroom suggests that there is value in the exercises. They lay a foundation which seems to aid the student in evaluating and absorbing the material which follows.

## The Need for Systems Thinking

United States industry is being challenged as never before. It faces the threat of loss of its dominant role in the world as the giant, efficient source of manufactured items. Mass production concepts were authored by Henry Ford and were refined for the better part of a century. But, they have begun to lose out in global competition with Japan and other, developing, industrial nations in the Orient.

---

## Exercise 1.1

Make a list of arguments you have heard which attempt to explain the industrial success of the Japanese in recent years.

---

## Theories about Japanese Industrial Success

There have been many theories which attempt to account for the loss of U. S. leadership in production of such commodities as television equipment, cameras, and microwaves. Even major commodities are not immune to foreign pressures. The production of steel and the building of ships has moved to the Orient. The manufacture of automobiles is in imminent danger of moving in the same direction. Many visits have been made to Japan, Korea, and Taiwan by political and industrial leaders. Much has been said and written about the probable causes of this ever-increasing manufacturing success in the Orient.

Theories are as plentiful as theorists. A partial list of theories includes:

- Japanese government sponsorship of industrial expansion
- Lower wages for workers
- Cultural tradition of a strong work ethic
- High levels of automation
- Unfair tariffs and exchange rates.

## The Systems Theory

Since there are so many theories, there might as well be one more on the list. The typical Japanese company has a practice of moving new management employees from department to department for the first five to ten years of their careers. This certainly gives them an exposure to the varying aspects of the operation of the business.

In addition, the Japanese are well recognized as being team players. They take extraordinary effort to seek agreement among all affected parties when a major change in operating procedure is contemplated. They discuss the change interminably. They then adhere to it rigorously when it is finally implemented.

These practices are clues to what appears to be a determination to refine the systems by which the business is managed. Japan is moving to "just-in-time" manufacture, and "just-in-time" delivery of materials to the assembly operation. This is a rethinking of the production system.

Japanese manufacturers are marketing automobiles with minimal buyer options and many built-in luxury features. This is the result of rethinking engineering, manufacturing, and marketing strategies and practices. It is the result of an effort to develop a single corporate strategy.

Automation is not itself a key strategy. The automation of any portion of the production process is simply a crystallization of a process which has already been restructured and simplified.

## Summary

The Japanese and others are doing many things which lead to success in the worldwide industrial marketplace. The single unifying principle in what they are doing is a rethinking of the way they run their business. They are doing it in a teamwork fashion. They recognize that the various parts of the organization are highly interdependent. Individual departments cannot perform their functions in ignorance of, or disregard of the other departments.

Each manager within an enterprise, Japanese, American, or other, is in the systems business, whether he or she realizes it or not. A significant difference between successful and unsuccessful competitors will be the degree of skill and dedication with which the systems of the enterprise are addressed.

This text is an attempt to develop an awareness of the need for systems skills, and then to assist management in beginning to develop the basic skills. The principles of information systems are applied to the concepts of CIM to assist those readers whose companies are embarking upon this new venture.

# 2

# *System vs. Computer*

## Introduction

There is a tendency for people to think "computer" when they talk about systems. The two concepts are quite different. The purpose of this chapter is to help the reader to clearly realize the difference. It will help the reader realize that it is prudent to simplify and refine a system (set of operating rules, procedures) before attempting to mechanize a system by application of a computer.

## Exercise 2.1

Write down what you think a computer is. Your list might consist of three quite different types of things:

- A definition of a computer
- A list of essential components
- A list of distinguishing capabilities.

## Computer—A Dictionary Definition

A definition of a computer according to Webster is: "An electronic contrivance which solves problems and does complicated calculations by processing data according to prescribed, programmed instructions; and then produces and/or retains the outcome of these processes."

## Computer—A Working Definition

*Figure 2.1* shows a schematic of the major components of a computer and how they relate. It is necessary to understand this in order to fully appreciate

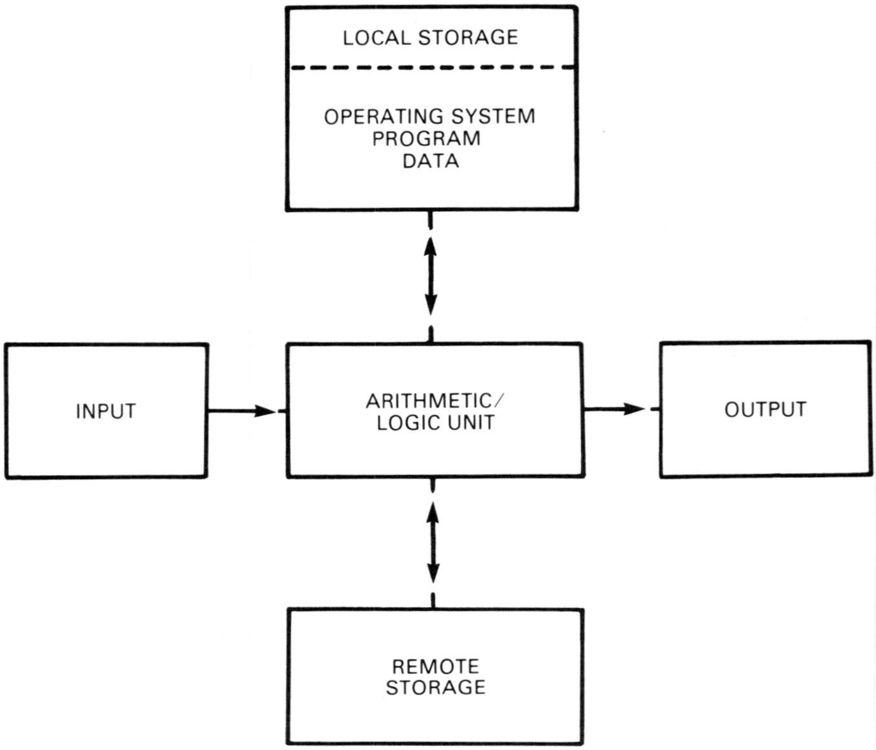


***Figure 2.1.*** Structure of a computer

those characteristics of a computer which provide it with its unique capabilities—capabilities which have been so valuable to the industrial world.

The heart of the computer is the arithmetic/logic unit which performs the computing functions. It is capable of performing the basic arithmetic operations of addition, subtraction, multiplication, and division. In addition, it can compare two bits of data to determine which is greater or if they are equal. As a corollary, it can examine a single bit of data and determine if it is numeric, alphabetic, or a special character such as a quotation mark. Not only does the arithmetic/logic unit make such comparisons, but it can be directed to perform different operations depending upon the outcome of the comparison.

All data comes into the computer through an *input unit*. This is an electronic device capable of codifying data in a form that is recognizable to the computer. The most common original source of input data is a typewriter-type keyboard on a terminal. Once the input data is captured electronically, it can be transmitted to any computer by a wide variety of high-speed input devices.

The input data is transferred through the arithmetic/logic unit to the memory of the computer. It is stored in a partition of memory called *local storage*. The memory of the computer also stores the series of instructions, a program, which tells the computer what to do.

There is a set of software or programs called the *operating system*, usually provided by the manufacturer of the computer. This software is stored in the memory and tells the computer how to perform its basic operations. They tell it how to "read" the input from a terminal.

A second set of software is the application program which tells the computer the specific job that it is to do at the moment. This might be to calculate a payroll or to compute the quantity of materials required to support a given level of production.

Finally, the memory of the computer contains any data resulting from the computations it performs under the control of a program.

The end results of the computation are transformed to a useful format, usually one which can be interpreted by people. This is done through an output device, such as a terminal screen or a printer.

If the quantity of input data is large, or if the results of the computation are voluminous; then the data might be stored on an electronic medium for later reference. This medium is called *remote storage*. A remote storage medium is often equivalent to an input or output medium.

## Essential Characteristics of Computers

There are three essential characteristics which distinguish the computer from other machines.

The first essential characteristic is the *memory*. The memory stores not only intermediate results, but all of the instructions (programs) by which the computer is directed to perform its functions.

The second essential characteristic of the computer is the *decision-making* capability imbedded in its arithmetic/logic unit. By means of this capability, the computer can execute different sets of logic depending upon the characteristics of the data which it is manipulating. For example, if the computer is calculating a payroll, it can deduct social security tax from an employee's paycheck, depending upon whether or not the employee has already paid the maximum amount of social security tax.

The third essential characteristic of the computer is the fact that it is *programmable*. It can be made to perform many different jobs through different programs. Once a payroll calculating program is read into the computer, it becomes a payroll calculating machine. When it is done with the payroll, a material requirements calculating program can be read into the computer. This makes it a totally different kind of machine.

## Comparison to a Calculator

The unique nature of a computer can be clarified by comparing it to an electronic calculator. The calculator can store only a limited number of constants or data values within its memory, but the computer can store vast amounts of data as well as programs. The calculator manipulates only numeric data, but the computer manipulates alphabetic data as well. Both machines perform basic arithmetic operations, but the computer can also perform varied functions depending upon logical analysis of data.

The calculator operates in essentially an arithmetic mode. The operator tells it in detail what to do by pressing the +, -, and other arithmetic operator keys in sequence with the entry of the data. The computer operates in an algebraic mode. The sequence of arithmetic operations is built into the program and is independent of the data. The computer can perform the same functions on any sequence of input data. The control of a calculator is by keyboard, for each individual calculation. The control of a computer is by program, developed once by keyboard, and automatically invoked thereafter.

The comparison of a computer and a calculator is summarized in *Figure 2.2.*

| | COMPUTER | CALCULATOR |
|---|---|---|
| **Memory** | Data and programs | Limited data only |
| **Data** | Alphabetic and numeric | Numeric only |
| **Operations** | Arithmetic and logic | Arithmetic only |
| **Control** | Program | Keyboard |
| **Logic Mode** | Algebraic | Arithmetic |

***Figure 2.2.*** Computer vs. calculator

## Flexible Machine

The computer is the most flexible machine ever invented. But, because of the difficulty of writing and debugging programs, it is the most difficult machine to flex. The computer is a marvelous machine when it is properly used, but it can be terribly misused.

One of the early uses of computers was to maintain mailing lists for magazines. Many a subscriber was mystified and frustrated when attempting to cancel a subscription or to correct a mailing address. The programmer of the computer had failed to realize that the customer would want to do these things.

If there is a change in the tax law, it is often far easier to give new instructions to a staff of payroll clerks than it is to develop and test new instructions for a computer.

The computer is not easy to flex, but once flexed, it performs its new functions with great speed and consistency. A cartoonist once pictured a frustrated person at the keyboard of a computer. The would-be programmer was shown as saying, "My computer keeps doing what I tell it to do instead of what I want it to do."

## Peripheral Devices

There are a great variety of input and output devices for computers. Those devices which can perform both input and output functions are candidates for use as remote storage devices. As a matter of reference, the most common devices are listed in *Figure 2.3* with an indication of their major characteristics. One of the most important characteristics is reusability, since there is often need to change or update data. For example, the master payroll record of an employee changes every time a paycheck is calculated. Each time the paycheck is calculated, there is a new year-to-date total for salary, income tax, and possibly social security tax.

Since this is a book about systems and not about computers per se, no more detail about the physical aspects of computers will be discussed.

| | INPUT | OUTPUT | CHEAP | FAST | HIGH VOLUME | REUSABLE MEDIUM |
|---|---|---|---|---|---|---|
| Punched Cards | X | X | | | | |
| Paper Tape | X | X | | | | |
| Magnetic Tape | X | X | X | X | X | X |
| Fixed Disk | X | X | X | X | X | X |
| Mass Storage | X | X | X | X | X | X |
| Laser Disk | X | X | X | X | X | |
| Floppy Disk | X | X | X | X | | X |
| Magnetic Strip | X | X | X | X | | X |
| Bar Code | X | X | X | X | | |
| Voice | X | X | X | | | X |
| Memory Chips | X | X | | X | | X |
| Optical Reader | X | | X | | | |
| Keyboard | X | | X | | | X |
| Mouse | X | | X | | | X |
| Analog Sensors | X | | | X | | X |
| Printer | | X | X | X | | |
| Video Screen | | X | X | X | | X |
| Microfilm | | X | X | X | X | |
| Analog Signals | | X | | X | | X |

***Figure 2.3.*** Input/output media

## Exercise 2.2

Write down on a piece of paper what you think a system is. It might help if you draw any distinction you feel appropriate between a system and a computer.

## System—A Dictionary Definition

A definition of a system according to Webster is: "An assemblage or combination of things or parts forming a complex or unitary whole."

## System—A Working Definition

A system is a collection of components working together to accomplish a common purpose.

*Figure 2.4* shows a schematic of the major components of a system and how it operates. The heart of a system is the process. Within the process a mission is fulfilled. Something is made, or something is changed or guided, or something is destroyed. But whatever is done, the purpose of the system is fulfilled.

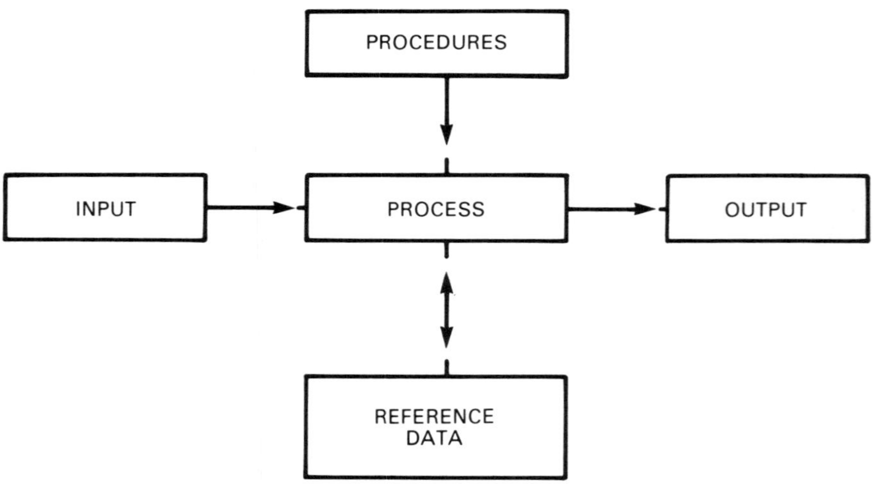


***Figure 2.4.*** Structure of a system

Like a computer, the system has to have something on which to operate. For that reason, there must be an input function. It delivers to the process the material and/or data which the process uses to perform its function.

In a similar fashion, there is output from the process. The operation of the process is not a random function, but it is guided and controlled by a set of rules or procedures.

Most processes require a set of reference data in order to operate. This data might be constant or it might change frequently. It tells the process the status of the environment in which the process is operating.

All of this probably seems to be rather abstract. It begins to take on concrete meaning when the concepts are applied to real systems as examples.

## Examples of Systems

There are innumerable systems which could be used as examples. To demonstrate the definition and structure of a system, four examples will suffice.

An example of an information system is a payroll system. The input could be time cards. The process is to calculate pay. The output is the paycheck. An example of a procedure is a rule regarding the payment of an overtime allowance. An example of reference data is federal tax tables. Obviously this system has a variety of procedures and reference data.

An example of a physical system is the human circulatory system. Input is digested food. The process is the exchange of energy-giving chemicals for waste products. The output is the waste products, which are transferred to another physical system. The procedures are internal mechanisms in the form of pulse and blood pressure. The reference data are the contents of the digestive system and the presence or absence of waste products in the tissues being served.

An example of a social system is the legislative branch of the U.S. government. The input is public opinion. The process is legislation. The output is new or changed laws. The procedures are the parliamentary rules by which the legislature operates. The reference data is the body of statistics and previous legislation which serves as a precedence.

An example of a mechanical system is the carburetor system of an automobile. The input is the pressure of a foot against an accelerator. The process is the delivery of a measured amount of fuel and air to the engine. The output is a mixture of gasoline vapor and air delivered to the cylinders. The procedures are the physical limits built into the throttle linkage and the fuel pump. The reference data are such things as the rpm of the engine and the temperature of the air.

---

## Exercise 2.3

1. What are the components of a class registration system in a college?
2. What are the components of the human body as a system?
3. What are the components of a hospital as a social system?
4. What are the components of a fountain pen as a physical system?
5. Write down a list of 5 to 10 systems which you can identify. Try to select at least one from each of the four types. Then identify the specific components of each.

---

## Essential Characteristics of Systems

There are two essential characteristics of a system. The first essential characteristic is that it is a combination of parts which work together.

The second essential characteristic is that a system has a unitary mission. It has a purpose. In the four examples of systems just mentioned, the purpose is evident in the output.

A system is an organized procedure for performing a function.

## Cautions

Even with the above definition and description of a system, there will be ambiguity every time a group of people talk about specific systems. The reason is that there is no size limit on a system. There are systems within systems. The circulatory system includes the heart, which is itself a system. The circulatory system is a subsystem of the human body, which is itself a system. The person who inhabits the body is a part of a larger social system. And on it goes.

A simple rule which can help to avoid ambiguity is to define carefully what you are talking about. Another simple rule is to always question the person who talks about a "computer system" when he or she is really talking about a set of software. Ask that person what the purpose of the software is, what the system is which the software is to be a part of. It is a usually a fatal mistake to apply a computer to a system until there is a good definition of how the system is to operate.

## Comparison to a Computer

The concept of a system is much broader than the concept of a computer. A bit of analysis, and a comparison of the two concepts should quickly reveal that a computer is one example of a physical system. Compare the diagrams in *Figures 2.1* and *2.4*. The comparison should also reveal that a system might or might not contain a computer as one of its components. Even an information system does not necessarily include a computer as a component. In the example of the payroll system described earlier, there was no reference to a computer.

---

## Exercise 2.4

Write down a list of the advantages which you feel might be obtained from the use of a computer. Why do businesses use computers—other than it being the modern thing to do?

---

## Advantages of a Computer

The primary advantages of using a computer are illustrated in *Figure 2.5*. The benefits of speed, accuracy, and repeatability all lead to an increase in profit. Profit is the primary purpose for which any business is organized.

**Speed.** A computer can make calculations faster than any other device known to man. Consider a rocket trip to the moon. An astronaut with a paper and pencil could perform all of the calculations necessary to make a mid-

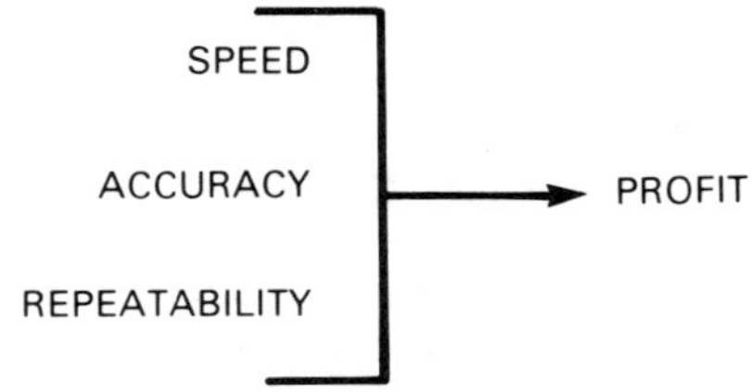


***Figure 2.5.*** Advantages of a computer

course adjustment in trajectory. But, the rocket would be far beyond the moon before the calculations could be completed.

**Accuracy.** A paycheck must be calculated with great accuracy, else the employee or the government will descend upon the employer with great wrath. Obviously, payroll calculation was an early application of the computer. This was particularly appropriate for companies with many employees to pay.

**Repeatability.** A corollary to accuracy is repeatability. The control of machine tools by computer has led to significant improvements in process control. *Process control* is a mechanism to provide feedback of process variation and to automatically make process adjustments. By this means, greater consistency of parts manufacture can be accomplished. The computer has been of great value when applied to process control functions. Often a computer has been specially designed for the purpose.

## Exercise 2.5

1. Try to think of systems from your own experience where each of the above three advantages led to the use of a computer. Or, have you seen systems where you feel that a computer could be profitably used?

2. Write down a list of dangers inherent in the use of the computer to enhance the operation of a system. Think of horror stories you have heard or of problems you have personally experienced.

## Disadvantages of a Computer

The disadvantages which are possible from the use of a computer stem not so much from limitations or deficiencies in the computer itself. They stem from lack of understanding or preparation by the people who apply the computer to the business function. To quote from the cartoon character, Pogo the Possum, "We have met the enemy, and they is us."

The following is a typical list of disadvantages which have occurred from unwise application of the computer.

**Bad Output from Bad Input.** It is not uncommon for insufficient production materials to be ordered because of failure of manufacturing personnel to report scrap. Excessive material has been ordered because people have reported an erroneous quantity of scrap. This type of error is the source of the phrase "GIGO—garbage in, garbage out."

**Loss of Personal Touch with Customer.** In the early days, computers were used to assist in handling customer orders for book clubs. A punched card was mailed to the subscriber each month offering a book for sale. If the subscriber wanted the book, nothing needed to be done. If the subscriber didn't want the book, he or she had to return the punched card. Many customers were alienated by a feeling that they were being treated as just another automatic component of the system. Then when the customers tried to cancel a subscription, they often found that the computer seemed to ignore their wishes and merely sent them a new card the next month. The problem was not with the computer, but with the rules built into the programs.

**Bad Output from Bad Program Rules.** As an example, a manufacturer developed a new, complex inventory-control system for indirect materials. Indirect materials are things not built into the product, but essential to the operation of the business—paper, soap, sweeping compound, etc. This material was stored in a central supply warehouse. It was disbursed to local supply cribs when orders were received from the local cribs. Reorder quantities from the suppliers were calculated monthly based upon the quantity in the central warehouse and the rate of ordering from the local cribs.

One winter there was little snow. This resulted in a surplus at the central warehouse of salt for melting ice on the drives. The central warehouse was crowded, so the manager asked his friends at the local cribs to order salt from him to make space available. They did as he requested. Nobody thought about the logic imbedded in the automatic inventory control system. Sure enough, a few weeks later a train car full of salt was delivered to the plant. After all, from the point of view of the computer, there had been a sudden upswing in the demand for salt and a sudden decline in the quantity on-hand at the central warehouse.

**Loss of Know-how or Creativity.** With the advent of computer graphics software, there is a strong drive within manufacturing industry to automate the design of some products. A company which manufactures hydraulic valves wanted to speed response to customer orders for custom valves. A computer application was developed to design valves to customer specifications based upon the rules which guided previous manual design. Although this has significant potential for labor saving and fast response, there is an imbedded danger. The designers could become unimaginative over time. They could automatically accept the computer-developed design, and they could even forget how to design new types of valves. The technology of the company would become frozen.

**Loss of Flexibility.** Over time, many companies have installed computerized attendance, labor, and payroll systems. In recent years, labor unions have become imaginative in demanding new benefits for their memberships. They have demanded things such as one hour of added vacation for each week worked without absence. It was not uncommon for the company labor negotiators to agree to some of the demands with a specific effective date to implement the demands.

Later, they would find out that the computer system could not be changed in time. Most companies have now realized that the company negotiator must consult with the Data Processing department before committing to any changes. They are thus avoiding an embarrassment and a significant increase in clerical effort, but they are also constrained in their freedom to react to change.

**Loss of Access to Records.** A Quality Control department maintained records of the quality of steel shipments from suppliers. A record card was kept on each receipt showing material chemistry, strength, and surface hardness. These cards were kept in file cabinets. It was tedious to search the files for a representative series of cards on a supplier. It was even more tedious to do a statistical analysis of supplier capability. A computer system was developed to mechanize the recordkeeping process and to prepare semiannual reports on each type of steel from each supplier.

After a massive record conversion effort, the system appeared to be working well. The original paper records were discarded. Shortly thereafter, a problem arose with a specific supplier. Quality Control ordered a special analysis to be performed, and found to its dismay that the system was not capable of performing the task. The need had never been defined. Quality Control had the option of paying for a full analysis of all suppliers, or of doing without the analysis of the supplier in question. The user had lost access to individual records—his own records.

**Loss of Capability to Perform an Important Business Function.** Many companies are using the computer to take customer orders for products, or to look up items in a computerized catalog. This provides excellent service to the customer and is a significant labor savings to the company. But, many such systems have been developed without any backup procedures. Computers and telephone lines are, after all, physical devices which can fail. In such a case, the company and the customer are out of business until the failure is repaired. At a minimum, the customer is irritated. Often the immediate sale is lost, and future sales to the customer are lost.

**LAW**

**Use it or Lose it.**

If a service is performed for people, they tend to come to expect it, to forget how to do it, and to cease to feel responsibility for it.

From these unsatisfactory experiences, a general law can be derived regarding human behavior as it relates to the application of computers to information systems. For the purposes of this text, a *law* can be defined as a likely pattern of behavior.

This is the first of a series of "natural laws" of human behavior relative to the management of information. None of these laws has been experimentally proven. All have been derived from broad experience in the development and operation of information systems.

The thrust of the law is that if a service is performed for people, they tend to come to expect it, to forget how to do it, and to cease to feel responsibility for it.

---

## Exercise 2.6

Identify examples of the Use it or Lose it law from your own experience. One starting example (not related to information management) is the child who never makes his or her bed because "Mom does it."

---

## Summary

A computer is an electronic device for processing data. The primary characteristics of a computer are:

- Memory
- Decision making
- Programmability

A *system* is a combination of things which work together to accomplish a single mission.

An *information system* is a system for managing information. The information does not necessarily have to be supported by a computer.

A *computer* is a system. A computer can be one of the elements of an information system.

The primary advantages of a computer are *speed, accuracy,* and *repeatability*.

There are potential disadvantages to the use of a computer, particularly if it is applied to ineffective information systems, or if its use is not carefully managed.

**LAW—Use it or Lose it.** A person who uses a computer system blindly will eventually lose control of the process which the computer is supporting.

# 3

# Industrial Applications

## Introduction

There is a tendency for people to think too narrowly when defining the need for a computerized information system. The usual intent is to build computer software to control the operation of some aspect of the business—payroll, material acquisition, billing, etc. The purpose of this chapter is to help the reader broaden his or her perspective when visualizing the potential application of a computer.

## Classical Management Model

The classical management model from a first year management course is shown in *Figure 3.1*. It is used to describe the sequence of activities by which a business is managed.

The normal activity is operating the business from day-to-day—making product, selling product, relating with the customer, receiving payments, and paying bills. The manager's responsibility is to see that these activities are done well and are done according to some set of prescribed norms. It sounds a bit like a system, doesn't it?

The daily activities are monitored in some fashion, preferably by a means which provides a specific numeric measurement of how the activities are being performed. These measurements are indicators of the volume of business conducted over a period of time, and the degree to which the prescribed norms were met. Examples include the volume of product manufactured, the amount sold, the amount of scrap, the cost of production, the amount of cash received for product sold, and the amount paid for materials and supplies.

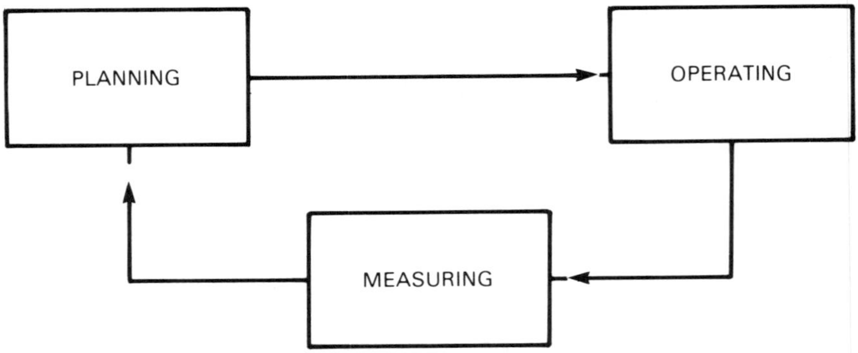


***Figure 3.1.*** Classical management model

The measurements are analyzed in the planning portion of the management cycle. Trends are plotted and analyzed, inefficiencies are observed and diagnosed, growth opportunities are projected. New and improved methods, and revised work norms are put into place to correct deficiencies and to seize opportunities. These new plans are the guide to the operating function, which begins the cycle all over again.

## Exercise 3.1

Make a list of the specific operating business activities which you feel are typical first candidates for mechanization—at least for some degree of computer aid in the performance of the task.

## Mechanization Emphasis—Operating Functions First

Historically, when a business looked for improvement opportunity from the application of the computer, it typically looked first to the operating function. It is there that tasks tend to be routine and simply defined. The primary rationale for the application of the computer was usually a reduction in work force, and a concurrent reduction in operating expense. It was expected that the reduction in normal operating costs would exceed the added cost of operating the computer. It was also expected that the change would provide a healthy return on the original investment in the computer and the software.

Early operating function candidates for mechanization have included:

- Maintaining inventory records
- Calculating material requirements
- Receiving production materials and supplies
- Paying bills and salaries
- Sending statements and monitoring accounts payable
- Maintaining bills of material and product catalogs
- Taking customer orders and scheduling delivery
- Keeping financial accounts, ledgers, budgets, etc.

The application of the computer did indeed bring significant improvements to the daily operation of businesses, but it also brought with it a number of significant problems. Where there was any inadequacy in the computerized version of a system, it was very difficult for the worker to find a way around the problem. It was also very difficult for the Data Processing staff to modify the programs in time to keep up with changes in the environment or with management directed changes in the procedures. The worker was often motivated to work against the system out of spite.

## Mechanization Emphasis—Measuring Functions Second

Once operating functions began to be supported by computer systems, it became apparent that the measuring portion of the management cycle was a convenient next opportunity for mechanization. After all, the data about the daily activities was already in the computer. It should be a relatively simple task to add up the volumes of activity and the amount of money entering and leaving the enterprise. It would then be another simple task to determine rates of production and sale, and the cost per type of activity. The final task would be to arrange the measurements into management reports to assist both the operating function and the planning function.

This arranging of summaries and totals of operating data into reports led into a general trend in the 1970s toward "management information systems." It was felt that detailed reports could be produced for first level management, more summarized reports for second level management, and even more summarized reports for higher levels of management.

Over time it was recognized that the image of a total management information system was far too idealistic. Many managers complained that they received too much data in their reports and too little useful information.

From this was born the concept of "exception reporting" whereby only significant information would be reported. This included things such as unusually high scrap rates, and aged accounts receivable. This began an unending debate about what parameters were appropriate for selecting the exceptions to report. It also led to a complaint by higher levels of management that trends of the business became lost in the myriad of details still reported. Top management also complained that they had lost the ability to make spot analyses of business trends by assigning a staff person to gather and arrange the appropriate data.

Finally, a significant uneasiness began to permeate clerical staff and lower levels of management. It seemed to them that the boss and upper management had too much detailed knowledge about how things were going. There was almost no place to hide mistakes or laziness. Big brother always seemed to be watching.

The mistake was in developing mechanized systems without considering psychological factors. Computers do not have a personality. People do. Their motivations and desires must be taken into account if the operation of the business is to proceed effectively. Later portions of this text will discuss these concepts in some depth.

## Mechanization Emphasis—Planning Functions Last

The planning function is the function which is most difficult to analyze and describe. The reason for this is that the planning function is a more creative type of work than operating or measuring, and it is less structured and less repetitive. For these reasons, it has been the last function to be addressed by efforts to apply the computer.

In recent years, significant efforts have been expended in industry to provide computer assistance for the planning function. This area of endeavor is not within the intended scope of this text. The reader who wishes to obtain more information on this subject should look for material on decision support systems and artificial intelligence or expert systems.

## Information Management Model

A more comprehensive business model is shown in *Figure 3.2*. It illustrates the flow of information in any business.

The typical business activity is the control of some function. Should a bill be paid? Should an invoice be sent? Should a new supply of material be

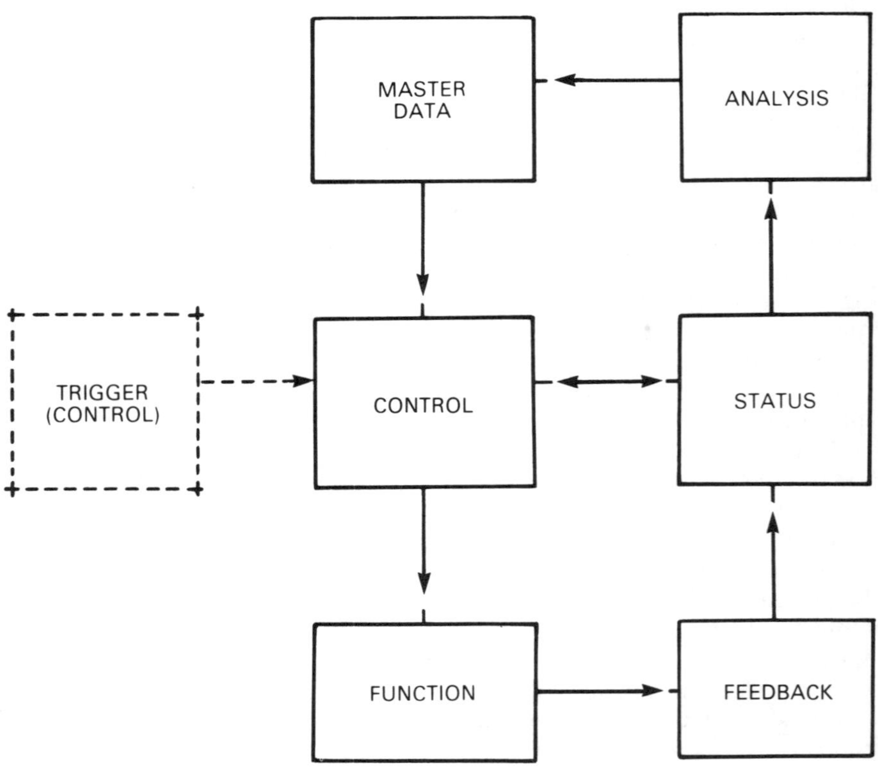


***Figure 3.2.*** Information management model

ordered? It is in the control and execution of such simple decisions that the computer has earned its place in industry.

For the control activity to operate, it needs knowledge of the status of the function being controlled. How much do we owe the supplier? Has the customer already paid his or her bill? How much material is on hand?

To maintain the status data, there must be some sort of feedback process in place. If a package of material and an invoice arrive from a supplier, more money is owed to the supplier. If customers have made a payment on their bills, that transaction must be recorded so that they aren't irritated with the receipt of a second, needless billing. If material is received, used, or scrapped, there must be a means for that fact to be posted against the status of the inventory record.

In addition, once an action message has been sent by the control activity, that fact must be recorded in the status record. If a payment to the supplier has been ordered, that fact must be posted against the account status. If a billing has been sent to the customer, that must also be recorded as status so that another billing is not sent out tomorrow. If an order is placed for material, a posting must be made to tell that there is more material ordered for delivery on a specific date.

The control activity needs more than status data in order to perform its function. It needs stable reference data against which to make its judgements and to place its orders for action. There must be a means of maintaining master data. What amount of credit is allowed for this customer? What is the customer's address? What is the discount allowed by the supplier? What is the supplier's address? Who is the supplier of the material which is needed? What is the supplier's address? What is the quantity which is usually ordered, and what are the price quotes from this supplier for various quantities of material?

On occasion, the operation of the whole cycle needs to be analyzed to determine if there is any reason to change the master data. Has this customer been paying bills regularly? Has this supplier been sending quality material on time, or has there been significant scrap and delay? Is there another supplier who might perform better and/or provide the material cheaper? Has the inventory of this item been high relative to the rate of use?

Finally, there is one outside activity which acts as a trigger function to cause the control activity to happen. Usually this trigger is the control activity of some related functional cycle. The sale of a product can trigger the consideration of sending a bill. The receipt of a load of material can trigger consideration of a payment. The use of production material to make a batch of product can trigger consideration to place an order for more.

All of these activities are systems and subsystems of a larger system. A specific example will illustrate this.

## Information Management Example

As an example of the information management module, consider the function "procure material." Refer to *Figure 3.3*. The material to be procured is production material which is to be used to manufacture product.

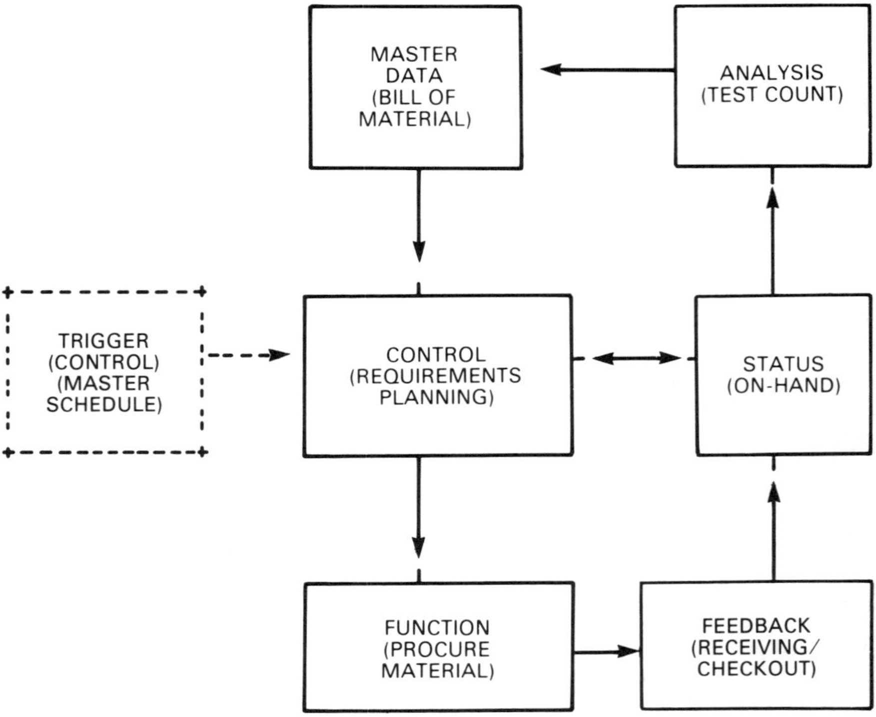


***Figure 3.3.*** Requirements planning model

The control function is requirements planning. It calculates the quantity of materials required for production. It extends the master schedule quantity of product to be produced (from the trigger function of master schedule) against the bill of material of the product (from the master data system). It then compares the total requirements against the stock on hand (from the status system) to determine the quantity to order.

The feedback system is an inventory posting system of some sort which records receipts and disbursements of the production material.

The analysis system is a sort of test count which periodically compares physical counts of production materials to the stock status in order to detect errors. Another function of the analysis system could be to determine if stock levels are too high or too low, depending upon supplier lead times and fluctuations in the rate of production.

## Intersystem Dependencies

Control systems cannot function properly unless they are supported by the other types of systems with appropriate timeliness and accuracy of data. For example, consider a requirements planning system which is processed daily. It would not be able to calculate accurately if it were supported by a status system which is only updated weekly. On the other hand, if the requirements planning system were processed weekly, there would be no need for the status system to be updated daily, unless the daily processing was for some other purpose. It is obviously very important for the bill of material system and the status system to be brought up-to-date immediately before the processing of requirements planning.

Control systems tend to "cascade" as trigger systems. That is, the processing of a control system triggers the processing of a dependent control system, which in turn triggers the processing of another control system. A market forecast triggers the master schedule, which triggers the requirements planning, which triggers the issuance of purchase orders to buy material, and triggers production orders to manufacture production parts and assemblies.

## Essential Databases

There are three types of data which are needed to support a full control system. These are illustrated in *Figure 3.4*.

The master database contains data which is reference data to the control function. This is data which has multiple uses in the enterprise, and is enduring. It doesn't change with any significant frequency. In the figure, the master data is bill of material data describing the structure of the product. The purpose of the master data system is to maintain the master database.

It is worth noting here that while system reference data is contained in the master database, system procedures are distributed in two other places. Some are imbedded in the programs which drive the computer as part of the control system. Others are located in written instructions and regulations which guide the people who operate the manual portions of the system.

The status database contains data which tells the status of the business entities being controlled, and possibly the status of related entities such as production machinery. This data changes with great frequency. In fact, it changes from minute to minute. The changes might not be posted to the records as frequently as the physical changes take place. This is no problem as long as the status database is updated before it is used to support the control function.

The status database is updated from two sources—the control system and the feedback system. In fact, the status database might be updated by a number of control and feedback systems. In *Figure 3.4*, the status system is the stock record or inventory record of production materials. It is updated by a system which reports receipt of material, by another system which reports consumption of material in built product, by a third system which reports scrap, and by a fourth system which reports shipment of service replacement parts.

The history database is composed of two types of data. One type is snapshots of status records at points in time, or copies of transactions which have been posted to the status database. The other type is summary data about what has happened in the status database over a period of time.

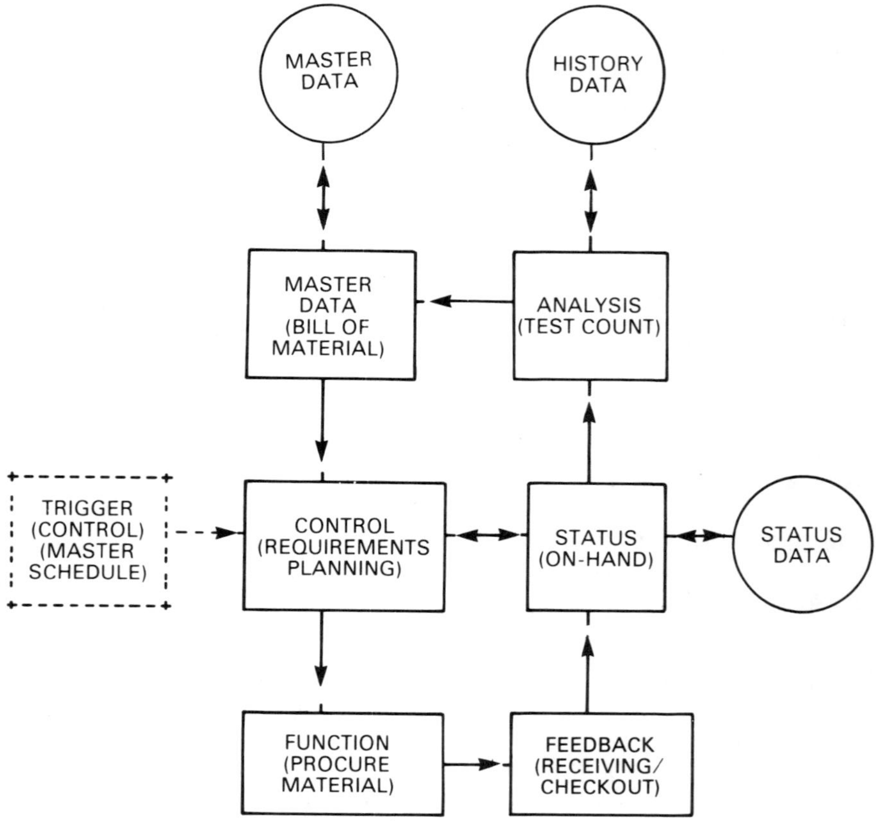


***Figure 3.4.*** Requirements planning databases

Generally speaking, the data in the history database is not changed once it has been recorded. However, on occasion, it is further summarized or purged when some of the data becomes so old as to be of limited value. The history database is loaded from the status database. In the example in *Figure 3.4*, the history data contains summary information about rates of use of parts in production, associated scrap percents, statistical stock on-hand quantities, stock turnover, and number of stock outs.

## Exercise 3.2

Compare the two models—the classical management model in *Figure 3.1* and the information management model in *Figure 3.2*. Correlate the functions between the models. List the subfunctions of the first model. Then list next to each of them, the subfunctions of the second model which seem to be equivalent.

## Exercise 3.3

If the requirements planning system in *Figure 3.4* were to be mechanized and processed weekly, which related systems would also have to be mechanized? What would be their required processing frequency?

## Typical Control Systems

*Figure 3.5* contains a summary of three other typical information management systems. There are many other examples which could be developed.

| BUSINESS | SCHOOL | BANK | INSURANCE |
|---|---|---|---|
| **Control** | Class Registration | Account Management | Writing Policies |
| **Master Data** | Course Catalog | Types of Accounts | Types of Policies |
| **Status** | Class Roster | Account Status | Customer Age, etc. |
| **Feedback** | Registration Card | Deposit and Withdrawal | Application Form |
| **Analysis** | Course Review | Account Audits | Actuarial Studies |
| **Trigger** | Semester Schedule | Bank Policy Change | Actuarial Changes |
| **Master Database** | Course Catalog | Types of Accounts | Types of Policies |
| **History Database** | Registered Requests per Course | Account Subscribers and Amounts | Policy Subscribers and Amounts |
| **Status Database** | Registration Records | Account Contents | Current Subscribers |

***Figure 3.5.*** Sample business models

## Exercise 3.4

From your own experience, develop several examples of control systems. Label the component subsystems, trigger system, and databases. Remember that the systems do not have to be mechanized. The trigger system might not be anything sophisticated, but might be something as simple as a customer walking in the door of a fast food restaurant. The databases might be complex computer databases. Or, they might be something as simple as a series of customer bills impaled on a metal spike in a country grocery store.

## CIM—A Working Definition

CIM is an acronym for computer aided manufacturing. It refers to the use of the computer to improve the operation of a manufacturing enterprise. So what is different about CIM? The computer has been applied to many manufacturing applications. The key is that CIM is the application of the computer to integrated systems within a manufacturing enterprise. The computer is not applied just to isolated tasks.

The managers of the enterprise rethink how the enterprise is to operate. They take into account the capabilities of the computer. They recognize that the various functions of the business are interdependent. After they have rethought the systems of the business, they set about the application of the computer as an aid to the operation.

## Subsets of CIM

There are a number of areas of specialized application of the concepts of CIM. The titles of these areas will be used throughout the text. They are defined here.

**Computer Aided Engineering (CAE).** This refers to the use of the computer to aid in the design of product. It also includes modeling and simulation of product performance, stress and fatigue analysis, and the integration of analysis and test data. CAE also includes the creation of product drawings.

**Computer Aided Design/Computer Aided Manufacturing (CAD/CAM).** This refers to the use of the computer to aid in integration of product design and process design. It is sometimes called *manufacturability*. The CAD label is essentially synonymous with CAE.

The CAM label refers to equivalent computer assistance within processing and production activities. The manufacturing applications use the electronic images and data from the engineering database as a starting point. This includes process planning, tool design, preparation of programs to drive numerical control machines, coordinate measuring machines, and robots. In addition to control programs for machining centers, it also includes the development and operation of manufacturing cells—sometimes called *cellular manufacturing*. In this concept, a series of machining centers are linked logically and physically. Once the production of a part has begun, the part moves quickly from machine to machine until it is finished. It is never stacked with other parts until it is finished.

**Material Requirements Planning (MRP).** This refers to the use of the computer to track and replenish materials inventories, particularly production materials. It includes the concept of dependent demand. The computer performs a breakdown of product bills of material to extend the quantities of prime product planned by a master production schedule. MRP includes a daily recalculation of material requirements based upon incremental changes in schedules or planned inventory status. In addition, it includes the adjustment of material requirements as actual customer orders are scheduled.

**Just-in-Time (JIT).** This refers to a refinement of MRP in which the procurement and manufacture of production materials is done in minimum lot sizes just-in-time to serve the needs of the assembly process. The theoretically ideal lot size is a single piece of production material. The JIT concept is enhanced, of course, by the CAM thrust toward cellular manufacturing.

**Group Technology (GT).** This refers to the gathering of parts, assemblies, and processes into families or groups with fundamental similarities. A group of production parts or assemblies with similar features tends to require similar processing steps. A group of production equipment with similar features can be used as alternates to produce a specific part or assembly. These groupings are based upon the use of classification and coding systems. Group Technology is essential to CAD/CAM and JIT.

**Computer Aided Process Planning (CAPP).** This refers to the use of the computer to develop process plans (production routings) for production parts and assemblies. The basis of CAPP is GT.

There are a number of new computer technologies which support CIM. These include computer aided graphics, numeric control, codification systems, expert systems, relational database languages, computer-to-computer communications facilities, and numerous commercially available applications, such as MRP systems. There is a danger in the use of these capabilities as isolated technologies to buy local advantages. This denies the strength and the value of the concept of CIM, which integrates systems while utilizing computer capabilities where appropriate.

## Planning and Control Systems

Many CIM applications are planning systems as described in *Figure 3.1*. In addition, many are control systems (*Figure 3.2*). The planning systems could be called *master data systems*, since they result in master data. This is true of applications which produce electronic product drawings. It is also true of applications which produce production routings. MRP and JIT are control systems by definition. GT is a master data system by definition. CAPP is a control system over the development of processes, but it results in master data. The software which uses the process data to operate a production cell is a control system.

## Summary

The *information management model* is a very useful model for analyzing information systems in a business. The model describes the flow of data to support key control systems within the business.

A *control system* drives some function of the business. It is activated by another triggering control system. A control system is also supported by a series of related systems, a *master data system,* a *feedback system,* a *status system,* and an *analysis system.*

Control systems cannot function properly unless the associated supporting systems are operated to provide data with appropriate *accuracy* and *timeliness.*

There are three types of data files or databases which are required to support a full control system—*master data, status data,* and *historical data.* The three have significantly different uses and different life styles. Master data is enduring and seldom changes. Status data changes very rapidly. History data is a store of past status data, unchanging, but growing in volume until old data is purged because it is judged to be of little continuing value.

Control systems tend to "cascade." For example, a market forecast triggers the master schedule, which triggers requirements planning, etc.

CIM is an emphasis on integration of the systems by which a manufacturing enterprise is managed. It is not a narrow application of computer techniques to the manufacturing process. CIM is an intelligent application of the computer to aid in the operation of refined planning and control systems.

# 4

# *Responsibilities of a Manager*

## Introduction

There is a tendency for managers to underestimate the importance of information systems and the development of improved systems, particularly improved mechanized systems. The purpose of this chapter is to make the reader aware of this tendency and the reasons for its existence. It is intended to help the reader gain insight into what is required to introduce improved methods and computer supported systems into the business.

## Management Attitude Toward Computers

Data processing and systems-oriented journals frequently print articles which complain about line management apathy toward the use of computers. They say, with a good deal of historical evidence, that managers have often abdicated their responsibilities and have expected the Data Processing organization to develop computer applications which will make their problems go away. This has been described as the first stage of computer use in a company. In later stages the managers develop more interest and commitment toward the development of computer systems.

---

### Exercise 4.1

Why do you think there is a tendency for management apathy toward the development of computer systems? List some of the reasons. Don't restrict your thoughts to deficiencies in line management, but think also about the data processors and the environment in which they exist.

---

## Management vs. Data Processing

If you found deficiencies in management, data processing, and the environment, you did your work well.

Data processing people are often at fault for lack of involvement with line management. There is something about complex electronic technology which generates a fascination that can become self-serving. Less mature data processors can be more interested in what they can make the computer do than in what management needs to have done. This is a common problem, even with data processors who have years of experience.

The data processor tends to use a lot of technical language. This is a turn off to users, who can feel that the data processor is talking down to them or trying to deceive them.

Finally, the development of computer applications is just now coming out of the realm of art and into the realm of systems engineering. Historically, most computer projects have cost twice the original estimate and have taken up to three times the estimated length of time to complete. The reasons for this and the cure will be discussed in later chapters.

The current business environment in the United States is based on precise budgeting and measurement of managerial performance on the basis of short-term objectives. The concept of management by objectives can be a deadly enemy to improvements in the systems of a business. Such improvements can be expensive and can take significant time to develop and perfect. It requires dedicated managers to make long-term investments when they are being measured only on short-term results.

Now that the blame has been spread around, it must be admitted that the major source of the problem is with the line managers. They can succumb to the short-term measurements of performance. Line managers can lack the training and skill required to make systematic improvements in the business. Or, they can just not be interested or have the time.

---

## Exercise 4.2

Make a list of what you think are the major responsibilities of a manager, any kind of manager. Think of generic responsibilities. Try to list about eight or ten of them.

---

## Typical Manager Responsibilities

No matter what responsibilities you wrote down on your list, they should all be found somewhere in the basic list shown in *Figure 4.1*.

The first responsibility is to run the shop. That is, the manager must see that the day-to-day activities are being performed. In a manufacturing company, the product must be built, sold, and shipped. In a fast-food restaurant, the door must be opened on time; the tables and counters must be

1. Run the Shop
2. Plan Physical Needs
3. Develop People
4. Keep the Customer Happy
5. Plan Improved Methods
6. Keep the Boss Happy

***Figure 4.1.*** Managerial responsibilities

cleaned; the food prepared, sold, and served; the remains must be cleaned up.

The second responsibility is to plan for any change in physical needs. In a manufacturing company, the master schedule for production must be adjusted to accommodate expected sales volumes; and materials must be ordered correspondingly. In a fast-food restaurant, the holiday crowds and the slack periods must be anticipated with corresponding adjustment to the ordering of food preparation materials and the scheduling of the work force.

The third responsibility is to develop people. In its broader sense it includes the recruiting, hiring, and training of people to do their assigned tasks. It also includes the identification and development of promising people to take on expanded responsibilities. The total management chain must be backed up by promising people who can carry on the business when the senior management is no longer there.

The fourth responsibility is to keep the customer happy. In its positive sense, it means presenting the company and the product to the customer in a friendly, comfortable, and professional fashion so that he or she is encouraged to do business with the enterprise. In a less positive sense, it means picking up the pieces when something has gone wrong and the customer has been alienated. This might include making repairs or offering replacement product. It might mean reducing or refunding charges. It might mean apologizing and promising that the problem will never be repeated.

The fifth responsibility is to plan improved methods. This is the systems business. It means developing new and better lines of products. It also means developing new and better ways of managing the business for greater efficiency and greater effectiveness. This is not a reaction to trends so much as it is a rethinking of how the business should be operated.

The sixth responsibility is to keep the boss happy. In its positive sense, this means seeing that the portion of the business for which the manager is responsible runs like a well oiled machine—meeting and exceeding production and performance norms. In a less positive sense, it means explaining to the boss about those things which have gone wrong, finding reasons why they were not the manager's fault, and promising to fix them promptly so that they will never occur again.

## Exercise 4.3

Study the definitions of the responsibilities of a manager. Then list them in the priority order that you think a poor manager might assign them. Consider a manager who is ill-trained, unskilled, or poorly motivated. How would he or she tend to allocate the working day among these responsibilities? The question is not so much one of how much time would be spent on each, but which responsibilities would tend to receive closer attention than others.

## Poor Managers

Exercise 4.3 has been performed by many managers and college students. The consensus of the priorities is listed in *Figure 4.2*.

| RESPONSIBILITY | PRIORITY |
|---|---|
| 1. Run the Shop | 3 |
| 2. Plan Physical Needs | 4 |
| 3. Develop People | 5 or 6 |
| 4. Keep the Customer Happy | 2 |
| 5. Plan Improved Methods | 5 or 6 |
| 6. Keep the Boss Happy | 1 |

***Figure 4.2.*** Priorities of a poor manager

The first priority is keeping the boss happy. Because the manager is not performing all of his responsibilities, he must pay close attention to the attitude of the boss. Otherwise, he might jeopardize his job security. He is never comfortable that the boss is happy, and might even go to the point of catering to the boss to try to distract him or her from observing or resenting the poor performance on other responsibilities.

The second priority is keeping the customer happy. Because the manager is not performing all of his responsibilities, he must also spend a lot of time talking with customers. He does this to keep them from reacting severely to the poor service which they receive from the area of the business under the manager's authority. Perhaps if he can keep the customers from making complaints to the boss, he won't have to spend so much time worrying about the boss's wrath.

Priority three is running the shop. Managers feel that if they watch the help more closely and keep the pressure on, not as many mistakes will be made in serving the customer. The poor boss is a very demanding taskmaster, since every lapse by an employee is a threat to his security.

Priority four is to plan physical needs. In those portions of the day that they can spare from watching over their staff, the poor managers work on the changes in supplies and staffing required for changing times. This type of manager usually tries to avoid criticism from the boss by ordering excessive supplies of material for slack periods, and by ordering inadequate supplies of materials for peak periods. After all, who could forgive running out of product when demand is low, and who could criticize if the business runs short of material when "nobody could guess that demand would be so great?"

There is a split of opinion as to the last two priorities. The race is a tie in that neither responsibility receives a great deal of attention from the poor manager. He has neither the time nor the inclination to develop people or to plan improved systems.

How can poor managers develop people when they have not been able to develop their own skills?

How can poor managers plan improved methods of running the business when they are unwilling or incapable of managing by the methods already in place? These, by the way, are the managers who ask the data processors to solve their problems. Before too radical an image is developed in the reader's mind, it must be stated in all fairness that "poor" is a relative term and applies in some degree to everybody.

### Exercise 4.4

Now that you have dissected the poor manager, consider effective managers—the managers who are adequately talented, trained, and motivated to perform responsibilities well. What are their priorities? How do they tend to ration their attention, if not their time? Make a priority list of the responsibilities in *Figure 4.1* to show how effective managers would see the priorities.

## Effective Managers

Exercise 4.4 has also been performed by many managers and college students. *Figure 4.3* is the consensus of the priorities.

There is a split of opinion as to the first two priorities. The race was a tie. The consensus was that both responsibilities are of vital importance to an effective manager and receive the manager's closest attention. The two top priority responsibilities are to develop people and to plan improved methods.

Since managers are skilled at their trade, they know what to look for in the next generation of managers. They pay close attention to attracting and

| RESPONSIBILITY | PRIORITY |
|---|---|
| 1. Run the Shop | 4 |
| 2. Plan Physical Needs | 3 |
| 3. Develop People | 1 or 2 |
| 4. Keep the Customer Happy | 5 |
| 5. Plan Improved Methods | 1 or 2 |
| 6. Keep the Boss Happy | 6 |

***Figure 4.3.*** Priorities of an effective manager

hiring good people who can be expected to advance through the ranks successfully. Managers also devote much time and attention to training others in their responsibilities. As they mature, managers train them to assume broader responsibilities.

Since effective managers are skilled at their trade and take pride in good performance, they are always looking for ways of doing things better. They are more than willing to look for improvements in the department's information systems. Managers are also willing to work with data processing and systems people to make the operation of the business more effective.

The third priority of effective managers is to plan physical needs to accommodate peak and slack periods. They are willing to accept a moderate risk of error in these plans, because they are comfortable in their position. There are few enough problems so they can afford a lost sale if the bottom line is more profit in the long term.

The fourth priority is to run the shop. Good managers do not hover over their people, but audit their work to determine if any corrective action is needed. Since they have paid close attention to selection of personnel and have trained them to operate by the best procedures (systems) they can devise, these managers are rather comfortable that the business will tend to run itself.

Priority five is keeping the customer happy. The majority of the time spent on this responsibility is in the realm of personal relations. The manager can afford to do this, since there are relatively few lapses in performance. This responsibility becomes a pleasant interlude to the daily activity whereby the manager can promote even more business.

The sixth responsibility is to keep the boss happy. If the boss has an ounce of brains in his head, he is already happy about the performance of the segment of the business under the responsibility of the effective manager. If the effective manager and the boss play golf together, it is because they are friends, not because one needs to impress the other.

## Quality of Management

It should be obvious that the priorities of the poor manager and the effective manager are in inverse order. Unfortunately, there is a rather large percentage of poor or relatively poor managers in the business world. To the extent that managers are less than fully effective (a nicer way of saying it), they are unlikely to emphasize personnel development or improved systems.

Since the purpose of this text is to improve management's ability to develop better information systems and to manage better through them, it is hoped that this exercise has had two effects:

- To sensitize some managers to the need to review their motivations, priorities, and skills
- To motivate the college student to gain the skills required to be an effective manager and to develop improved systems.

## Summary

Systems improvements receive little attention or cooperation from managers who are not motivated or skilled in systems concepts.

The practice of management by objectives tends to motivate short-term approaches to systems development. This can be a deterrent to creative thinking.

The effective manager emphasizes those things which put in place a well-functioning operation—developing people and planning improved methods (systems).

The poor manager tends to spend the majority of his time picking up the pieces after operational failures which result from a lack of skilled staff and well-structured systems.

Managers who improve the business spend the time to acquire systems skills and to apply them. They pay close attention to personnel development and to systems improvements.

# 5

# *File vs. Database*

## Introduction

There is a tendency for people to use the label "database" casually for any collection of data. So far, the label has been used that way in this text. The purpose of this exercise is to help the reader realize the difference between a file and a database, and to have an appreciation of their relative advantages and disadvantages.

## Exercise 5.1

Write down what you think a file is. Don't necessarily think only in computer terms.

## File—A Dictionary Definition

A definition of a file according to Webster is: "a line of things arranged one behind another."

## File—A Working Definition

By the dictionary definition, a queue of people waiting for a bus is a file. A set of patient folders on a shelf in a doctor's office is a file. A stack of customer bills skewered on a spike in a country grocery store is a file. And, a set of computer records about an aspect of a business is a file.

*Figure 5.1* summarizes the fundamental characteristics of a file. It refers primarily to a file of data, whether in computer form or in written form.

A file is a set of records which is organized in a specific sequence by the use

| CHARACTERISTICS OF A FILE |
|---|
| 1. Sequential |
| 2. Singular Format |
| 3. Singular Purpose |

***Figure 5.1.*** Characteristics of a file

of an identifier or controlling key, such as employee name or identification number.

Each record in a file honors a specific record format wherein the bits of data are arranged in similar fashion from record to record. Standard forms are developed to discipline the data in a paper filing system.

Finally, a file is organized to satisfy a single primary business purpose. The files in a doctor's office are arranged by customer name so that the correct folder can be pulled when a patient is scheduled to visit the doctor. The data in the file is arranged on formatted pages so that the doctor can find the specific data needed. The purpose of the file is to provide convenient reference to the case history of individuals.

The stack of customer bills on the spike in the country store is arranged in a time sequence. The store manager knows that the oldest bill is the one on the bottom. This is a simple case of aged accounts.

## Computer File Structure

*Figure 5.2* illustrates a computer record in a file used to keep track of enrollment in the courses of a college. The key to the record is the course number. The record also contains the name of the course and the identity number and name of each student who is enrolled. The purpose of the file is primarily to print a roster for each course.

| COURSE NO. | COURSE NAME | STUDENT NO. | STUDENT NAME |
|---|---|---|---|

***Figure 5.2.*** File of course membership

The file is stored on magnetic tape. When it is used, the records must be read sequentially.

Note how the structure of the record causes a significant amount of redundant data. If there are thirty students enrolled in a course, then thirty records contain the same course number as well as the course name. If a student is enrolled in five courses, then there are five records with the same student name and identification number.

Since the file is sequenced by course number, it takes only one pass through the file to print a course roster. It would not be convenient to use the file to limit the number of students in a specific course. The file would have to be read sequentially up to the records containing the course number in order to determine if a requested registration could be allowed. This is obviously impractical, so the most common technique has been to keep manual records of the number of registrations. The registrations are manually posted on the printed course roster.

In the 1970s, random access storage devices came into use. They provided a mechanism for more effective use of the computer to support multiple business functions. More on this will be discussed later.

## Complex Computer File Structures

*Figure 5.3* shows a more complicated file which includes two types of records. The first type is indicated by a "1" in the field called Rec. Type, and the second type is indicated by a "2" in the same field. When the computer reads a record, it first examines the record type to determine what contents to look for. When it finds a record type 1, it knows that it has found a student record. Notice that with this more complex file structure, the amount of redundant data within the file is reduced. The student name and identification number are present in only one record.

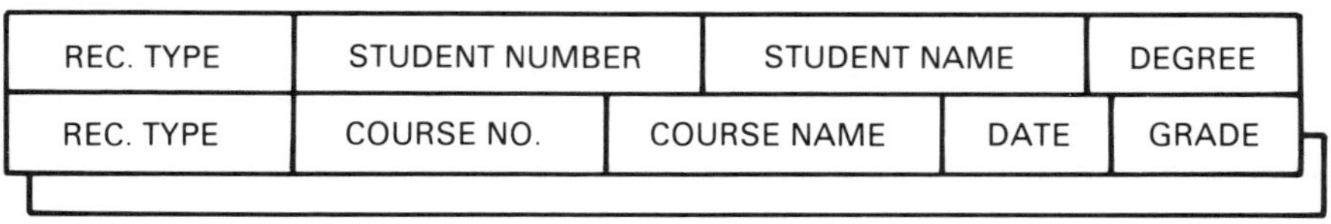


***Figure 5.3.*** File of student records

All of the student records are in sequence by student identification number. The sorting convention of the file is that all enrollments for a student are in sequence by course number behind the student record. The computer can read consecutive records after a student record, knowing that until it encounters another record type 1, it is reading course enrollments for the student in the last type 1 record read.

The purpose of the file is to print a course roster for students. The file could not easily be used to print a course roster for each course. It would have to be resequenced. It is even less serviceable than the previous file for limiting the number of registrations in a course, since the whole file would have to be read in order to count the number of students in a specific course.

Although sequential computer files are very handy mechanisms for serving their primary purpose, they are awkward at best when used to serve secondary purposes. For this reason there is a need to maintain redundant data in a number of files so that the files can be processed efficiently. This in turn brings potential problems with keeping the separate files updated together so that the data is consistent. The data processor refers to the files as "being in synch."

## Exercise 5.2

Think of files you feel might exist to serve a business function. It might be easier to think of the function to be served and then to think of the appropriate file. Also list data fields you think might be in the files.

## Typical Files and Their Uses

The concept of computer files began when records were maintained on punched cards. The concept remained the same when magnetic tape files were introduced. In each of these cases, the files are sequential. The computer must read each record from the beginning of the file until it reaches the record of interest. For this reason it is seldom that a file passes through the computer unless all of the records are to be used. An example is the printing of a full course roster or the printing of a full student roster.

*Figure 5.4* illustrates a number of example files with their typical contents and uses.

| FILE | USE | CONTENTS |
|---|---|---|
| Payroll | Write Checks | Employee I.D., Rate, History |
| Accounts | Write Bills | Customer, Credit, Invoice |
| Inventory | Keep Status | Items, Quantity, Value |
| Class | Registration | Courses, Students, Quantity |

***Figure 5.4.*** Examples of files and uses

## Exercise 5.3

Refer to *Figure 2.3*. Which of the input and output media are designed to be processed only in sequence?

## Exercise 5.4

Write down what you think a database is. In this case, you must think in computer terms because the concept of a database exists only for computer processing.

## Database—A Working Definition

A *database* is an organized collection of logically related data about a single type of entity, intended as a common reference source for multiple purposes. This is a rather complex definition. It needs to be looked at in pieces.

An entity is a thing about which management maintains data. Management maintains data about parts, production machinery, and customers. Parts, machines, and customers are entities. In a college environment, entities include courses, students, classrooms, and teachers.

A field of data about an entity is called an *attribute* of the entity. Entities and attributes of entities are recorded in computer records as data fields. A record can have a field which contains the entity "student" (probably recorded in the form of a student identification number) and the attributes "student name" and "degree which is being pursued."

A database is intended to be the single authoritative source of data about the entities. The database replaces the need to have many different files with different collections of redundant data about the same entities. There are many data files because there are many different business purposes to be served.

The records in a database can be read by the computer in sequential fashion just as if the database were a file similar to the one in *Figure 5.3*. Indeed, this is often done. But one of the strengths of a database is that the records can be read in random order. That is, the computer can go directly to the record for student number 12364 without reading all of the records in front of the one desired. This is called *random access*.

A similar random access is possible with paper files. A nurse doesn't look at all patient folders in sequence to find the one wanted by the doctor. He or she has the folders arranged to quickly find the one that is wanted. The color codes on the edges of such folders indicate the first two letters of the patient's last name.

As an analogy for sequential and random access, consider the devices on which music is recorded. A cassette tape is a sequential device, since the cassette player must read past all songs from the beginning of the tape to find the one the listener wants. A phonograph record can be accessed either sequentially or randomly. The record can be played from the beginning, or the listener can place the needle in front of the desired song.

*Figure 5.5* summarizes the primary characteristics of a database.

| CHARACTERISTICS OF A DATABASE |
| --- |
| 1. Authoritative Data Source |
| 2. Multiple Purposes |
| 3. Random Access |
| 4. Complex Structure |

***Figure 5.5.*** Characteristics of a database

## Hierarchical or Tree Database Structure

*Figure 5.6* illustrates a database about the entity "student." It is similar to a file like the one in *Figure 5.3*, but it is also different in that the structure is more complex.

The basic record of personal data about the student is called the *root segment* and is identified by the *root key*—the student identification number

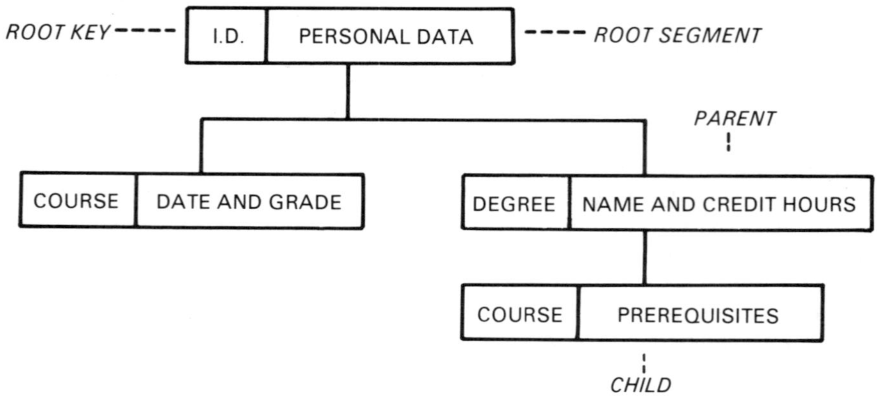


***Figure 5.6.*** Hierarchical or tree database structure

in this instance. The segments or records about the courses in which the student is registered or has completed are the next segments in sequence. They are *children* of the root segment, which is a *parent* to them. The course segments are sequenced by course number.

The next records in sequence are the *degree segments* which are sequenced by degree code. After each degree are the segments which list the prerequisites that the student must complete before earning the degree. Again, the prerequisite segment is a child of the degree segment. The degree segment is a parent to the prerequisite segment.

The structure of a hierarchical database is such that there need not be any redundancy of data within the database except for the keys to child segments. John Jones took Industrial Engineering IE409, so "IE409" is in a field in a course segment, child to the root segment for John Jones. It is also in a child segment of any other entity (student) who took the course or who is registered in the course.

If a counselor wanted to know what remaining requirements John Jones must complete in order to earn his Electrical Engineering degree, the counselor could enter a query on his terminal. This presumes that a program exists to answer such a query. The computer would ask for the identification number of the student and the identification number of the degree. How the counselor knows these numbers is a problem for a later chapter.

The computer would go directly to the root segment of the student. The computer would then read all of the succeeding segments about that student (a little bit of sequential processing) until it found the segment containing the degree of interest. The computer would then read the segments immediately following until it came to a segment which was of a different type. All of these intermediate segments are prerequisites for the specified degree of the specified student.

It should be obvious that this type of database structure is far more powerful than the simple file structure. It can readily answer many different types of questions, such as:

- What degrees is Susie Strong working toward?
- What are the courses that Tom Turner has completed?
- In what courses is Jane Johnson registered?

This type of database structure also has its limits. If the counselor should ask for the names of all students who are working for a bachelors degree in Industrial Engineering, the processing could take a long time. It is too technical for this text to explain in detail, but there would need to be a number of special characteristics built into the database to answer such a question. A simple rule can clarify what questions can be readily answered in a specific hierarchical database. Questions can be readily answered if the sequence of the data search is from root to parent to child. Searches are very inefficient if the question requires a search proceeding from child to parent.

## Relational or Flat File Structure

Another more modern type of database is a relational database such as the one illustrated in *Figure 5.7*. It looks very much like the series of independent files in *Figure 5.2*, but the files are logically linked within the computer. Given the keys associated with any type of query (request for information), the specific records can be accessed without long sequential reading processes. Obviously, this type of database structure is the most versatile of the types discussed in this chapter.

The example relational database in *Figure 5.7* contains the same data as the hierarchical database in *Figure 5.6*. There is a bit more data redundancy,

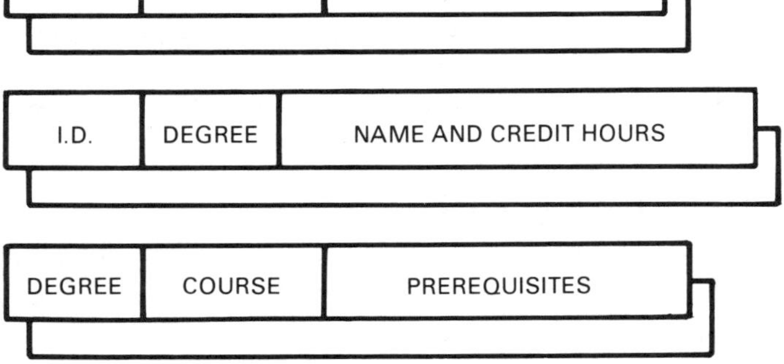


***Figure 5.7.*** Relational or flat file structure

since each of the records has a key (student identification number) or a string of keys (degree, course number). This is a slight price to pay for the versatility of the structure.

## Relative Characteristics

The relative characteristics of files and databases are listed in *Figure 5.8*. The only characteristic not previously discussed is the multiple sources of data in a database. Since a database is a comprehensive fund of data about an entity, the source of that data can be anywhere that there is activity involving the entity.

| FILE | DATABASE |
|---|---|
| Single Use | Multiple Uses |
| Single User | Multiple Users |
| Sequential Processing | Random Processing |
| Batch Processing | Transaction Processing |
| Single Data Source | Multiple Data Sources |

***Figure 5.8.*** File vs. database comparison

The students themselves provide the personal data for the root segment when they enroll in the college. The registrar's office is the source of the course enrollment for the current semester. The teachers are the source of the grades for completed courses, and the department head is the source of the total set of prerequisites for a degree. The list of prerequisites is reduced one by one for the student as prerequisite courses are completed with a satisfactory grade.

## Exercise 5.5

Refer to *Figure 2.3*. Which of the input and output media are designed to be processed randomly as well as sequentially?

## Exercise 5.6

Make a list of what you think are the relative advantages of files and databases. If you think carefully about the differences between the two types of data structures, you should be able to deduce some resulting relative advantages of each over the other.

## Right Tool for the Right Job

A surface impression would suggest that a database is always preferable to a file. This is not so. *Figure 5.9* is a list of relative advantages.

## Advantages of a File

A file is a great device for a simple, straightforward processing job if there is little likelihood that a different use of the file might develop. As an example,

| ADVANTAGES OF FILES |
| --- |
| Simple Keys and Logic |
| Efficient Processing for a Specific Function |
| Simple Security Control |
| **ADVANTAGES OF DATABASES** |
| Availability of Related Data |
| Developed Data Accuracy through Use |
| Overall Processing Economy |
| Inquiry Capability |
| No Need to Change Programs for Database Changes |
| Ease of Addition of New Segments—Growth |
| Data Storage Economy—Little Redundancy |

***Figure 5.9.*** Relative advantages of files and databases

consider a checkbook as a simple file. It is quite satisfactory as a chronological record of when expenditures are made. As long as there is no need to summarize similar types of expenditures, the sequential file is adequate.

A file is far simpler for programmers to use when they write the logical steps which result in programs. They access records sequentially by simple keys and simple logic.

As long as the use of a file requires sequential processing of the whole file, the processing will be accomplished faster and cheaper than it would be if the data were in a database structure.

If a set of data about an entity is of a highly sensitive nature, the security of the data from unauthorized access can be most readily assured with a file structure. The medium on which the file is recorded can be physically removed from the computer and stored under lock and key when not in use.

## Advantages of a Database

A database has many more advantages. Maybe it would be more accurate to say that there are many more occasions when a database is a preferable structure for data about an entity.

When there is a need for a variety of information about an entity, it is easier to access a single database rather than to try to combine the data from a number of files.

When data is in a database, it is used for a variety of purposes. When data is used by a number of people, any deficiency in the accuracy of the data is more likely to be observed. When data is inaccurate, it causes an inconvenience which is sometimes serious to the user. When this happens, the user is likely to complain and the data is likely to be corrected. For this reason, the contents of a database are more likely to be accurate than the contents of a file. There is an additional advantage of databases over a series of files which must be combined for a task, since the contents of a database are always in synch.

Storing all of the data about an entity in a single structure avoids the need to sort files to perform different tasks. It avoids the need to update separate files containing different sets of attributes about an entity. For this reason, a database is more economical than a file when there are a number of different uses for the data.

By definition, a database is built to support direct inquiry about a single entity, while a file is built to process all included entities sequentially.

When the structure of a file is changed, such as adding a new attribute or changing the field size of an attribute, all of the programs using that file must be changed. On the other hand, for a database, it is a general rule that only those programs which access a changed attribute need be changed.

When new sets of data need to be recorded about an entity, it is far easier to add them as segments to a database than it is to add them to files or to create a new file.

Since a database minimizes the redundancy of data which must be stored for computer use, the database structure is usually less expensive in terms of data storage medium costs.

---

### Exercise 5.7

Now that the relative advantages of files and databases have been explored to the general advantage of the database, extend your imagination and logic to try to list any disadvantages you think might be associated with databases. Write them down in a list.

---

## Databases are Mixed Blessings

Although databases have many advantages, there is a price to pay. There are significant added complexities, and the potential for significant error in the use of a database. When Detroit added the automatic choke to the automobile, they made it far easier for the driver when everything worked well, but they also made it exceptionally difficult for the driver when the choke didn't work correctly.

Bad data affects everyone. When erroneous data is placed in a database, it can have a negative impact on anyone who uses it. On the other hand, the more people who use a bit of data, the more likely it is that an error will be detected and corrected. This will be seen later in a number of the case studies.

If all the data about an entity is in a single database, summary reports about that data by different departments are more likely to be consistent. In a business which operates from different departmental files, the chief executive is likely to hear conflicting reports from the different departments. Sales for the month will be reported by the Sales department and by the Accounting department from different files which are likely to be out of synch.

In a database environment, new data is entered into the database from the place where it occurs. Product failure in the field is recorded, for example, by the customer contact person, possibly a salesperson. People seem to have a reluctance to provide data for the use of others when the data is of no use to themselves. As an example, a Field Service department needs to know exactly when a product change goes into effect in the factory. The Assembly department is the best source of that information, since they are the ones who implement the change. But the information is of no use at all to the Assembly department. Therefore, there is no real incentive for the Assembly department to interrupt the normal flow of work in order to write down the information for someone else.

With a lot of different segments of data in a single structure, the access to a specific set of data can involve a complex bit of logic including a number of keys. This is more true about the hierarchical database structure than it is about the newer, relational database structure.

The development of a database is a very large undertaking. It is usually initiated when a new, significant demand is placed upon the data about an entity. Since the data in a database comes from a variety of sources, it takes the cooperation of a number of departments to define the needs and the structure of the database. The department which has the immediate need has every reason to become impatient. They are prone to ask, "Why are you delaying the response to my need while you develop some idealistic new concept which you tell me is of great value to others who have no pressing new needs?" Although the answer to this question is simple in theory, it is difficult to accept in the real world, especially since management, including Data Processing, tends to be measured on short-range objectives.

Since management is closely budgeted and is measured on short-range objectives, there is usually a difficult question regarding who is to pay for the development of the database. It costs more than the value it offers to any single department. The only answer is that the Data Processing department bears the major expense and has the support of top management.

When a commitment is made to develop and install a database, a question arises of what to do with the old data files which the new ones theoretically make obsolete. There are many programs which are built to access the old files. The effort to convert these programs to use the new database could be very large and prohibitive. For this reason, a new database is usually linked to the old files. One updates the other. This is done until there is a need to change the old programs. This is used as an incentive to eliminate a file. For a long time, the business is in the position of wearing a belt and suspenders when it comes to storing and maintaining data. This eats up much of the expected economy from database use.

Who owns the data in the database? This is a very tricky question, since someone must be accountable for the quality of the contents of a database. Since a number of departments are maintaining the data, each can generally blame another if anything goes wrong. Where responsibility is divided, there is usually little sense of personal responsibility. Who owns an inventory record when Material Control posts the receipt of material from suppliers and the Manufacturing department posts the use of the material in product?

It should be obvious that when all of the data about an entity is in a single database, it is difficult to protect selected segments of that data from unauthorized access. The Accounting department certainly wants to protect payroll data about an employee when it is in the same database as attendance data, which is of general interest to the Personnel department and to the factory.

Files are often copied after being updated in order to provide a backup in case of damage or loss. A database is also subject to damage or loss. Since a database is much larger and is updated constantly, there is a serious logistical problem of when and how to do a backup. On the one hand, the backup process can be expensive and time-consuming. On the other hand, there is a greater likelihood of damage, and it requires a longer time to recover from a loss of data.

If the computer and the data storage devices are not of adequate speed and capacity, there can be a problem of competition for access to a database. Fortunately, the rate of development of improved computer hardware is faster than the rate of development of databases.

> **LAW**
>
> **Data Accuracy is Proportional to its Visibility.**
>
> Data inaccuracies are only identified during use, and are only corrected as necessary for known immediate uses.

This law states that data inaccuracies are only identified during use, and are only corrected as necessary for known immediate uses.

The validity of this law should be self-evident from the sequence of thought in this chapter. As the pressures for economy increase in a highly competitive world (especially in manufacturing), the truth of this law will become increasingly evident. Management will not be able to afford the time and expense to maintain accurate records unless there is a commensurate return on the investment. The problem of interdepartmental conflict will become more severe if the department making the investment is not the department reaping the benefits.

## Exercise 5.8

Can you find examples of this law from your own experience? A little reflection should reveal numerous examples.

## Exercise 5.9

There is a database within your company about the entity "final product." In the database there is a field labeled "date of sale." List on a piece of paper the definition of that field as you think it would be viewed by the Sales department, the Accounting department, the Field Service department, the Order Entry department, and the Shipping department. If you have difficulty, refer to the descriptions of the departments in Appendix B.

**LAW**

**Data is in the Eye of the Beholder.**

Data takes on the bias of the originator and of the user.

According to this law, data takes on the bias of the originator and of the user.

From the exercise just concluded, you should have gained the firm opinion that the above law is valid. Each department views the field, "Date of Sale," from a perspective of the function of that department.

Sales is concerned about the date on which a commitment to buy was made by the customer—for the purpose of meeting sales goals and obtaining sales commissions.

Accounting is concerned about the date on which a financial obligation was incurred by the customer—for the purpose of cash management.

Service is concerned about the date the customer takes title to the product—for the purpose of monitoring warranty.

Order Entry is concerned about the assigned priority of build and/or shipment of the product—for the purpose of managing finished product inventory and the scheduling of product assembly.

Shipping is concerned about the date when the product must be prepared for delivery to the customer.

Although some of the dates as viewed by the various departments can be the same calendar date, there is a significant likelihood that some of them are indeed different calendar dates. The only way that all of these diverse viewpoints of "date of sale" can be rationalized is to have several distinct fields in the database to record those dates which are indeed different. Otherwise, reports to upper management will be as conflicting as if each department had its own private file.

## Relational Database—Key to CIM

Much of computer integrated manufacturing (CIM) is based upon the use of group technology (GT). In order to manage things through the use of a computer, the characteristics of the things must be identified to the computer. This is done through classification and coding systems. These systems are described in some detail in Chapter 18.

The encoded data about manufacturing entities must be stored in a database for convenient random access. There is data about parts, features of parts (e.g., holes, surface finishes), production machines, cutting tools, holding fixtures, and inspection tools. As the volume and variety of this data grows, the database must be able to flex without causing the need to rework application programs. The reasonably new concept of relational databases fits that need admirably.

It is important to note that CIM is a management strategy and not a magical set of computer applications. The computer applications will be developed over many years based upon redefinition of business practices, implementation of new technologies, and experience in the application of both. The databases and the computer programs must be capable of lasting through the evolution without continual rework. The relational database offers a significant step forward in flexibility to support future change.

## Graphics—A Different Kind of Data

Most traditional data in a database is organized in segments or records in a fashion analogous to transactions. The records are rather brief and simple. The access to data is record by record.

The graphic images of parts and tools are stored as masses of data with complex relationships. A hole in a part, for example, is not necessarily stored as a record about a hole. The hole is described as a series of lines and coordinates in several orthographic views. It is also stored as text and encoded data in various locations over the surface of the electronic "drawing." The draftsman and the processor don't access the record for the hole, but the record for the part. They then "point" to the hole with a wand or the cursor.

The computer record for an item in inventory might consist of 50 to 100 characters of data in a database. The computer record for a part drawing is a file which is a complex of interrelated data of a volume from 50,00 to 500,000 characters. This volume of data and complexity of data structure require new data management disciplines. A database about parts can contain data which is like a catalog to the drawing files; but the drawing files must be stored under separate disciplines, similar to those which apply to the storage and retrieval of computer programs.

The retrieval and use of drawing data is also different from the retrieval and use of conventional data records. A transaction such as an inventory transaction is normally processed in two to five seconds. This is an adequate response before the user is ready to enter another transaction.

If an engineer wants to look at a drawing, it can take from 30 seconds to several minutes for the thousands of characters in the drawing file to be obtained from secondary storage and moved to the computer where they can be operated upon. Then, when the engineer inputs commands to alter the drawing, he needs computer response times of less than a second. The reason for this is that the engineer has a pattern of activity in mind. To draw a hole, he must perform a sequence of steps. If the response time of the computer is slow, he becomes frustrated waiting for it, and can then become distracted by delay and make errors in the series of steps.

## Summary

A *file* is a set of records which is organized in a specific sequence by the use of an identifier or controlling key, such as employee name or identification number.

A *database* is an organized collection of logically related data about a single type of entity, intended as a common reference source for multiple purposes.

There are two types of database structures, a hierarchical or tree structure, and a newer relational or flat file structure. The relational structure is more versatile.

Both files and databases have their relative advantages. The database is generally the more effective tool if the data about an entity is used for a variety of purposes.

**LAW—Data Accuracy is Proportional to its Visibility.** Data inaccuracies are only identified during use, and are only corrected as necessary for known immediate uses.

**LAW—Data is in the Eye of the Beholder.** Data takes on the bias of the originator and of the user.

CIM is dependent upon relational database capabilities. The flexibility of relational databases protects both the data structures and application programs from the need to be revamped as concepts of CIM are implemented over many years.

Graphics data has significantly different characteristics from ordinary alphanumeric data. It must be stored under different disciplines. The computer response times required by the users are also different.

# 6

# Case: Production Routing

## Introduction

There is a tendency for people to think that all data in a computer system is highly disciplined and available to serve any newly identified need. This is not necessarily so. The purpose of this chapter is to help the reader realize that there are limits to data quality and availability. The discipline of data depends upon the foresight with which a system and database are planned. It also depends upon the immediacy of need of the data entered into the system.

## Foundation of Cases

The case studies in this chapter and in the rest of the text are based upon experiences which are typical of the mobile equipment manufacturing industries in the United States. Up until the 1960s, mobile equipment was produced on assembly lines at a stable rate and stored as finished inventory. As customer orders arrived for specific configurations of product, units of finished product were moved to assembly bays. Optional and customized materials were marshalled at the bays, and the products were configured to suit the customer orders.

All of the systems (procedures by which the business was managed) were developed around the concept of build-to-stock and retrofit to customer order. The systems were manual, being developed in the 1940s and 1950s before computers came to be widely used. The systems were well adapted to the needs of the business. They relied on manual records and the limited form of mechanical computation capability which existed at the time.

During the late 1960s, the business changed in two ways. The marketplace demanded a variety of products, requiring an ever-growing variety of product options. And, the computer came into general usage. The new demand for product caused the industry to move gradually into a build-to-order method of operation. More product was assembled on the assembly line with specific customer ordered options, and less product was assembled to stock. In fact, the building of stock product resulted from an effort to keep manufacturing and assembly labor at constant levels when customer orders were at a low ebb. The availability of the power of the computer led to a variety of computer applications to "shore up" the build-to-stock systems, to make them more compatible with a build-to-order operation.

Many of the computer applications did not reflect true changes in the systems by which the business was managed. They were "band-aids" to overcome the most pressing problems resulting from the change in the product build strategy.

The cases in this text provide the reader with an opportunity to observe and analyze the need for change, and the information management errors which were made during the change. It is always easier to detect errors in retrospect. One has had the opportunity to learn from the errors, and from the solutions developed by those who went before.

## PRODUCTION ROUTINGS

A *production routing* is a recipe (like a cake recipe) for the manufacture of a component of a product or of a subassembly of a product. It describes the process through which the material passes over a series of machines or workstations.

Historically, the production routing does not describe the assembly of product on an assembly line. It does, however, describe the assembly of parts which are permanently fastened together, such as through welding. Often such an assembly is then passed through a subsequent series of machining and processing steps.

### Description

A typical production routing is shown in *Figure 6.1*. The figure shows only a subset of the most frequently used data on a routing. In practice, a routing can contain much more data and can be much more complex.

At the top of the routing is descriptive data about the part for which the routing serves as a manufacturing recipe. The descriptive data includes the name and the part number of the part. The typical lot size is shown, since the processing steps were designed to be cost-effective at a specific level of production. Finally, the indicative data includes the type of raw or rough material from which the part is to be made. A more complete routing might include information about the specifications of the raw material, and a description of the location to which the finished parts are to be delivered.

The middle section of the production routing contains indicators which tell the change level of the routing information. The Design Engineering department released the part at Engineering change level 0. Since then, for various

| PART NUMBER: 124876 | | | STANDARD LOT SIZE: 500 | |
|---|---|---|---|---|
| PART NAME: Lever | | | RAW MATERIAL: .75 bar | |
| ENG. CHANGE: 3 | | | | |
| MFG. CHANGE: 5 | | | | |
| OPER. NO. | MACHINE | SETUP TIME | PIECE TIME | DESCRIPTION |
| 010 | M1476 | 2.0 | .1475 | Saw to 18.0 length |
| 020 | M2746 | 1.0 | .0735 | Press flat on end |
| 025 | M3423 | 2.0 | .1830 | Drill 0.50 dia. hole |
| 030 | M8852 | 0.5 | .3250 | Turn thread |
| 040 | M9273 | 0.0 | .0080 | Wash |
| 050 | M2137 | 1.0 | .0445 | Heat treat |

***Figure 6.1.*** Production routing

reasons, the design of the part has been changed three times. The Production Engineering department released the production routing at Manufacturing change level 0. For various reasons, design changes or process improvements, the production routing has been changed five times.

The bottom portion of the production routing contains a description of the processing steps by which the raw material is transformed into the finished part. A piece of the bar is sawed off and is pressed flat on one end; a hole is drilled, and screw threads are machined in the hole. Finally, the part is washed and heat-treated to improve its wear qualities.

The operations are numbered by tens to make it easy to insert new operations if needed. Operation 025 was added after the first release of the production routing.

The machines over which the part is processed are identified by an identification number. In a complete routing, the physical location of the machine in the factory is shown, in addition to a classification code indicating if the machine is one of a group of machines which can be substituted for one another.

The time required to set up the machine is shown in hours. The setup process consists of installing and adjusting specific holding fixtures and cutting tools on the machine. The setup time also includes the amount of time it should typically take to remove the fixtures and cutting tools from the previous job, whatever it happens to be.

The piece time is the portion of an hour it takes to process a single part over the machine. The time includes consideration of the effort to unclamp and remove the previous part, to place and secure the new part, and to machine the new part. This is an area of the production routing which can become complex, since some machines can produce several pieces at the same time; heat-treat machines take time to come to temperature; and heat-treated parts take time to cool off. If a machine requires more than one operator to set it up or to produce the parts, there could be another set of time standards on the routing to distinguish between the load on the machine and the load on the operator.

Finally, a free-form verbal text is included to describe each operation. This description often includes a listing of the tools to be used in the operation. It also lists the parts which are fastened together in an assembly operation, such as through welding. Other possible information in this portion of the routing might include tool adjustment instructions and inspection instructions.

## Purpose

The production routing was traditionally prepared to direct the installation of the production facilities required to make the part. This included new or rearranged production machinery, new or increased quantities of cutting tools and inspection tools, and any new fixtures or holding devices.

The production routing was not normally maintained with any degree of priority or urgency when experience on the shop floor disclosed that different tooling or times were appropriate. The shop practice would change as needed, but the routing was not necessarily changed accordingly.

The times on the routing for machine setup and part processing were intended by the Production Design department to be within 5 to 10% of the time it should typically take the typical machine operator to complete the work. If the operator found a faster or more convenient method of doing the work, he/she was free to do so, as long as the boss didn't mind, and as long as the final part met the inspection criteria. This improvement in method was seldom reported to Process Design, so the routing was not updated to reflect the improvement in method.

## Preparation

The preparation of the production routing was a manual process (*Figure 6.2*). The processing engineer wrote the information on a blank routing form. When it was completed to his/her satisfaction, it was passed to a clerk typist so that it could be typed on a standard routing form on multilith master paper. The resulting copy was proofread by the processing engineer to ensure that the typist had made no errors.

Obviously, a production routing was prepared in advance of introduction of the process to the shop. The routing would then need to be put into use (made effective) at the appropriate time, such as when all of the necessary tooling had been put into place. Since the system for preparing production routings was manual, the most convenient change control device was to store the new multilith copy of a production routing in the processor's desk until the time came for it to become effective. This was known as desk drawer change control.

When the routing was put into effect, multilith copies were made and distributed to all locations where needed. The master copy was stored in a filing cabinet with all of the other routings currently in effect.

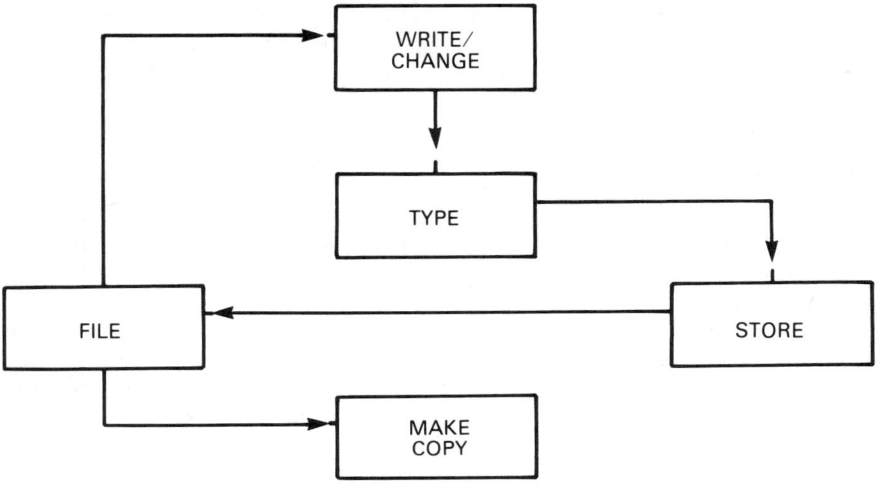


*Figure 6.2.* Production routing preparation

## WORK ORDERS

A *work order* is an authorization for the factory to produce a specific quantity of a part by a particular time. It is an order to do some work—to make a batch of parts, for example. The build-to-order factory found it most convenient to make parts in batches or lots.

The work order was produced in a simple fashion by adding two fields of data to a copy of the production routing—the lot size and the due date. Note in *Figure 6.3*, that the order is for the production of 530 pieces of lever 124876

| **PART NUMBER:** 124876 | | | **STANDARD LOT SIZE:** 500 | |
|---|---|---|---|---|
| **PART NAME:** Lever | | | **RAW MATERIAL:** .75 bar | |
| **ENG. CHANGE:** 3 | | | **PRODUCE:** 530 | |
| **MFG. CHANGE:** 5 | | | **BY DATE:** 4/87 | |
| **OPER. NO.** | **MACHINE** | **SETUP TIME** | **PIECE TIME** | **DESCRIPTION** |
| 010 | M1476 | 2.0 | .1475 | Saw to 18.0 length |
| 020 | M2746 | 1.0 | .0735 | Press flat on end |
| 025 | M3423 | 2.0 | .1830 | Drill 0.50 dia. hole |
| 030 | M8852 | 0.5 | .3250 | Turn thread |
| 040 | M9273 | 0.0 | .0080 | Wash |
| 050 | M2137 | 1.0 | .0445 | Heat treat |

*Figure 6.3.* Work order

by the first of April, 1987. The lot size which was ordered could be quite different from the standard lot size, because the order was for the quantity expected to be used over a given period of time, usually a month. The standard lot size was just an estimate for the purpose of designing a cost-effective production method.

## Preparation

When a set of work orders was to be issued (usually once a month), multilith copies were made of the associated production routings (*Figure 6.4*). The lot size and due date were added, and the resulting work order was sent to the shop.

A copy of the work order was delivered to each foreman in the shop. He/she received a copy of the work order for each part or subassembly which his/her machine line worked on. If a production routing prescribed the movement of a part over machines in three different machine lines, then three copies of the work order were sent to the factory.

The routing not only showed the foreman what quantity of parts had to be produced by a specific date, but the routing was a reminder of the processing steps for which he/she was responsible. Finally, it showed the foreman where

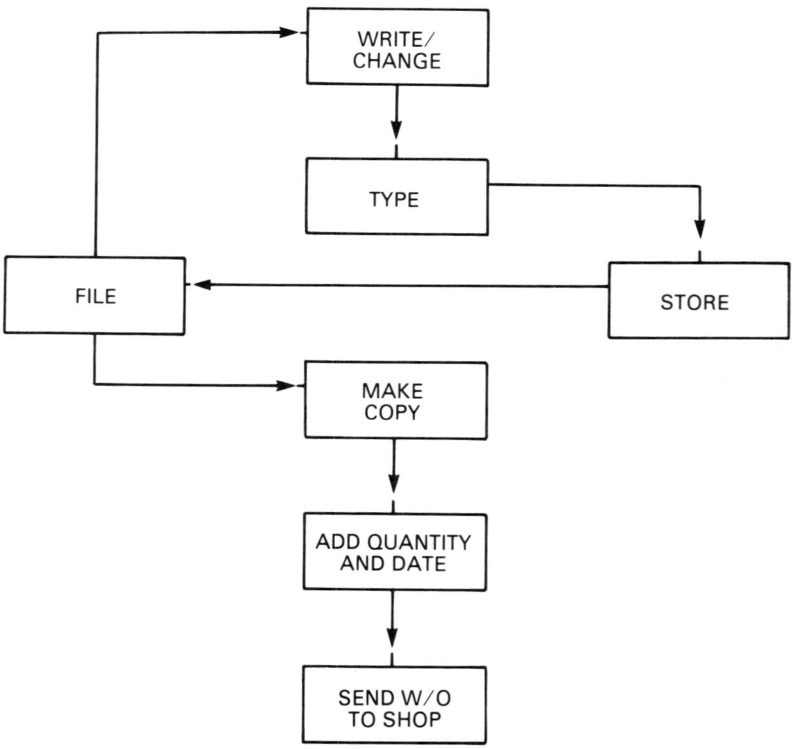


***Figure 6.4.*** Work order issue

to look for incoming material, since operations performed on other machine lines were also shown on the routing.

The reverse side of the routing contained a formatted "scratch pad" which made it relatively simple for the foreman to record daily progress in completing the work order.

## Exercise 6.1

Write down on a piece of paper the uses to which you think the data on a production routing or a work order could be put. Don't limit your thinking to the factory, but also consider the possible uses in the office and in support areas which provide materials and tooling. Indicate whether the use requires only the data on the production routing, or also requires the added two fields of data on the work order.

## Exercise 6.2

*Figure 6.5* shows some of the possible uses of the data on a production routing or a work order. The abbreviation "p/r" indicates a production routing, and the abbreviation "w/o" indicates a work order.

What characteristics of a computer make it a possible tool for accomplishing some of the uses which you have just listed?

| USE | TYPE |
|---|---|
| Calculate Costs | P/R |
| Calculate Load | W/O |
| Order Production | W/O |
| Order New Tooling | P/R |
| Plan Materials | W/O |

***Figure 6.5.*** Uses of production routing (P/R) and work order (W/O)

## Exercise 6.3

Of course, the computer is strong on speed and accuracy. The more data a person has to manipulate, the longer it takes, and the more likely the person is to make an error.

Extend the list from Exercise 6.5 to indicate added parameters for each possible use of production routings or work orders. Make headings labeled "quantity," "calculation," and "accuracy."

For each use, write down on the list whether the quantity of documents (p/r's or w/o's) required is "all," "some," or "one." Write down the type of calculation you think would be needed: "complex," "simple," or "none." Finally, write down the accuracy of calculation which is required: "accurate," "approximate," or "n/a" (not applicable).

## Exercise 6.4

*Figure 6.6* shows the results of Exercise 6.3 based upon the operating practices of one large manufacturer. The results are not absolute. They are only an indication of the possible advantages to be gained from the application of a computer to facilitate the use of production routings or work orders for the desired purposes.

Based on the results of Exercises 6.1 through 6.3, try to determine which uses have the potential of justifying the application of a computer.

| USE | TYPE | QUANTITY | CALCULATION | ACCURACY |
|---|---|---|---|---|
| Calculate Costs | P/R | Some | Complex | Accurate |
| Calculate Load | W/O | All | Complex | Approximate |
| Order Production | W/O | One | None | N/A |
| Order New Tooling | P/R | One | None | N/A |
| Plan Materials | W/O | All | Simple | Accurate |

***Figure 6.6.*** Characteristics of uses of P/R and W/O

## Potential Computer Applications

A computer could be a useful tool for the calculation of expected production costs from the use of production work orders. To calculate the cost of a single piece part, only a single routing is needed. But to calculate the cost of a welded assembly, data is needed from a number of routings—the routing for the assembly and the routings for the component parts of the assembly. The results of the calculation should be accurate to support the accurate pricing of the parts. The calculation of cumulative costs through the assembly of a number of items can be a bit complex.

The calculation of expected factory load from a set of work orders does not need to be extremely accurate, since personal performance of the machine operators is only expected to be within 5 to 10% of the planned time. But, all open (issued, but not yet completed) work orders are needed to perform the calculation. It also becomes rather complex to accumulate the burden of the various operations over the various machines. This becomes especially complex if there are machines which can be substituted for one another. The complexity and the volume of calculation would tend to justify the use of a computer for this function.

To order the production of a part, only a single work order is required. There is no calculation. The use of a computer is clearly not justified in this case.

The processing engineer uses a single production routing as a basis for ordering the design and/or procurement of new production tooling. There is no calculation required. Again, the use of a computer is not justified.

In order for the Material Planning and Purchasing department to order rough production materials, it needs the lot sizes and due dates of all work orders which are scheduled for issue. Although the calculation is relatively simple, the results must be accurate. The calculation involves an accumulation of quantities for any rough material which is used for several different parts. The use of a computer could be justified here.

Note that in the above discussion it is said that the use of a computer could be justified. The decision depends upon several factors. How many documents are involved? For a large company, "all work orders" could mean thousands of work orders. For a small company, "all work orders" could mean tens of work orders.

Even though one function does not justify the use of a computer, the accumulation of potential advantage from a number of functions could tip the balance. For example, if the work order is mechanized to support the planning of materials, the necessary data to support the calculation of rough material requirements is already included in the form.

## Rule of Thumb for Applicability of a Computer

The discussion on potential computer applications leads to a good rule of thumb. The use of a computer tends to be justified where data is used and reused in a variety of combinations for a variety of purposes. This sounds similar to the concepts behind a database, doesn't it?

## Case: Burden Calculation

*Figure 6.7* shows the flow of data involved in the use of a computer to support the calculation of work load or burden for a factory. The application was mechanized for several reasons. The volume of manufactured parts was very large. Therefore, the number of production routings was very large. In addition, burden was desired not only for the machines in the factory, but also for the various labor skills required to operate the machines.

The desired information was not the current load in the factory, but a projection of potential future workload. For this purpose, all production routings were used, as well as a projection of the quantity of each part number required for a given production schedule expected for a given future month. The load was calculated for machines and labor grades. In addition, the quantity of rough and purchased finished material requirements was calculated.

The change control of the routing was the same as described earlier—desk drawer control. When a routing was made effective, the contents of the routing were added to a magnetic tape file for use to calculate the burden. Any obsolete routing was deleted from the file.

When burden was to be calculated once each quarter, the routing file was processed against the estimate of future requirements.

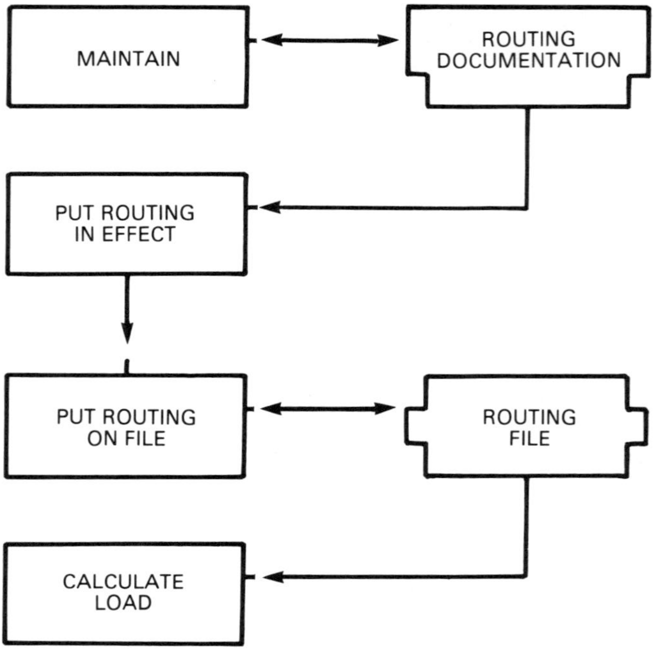


***Figure 6.7.*** Load calculation

---

## Exercise 6.5: Burden Calculation

Do you see any potential deficiencies in the system for burden calculation based upon the description in the section on burden calculation? Is all of the needed data available? Is it of the necessary quality? List any deficiencies you perceive to be possible. Also try to determine what might be done to overcome the deficiency.

---

**Problem 1.** The only routings in the tape file are those which are in effect. Therefore any calculation of future burden based upon expected but not released work orders is subject to error.

**Problem 2.** Future product and future changes to product would be in the master schedule used in the material requirements projection, but the process for manufacturing these components might not yet be documented.

***Solution 1.*** The computer system had to be upgraded to include future effective routings with a date control of effective changes.

***Solution 2.*** Temporary production routings had to be developed, based upon rough estimates of the processing steps and processing times for new or changed components. These were usually based upon the production routings of similar parts already in production.

## Case: Production Line Scheduling

*Figure 6.8* is an expansion of the flow of production routing data. It includes the support of a computer application to schedule the flow of work order operations in the shop. The intent was to optimize the flow of work in the shop. One objective was to avoid bottlenecks where a fast machining process might be starved for materials by a slower machine. Another objec-

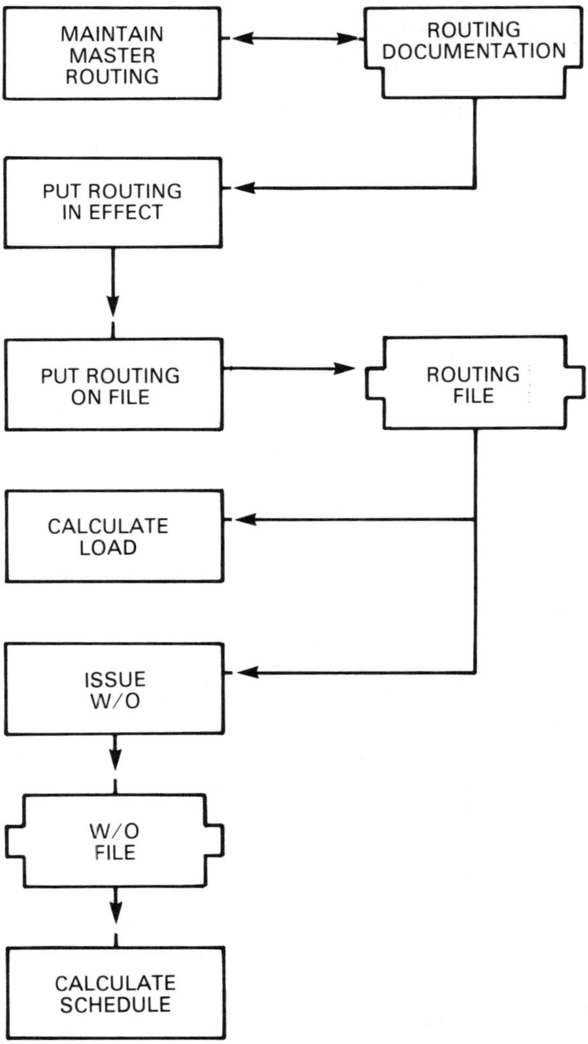


***Figure 6.8.*** Production line scheduling

tive was to spread work among similar machines wherever possible. A third and most important objective was to complete all production parts on time as authorized by the work orders. Not all areas of the shop were scheduled, only those where the flow of work was difficult for the foreman to manage through manual work scheduling techniques.

After the work orders were issued by adding the quantity and due date data to the production routings, the resulting work order data was also retained on a disk file to support the production line scheduling application. In fact, there were two files which were used, the routing file and a brief file containing the quantity and due date data from the work orders.

The calculation of the production line schedule took into account all open work orders. It also considered the degree of completion of the various operations at the time of the calculation. In addition, it was necessary to take into account the availability of production machines, tools, and rough materials. This data was manually recorded from the shop floor immediately prior to the calculation.

---

## Exercise 6.6: Production Line Scheduling

Do you see any potential deficiencies in the system for production line scheduling? Is all of the needed data available? Is it of the necessary quality? List any possible deficiencies which you perceive. Also try to determine what might be done to overcome the deficiencies.

---

**Problem 1.** The times on the work orders were unreliable. Because the routings were not kept current with the shop, and because the calculation of burdens required only approximate accuracy, erroneous times had not been detected and corrected. A common error was recording 0.1 hour of setup when 1.0 was intended. The result of this error was insignificant to burden calculation, since only approximate accuracy was required, but it caused significant inaccuracy in the resulting work schedule.

**Problem 2.** The foreman tended not to follow the calculated schedule. The foreman was measured on performance, calculated as the number of labor hours it required to produce a given amount of work. Performance was expressed as a percent of the expected standard hours calculated from the work order. It didn't take long for the foreman to realize that his performance would suffer unless he sought out those operations where his experience told him that he could beat the standards. He called these "gravy jobs." This, of course, frustrated the intent of the calculated schedule.

**Problem 3.** The manual process of reading the status of work on the shop floor was time-consuming and error-prone. The resulting error hindered the calculation of a reliable schedule. It motivated the foreman to use the short list as a priority setting device, rather than follow the calculated schedule. The short list was a list of those parts which were in short supply for product assembly.

***Solution 1.*** The production routing of each area to be scheduled was reviewed against current shop practices to identify and correct all data deficiencies. It became necessary to change the standard procedure of only updating a routing with the implementation of new or changed production processes. The production routing had to be updated when any deviation was implemented in actual factory practices.

***Solution 2.*** The primary measurement of the foreman had to be changed to one which would motivate him to follow the schedule. The obvious answer was to measure the foreman on the extent to which he followed the schedule. This was a difficult change for upper management to accept. All previous experience in evaluating a foreman was by the performance measure. If this doesn't seem reasonable, ask the following question. How long would it take you to learn to comprehend temperature in Celsius measure with 22° being a comfortable air temperature, and 37° being the normal body temperature?

***Solution 3.*** The answer to this problem would be to have automatic feedback of the status of work and supplies from the shop floor. It was many years before this solution could be implemented due to economic and technical constraints. It was justified on the basis of its value for work measurement, rather than its value for providing data to support shop scheduling. The use of the data for one purpose enhances the value of its use for another purpose. This is in accord with the rule of thumb for applicability of a computer.

## Case: Performance and Data Collection

*Figure 6.9* shows the flow of work order data expanded to include additional uses. The work order file (quantity and due date) was now expanded to include all of the routing data. The file was used by the computer to produce reporting cards for use in the shop to report the progress of operations.

The report card was inserted into a shop floor terminal to automatically report the beginning or completion of a setup. It was inserted into the terminal and a quantity was entered into a keyboard to report the completion of any portion of a lot size across an operation. A personal badge was also inserted into the terminal by the operators to report their arrival or departure from the work area and to identify who was reporting work completed.

The report of completed work, including setups and partially completed operations, was matched against the reports of attendance to calculate individual and group performance. This report was used daily by the foreman to evaluate work effort.

---

## Exercise 6.7: Performance and Data Collection

Do you see any potential deficiencies in the system for performance and data collection? Is all of the needed data available? Is it of the necessary quality? List any deficiencies which you perceive to be possible. Also try to determine what might be done to overcome the deficiencies.

---

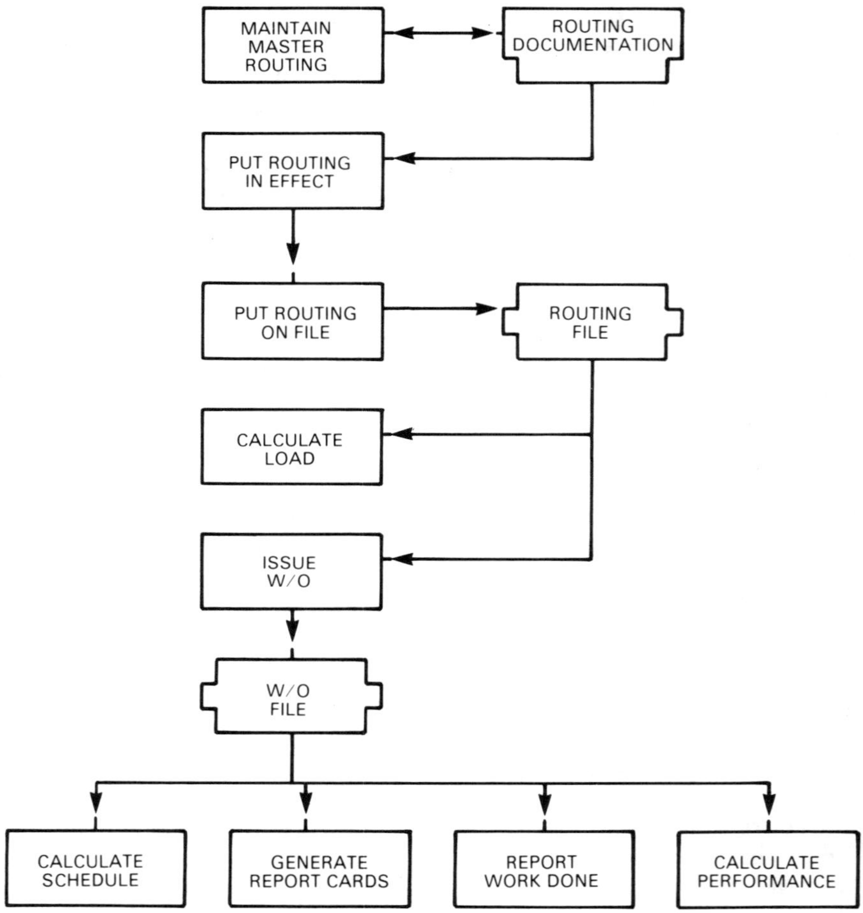


***Figure 6.9.*** Performance and data collection

**Problem 1.** The requirement for accuracy of work order times was even more stringent when the data was used to calculate a daily measurement of individual performance. Any low performance which could be blamed upon data errors resulted in protests from the workers, and from the foreman. Of course, any error in the opposite direction was rarely reported.

**Problem 2.** The worker was told one time standard by the work order paper, but could be told a different time standard by the report card. The reason for this was that there were dual sources for the data.

***Solution 1.*** The time discrepancies had to be manually reviewed and corrected again, just as they were for shop scheduling. Since scheduling was not done for all parts, the unscheduled parts had a greater amount of error to correct.

***Solution 2.*** The error potential from manual transcription of data had to be minimized. For this reason, the work order system was modified. It was changed to print the work order from the routing file in place of printing it from a multilith copy of the paper routing. Thus, when an error was discovered and corrected, the correct time appeared in both the work order and in the report card.

## Case: Tool Usage Analysis

*Figure 6.10* shows the expanded flow of data which would be required to support a requested computer application to project the expected amount of tool usage in the shop. It was desired to more accurately control the volume of durable tools, such as fixtures, and of perishable tools, such as milling cutters.

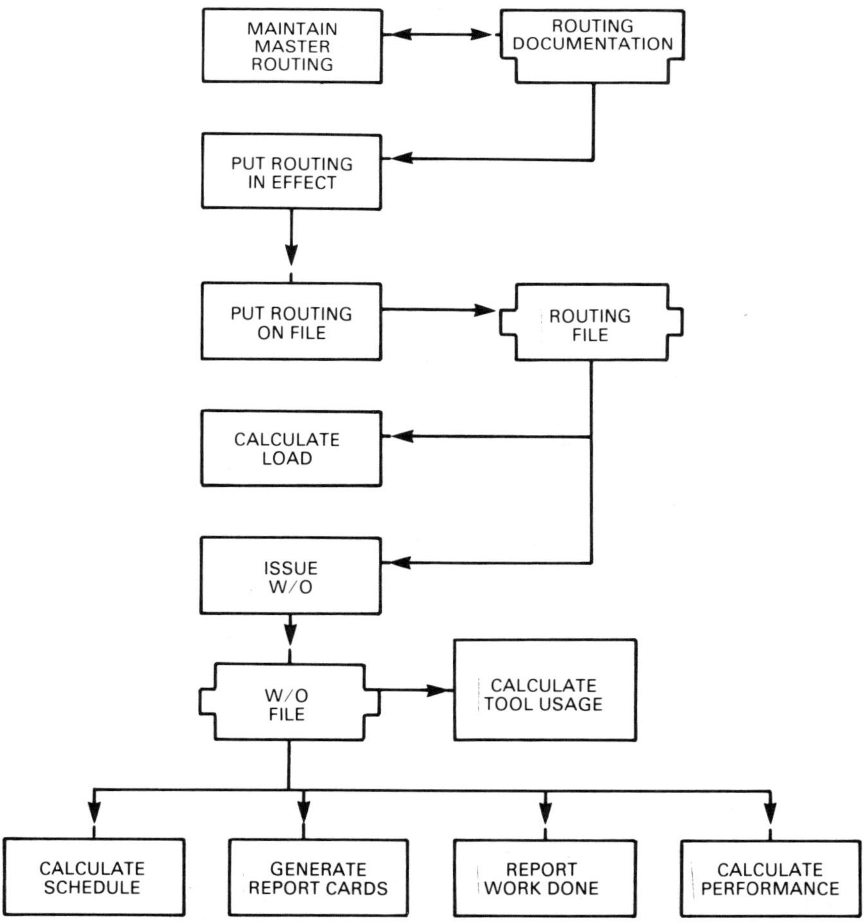


***Figure 6.10.*** Tool usage calculation

The projection was to be based upon the need for a given durable tool by different operations at the same time, as determined by a calculated production schedule. The basis of burden for perishable tools was to be the historic rate of consumption in the completion of past work orders.

---

## Exercise 6.8: Tool Usage Analysis

Do you see any potential deficiencies in the proposed system for tool usage analysis? Is all of the needed data available? Is it of the necessary quality? List any deficiencies which you perceive to be possible. Also try to determine what might be done to overcome the deficiencies.

---

**Problem 1.** The basic tool data was not recorded on the paper routing or in the routing file in a disciplined fashion, but only in the operation description as free-form text. This made it virtually impossible to deal with the data by computer for calculation purposes.

***Solution 1.*** The tool data would have to be recorded in the routing file as disciplined data. This means that special fields would have to be set aside on the form and in the data file to list the tools required.

> **LAW**
>
> **Data is Only as Accurate as its Use Requires.**
>
> It is unlikely that data will be any more accurate than required for its immediately intended use.

This law states that it is unlikely that data will be any more accurate than required for its immediately intended use. People are unwilling to make the extra effort to ensure data accuracy for some future potential function if there is no immediate benefit, or if there is no penalty to be paid for not providing the desired data. If the results of data inaccuracy are immediate and painful, then the data will be corrected.

It should be obvious from the described cases that this law is valid.

---

## Exercise 6.9

Can you illustrate the law, Data is Only as Accurate as its Use Requires, from your own experience? It applies to many circumstances, whether a computer is involved or not.

---

> **LAW**
>
> **Manual Data Transcription is Error-prone.**
>
> The manual transcription of data from one medium to another is subject to some degree of error.

According to this law, any manual transcription of data from one medium to another is subject to some degree of error. This is true enough in an office environment, but is amplified in a noisy and distracting environment such as a shop floor.

Experiments have demonstrated that error rates in a shop floor environment can be as high as 6%. That is, if an inventory count is made and reported, there is a 6% chance that the wrong part number would be written, a 6% chance that the wrong storage location would be written, and a 6% chance that the wrong quantity would be written.

---

### Exercise 6.10

Consider that you are taking inventory of production materials on the shop floor. You are counting and recording the quantity of parts in bins. You report the quantity of part 124876 in two different bins. Presume that you make an accurate count in each case, but you are subject to normal data transcription error when recording the results.

1. What are the chances that the resulting records are correct for each bin? What is the chance of accuracy for the total bin inventory of the part?
2. What is the probability that there will be a resulting error in the record of some other part?

---

**LAW**

**Mechanically Available Data Generates New Uses.**

The eventual volume of use of a database is about twice that which is normally anticipated when the database is first established.

The thrust of this law is that if a fund of data is available in mechanized form, its presence will cause someone to have an idea for new uses to which the data could be put. The series of described cases are an illustration of this law. In practice it seems that the number of uses is about twice that which is envisioned when the data is first captured in mechanical form, especially if it is stored in a database structure.

Can you think of examples of this law from your own experience?

## The Production Routing Database System

The production routing in the case study gradually evolved from a paper form of relatively little function to a database application with a great deal of function. It might be instructive to examine the differences.

The paper routing contained a reasonable amount of data about the processing steps for a part. The data was arranged for convenience of visual use by the processor and the production foreman. The original data files were designed to store the data in similar fashion. But, as the computer applications evolved around the production routing file, it became necessary to arrange the data quite differently. It was arranged to make it convenient for the computer to access data. The paper routing was only one of many outputs of the system.

Data which had no specific discipline had to be reorganized to make it understandable to the computer. The undisciplined description of the operations and required tools is an example.

As the routing became a database, the door was opened to significant new uses, including functions which required data never typed on the original paper production routing. This included delivery location, inspection instructions, inspection tools, bin locations, weld specifications, instructions, and quantities. It also included identification of alternate processing centers, numerical control programs, coordinate measuring machine programs, and packaging materials and instructions. It can include just about anything that might in any way be associated with the production of component parts and subassemblies.

## Production Routing in CIM

The paper production routing in computer integrated manufacturing (CIM) is dead. So is the paper work order, as will become apparent. The production routing has become a process database or a manufacturing plan database.

The just-in-time concept will lead to the assembly of component parts into modules which will in turn be assembled into larger modules. The final product might or might not be assembled on a moving assembly line, but it is certain that fewer components will be stocked at the location of the final assembly. The assembly process will gradually merge into the manufacturing process. Just-completed gears will be installed onto just-completed shafts. The just-completed shaft assemblies will be installed into just-completed transmission housings. And so it will go.

This radical change in the production process will remove the need for, or value of, separate databases for parts and line assemblies. The single manufacturing plan database will contain any process-related data which is of value. As individual factory functions are placed under computer control, the need for anything like a paper routing is reduced. The paper, if needed at all, is used to install the processes, not to operate them.

## The Manufacturing Plan Database

The manufacturing plan database describes the production process for the benefit of the processor, the tool designer, the scheduler, the foreman, the engineer who installs machines, the part programmer, the inspector, and the computer which controls any aspect of a production process. The database contains all data required for these functions. It probably doesn't contain graphics data or part programs though it does certainly contain a record telling what versions of graphics images and parts programs are current and planned. It also holds data which tells where these files are stored.

The process plan will be organized on any of one to three levels, depending upon the degree of sophistication of the production processes involved.

The first level of process description is an atomic level in which the separate processing steps are described with standard terminology and specific variable data. The phrase "cut to length" is an example of a standard text (probably represented in the computer by a shorthand code). The specific variable data is the particular length of stock to be cut for the part in question.

Note that the operation description does not specify what type of machine is to be used. The description will probably also contain a tolerance dimension for the cut length. The size of the stock, the length of the part, and the tolerance for the length are all parameters which describe the capabilities required in the equipment which will be selected to perform the operation.

The second level of process description is a list of the cells which have the capability of performing the full set of operations to produce the part. If a cell does not have a machine capable of producing a length of part as described in the cut to length operation, that cell is not on the list. The times and costs associated with production of the part are recorded along with the identification of the capable cells. Different cells have different production efficiencies for a specific part.

The third level of process description is a list of the alternate machines within each cell which can perform each specific operation to required tolerances. Time and cost variances from the ideal are recorded.

The obvious intent of such a database is to provide flexibility in the production of parts and assemblies. The most cost-effective process will be selected for a given production task as long as the equipment is in an operational status and is not overburdened. If either criterion is not met, the best available optional process will be selected.

## The Manufacturing Capability Database

The "issuing of work orders" in a CIM factory is really the assignment of work to the most cost-effective and time-effective cell and machine within a cell. For this reason, the Manufacturing Plan Database must be supplemented with a Manufacturing Capability Database.

The Manufacturing Capability Database contains parameters describing the capability, burden, and availability of production facilities. It is organized on two levels.

The first level of manufacturing capability is a description of the capabilities of manufacturing and assembly cells. It includes data regarding the size of objects which can be handled and the accuracy of dimensions which can be produced.

The second level of manufacturing capability is a description of individual machines within cells. It includes data regarding the size of objects which can be handled, the part features which can be produced, the speed and feed ranges that are most effective, and the tolerances which can be met.

This database has more value than just driving production. The tolerance and cost capability parameters will serve as reference data to the design engineers as they design new products. The design engineers will be aided in the design of parts which can be produced at a profit. This is an example of the concept of *manufacturability*.

## Summary

The economics of data use in computerized form depend upon the data's value to speed calculation and to enhance the accuracy of calculation. The greater the volume of data to be processed, the greater the potential of cost avoidance and error avoidance.

Rule of thumb—The more data that is used and reused in various combinations for various purposes, the more likely that computer use is justified.

**LAW—Data is Only as Accurate as its Use Requires.** People are unwilling to provide data for another part of the organization unless they receive a reward or a punishment based upon the accuracy and the timeliness of the data.

**LAW—Manual Data Transcription is Error-Prone.** The manual copying of data is subject to error, especially in a noisy and distracting environment.

**LAW—Mechanically Available Data Generates New Uses.** The eventual volume of use of a database is about twice that which is normally anticipated when the database is first established.

In CIM, the production routing will be replaced by a *Manufacturing Plan Database* and a companion *Manufacturing Capability Database*. These databases will support the assignment of production tasks and the computer control of production processes where appropriate. The capabilities of the production processes, as described in the second database, will be used as reference data to aid in the cost-effective design of new parts and assemblies.

# 7

# *Project Phases*

## Introduction

There is a tendency for people to take on large projects without an adequate perspective of the amount of work to be done, or of the possible complexities which are yet to be discovered. The purpose of this chapter is to help the user realize this tendency, and to recognize the advantages of addressing a project in phases. This is particularly appropriate for projects to develop mechanized information systems.

## Manufacturing Systems

As the reader might have deduced from the previous chapter, manufacturing management is inclined to view systems as their property, and not the property of the company. In this they are really no different from the management of most any other functional area. The systems are usually viewed as departmental systems, without much perspective on how they serve the business as a whole.

The work flow in a manufacturing company is not managed by independent systems, nor by several sets of integrated systems, but by one overall system structure. If there were no overall system structure, the business could not function.

The ideas of these last two paragraphs seem to be diametrically opposed. Not so. There is an overall system structure in any reasonably successful business. The fact that it exists does not imply that it is perceived by the average line manager, or by any manager for that matter. No manager sees the whole systems structure of the business. The typical manager perceives an "environment," not a structure.

In the typical business, departmental systems are interfaced where they are not integrated. Each department makes up in its own way for the inadequacies in the information provided to it by neighboring departments. This compensation becomes a habit over time. Unanswered complaints die away, and alternate methods are found to satisfy departmental needs. Sometimes this takes the form of extra effort to correct errors and to add missing information. Other times, unfortunately, the alternate method involves development of a second, redundant source of the needed information. This is especially unfortunate when the responsible source of the information continues to expend the effort—and money—to provide information which is not used or usable.

There is a wealth of opportunity for intelligent and efficient management of information within a manufacturing company. This is because the manufacturing process is an additive process. Data can be added to a database as work progresses through various functional areas. Consider the product development cycle. The specifications of a product lead to the design of a product, which leads to the design of the production processes for the product, which leads to the inspection and testing procedures for the product. This is also true about the production cycle. A master production schedule leads to the material requirements planning process, which leads to the materials management and distribution process, which leads to the machining and assembly functions, which finally lead to the product sale and shipment functions. A manufacturing company is naturally suited for the use of database concepts. But the development of database systems (obviously, mechanized systems) poses serious project management challenges. The development projects are usually large and complex.

---

## Exercise 7.1

Write down a list of 10 or 15 major activities which would have to be performed by a person who decided to build a custom-designed house. The process begins with the concept and concludes with moving in and keeping the house in a state of good repair. In the interim, there is the need for site selection, architect, contractor, etc.

---

## House Building Phases

The phases of development of a house can serve as an analogy for the phases of development of an information system. One example of the phases usually included in the building of a house is shown in *Figure 7.1*. It is by no means an authoritative list, but a reasonable example.

1. Concept of the Type of House
2. Evaluation of Economic Feasibility
3. Description to Architect
4. Site Selection
5. Design by Architect
6. Bids by Contractors
7. Construction
8. Moving In
9. Correcting Discrepancies
10. Ongoing Maintenance

***Figure 7.1.*** House building phases

## Exercise 7.2

Why do projects such as the building of a house or the building of a mechanized information system tend to be managed in phases? What is it about such projects that leads to a phased approach to the development effort?

## The Need for Phases

The reasons for breaking a project into phases are shown in *Figure 7.2*. Reference to the house building tasks in *Figure 7.1* should help to illustrate the concepts.

1. Complexity
2. Differing Skills
3. Progress Checkpoints
4. Cost/Benefit Analysis

***Figure 7.2.*** Reasons for project phases

The very complexity of a project can make it necessary to break it up into phases so that the work can be comprehended and planned. The most complex project can be handled if it is broken down into manageable tasks.

Totally different skills might be required at different times in the progress of a project. The completion of work of one type makes it possible to begin work of a different type. The house building scenario illustrates the point.

Once the potential house owner has completed the description of the basic requirements, the architect has the information required to design the house. Once the architect has designed the house, the necessary information is available for the contractors to prepare bids, and then for a single contractor to build the house. Obviously, there are natural break points in the information flow (or sometimes in the material flow) where one phase of activity is completed and another is able to begin. Usually these phase break points occur where skill needs change.

A project which is exceptionally long can easily be far out of control without being detected. For this reason, prudent managers break work into phases—sometimes arbitrary phases. They do this so that there are points in time where specific, measurable tasks are to be completed. The key idea here is to have clearly identified and tangible products or deliverables (material or information) which serve as tangible demonstrations of work completion—checkpoints of progress.

The larger and the more complex that a project is, the more difficult it is to reliably determine either the required investment or the expected return. If a project is broken into phases, the completion of each phase provides a new opportunity to reassess the economics of the whole project with refined information.

---

## Exercise 7.3

How long do you think a project or a phase should be in terms of calendar time? What factors do you think determine the practical limits of the length of time a specific package of work can be allowed to take?

---

## Phase Length Factors

If a project or a phase of a project is too long, then there is the possibility that the requirements can change. It is not uncommon for a manager of a function to sponsor the development of a new computer application and then be moved to a new assignment before the software is finished. The replacement manager often has his or her own ideas on how to operate the function. It is not uncommon for the software development project to be significantly redirected, or even cancelled.

It is not only management which can change. The environment also changes. The product of a lengthy project can be obsolete even before it is delivered. This is not a trivial point. The business environment is changing faster than it ever has before.

The longer a project or a phase of a project is, the more likely that there could be turnover in key personnel. This can result in a significant loss of continuity. If there is turnover at the completion of a phase, at least there is a completed set of material to pass on to the new staff for the next phase.

Reasonably spaced phases of a project can provide a convenient means for tangible measurement of progress. The completion of a defined package of work (a deliverable) makes it possible to measure performance and to review plans and schedules for future effort.

The longer a project takes, the more likely that the sponsor of the project can become uncomfortable about the likelihood of the final product meeting his or her expectations. If some usable amount of the final product can be delivered early, it can be a significant confidence builder. This is not so much a phase of a project as it is the delivery of a usable module of the final product.

## Rule of Thumb for Length of a Project or Phase

Some dimensions can put these cautionary statements into perspective. Experience has demonstrated that an information systems project must generally be completed within eighteen months. If not, it is subject to changing requirements fróm changing management or changing environment. Indeed, if a project takes as long as five years, it is possible for changes to be of such magnitude that new changes will be demanded before the first are completed. An endless cycle of change is theoretically possible.

A general rule of thumb for the length of a phase of a project is six months.

If it is necessary for a project or a phase to be longer than eighteen months or six months respectively, then it is prudent to attempt to define and deliver usable modules.

## Phases vs. Modules

Phases are discrete steps toward an end goal of completion of a project. Modules are delivered, usable subsets of the final product. The difference is illustrated in *Figure 7.3*. In the figure, each of three modules is developed in a series of phases, probably similar sequences of activity. There are not only three series of phases, but there is also an ongoing task of planning and coordinating.

A practical example might be a complete information system (*Figure 3.4*). A first module could be the bill of material system. A second module could be the inventory on-hand system. A third phase could be the requirements planning system. A fourth phase could be the test count system. Note that the

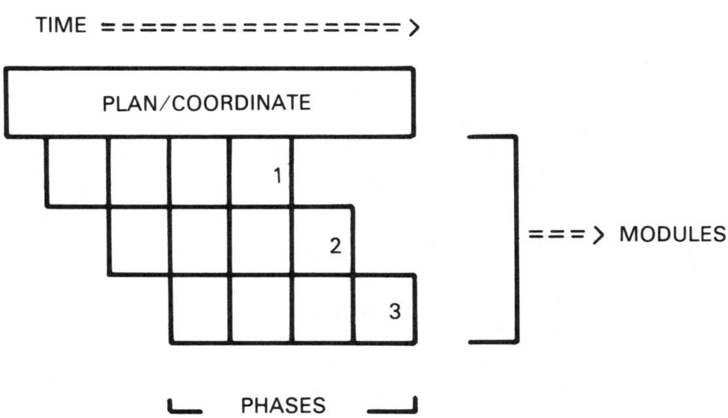


***Figure 7.3.*** Phases and modules

first module can stand alone, the second module uses the output of the first, the third uses the output of the second, and the fourth uses the output of the third. Indeed, the fourth module is of no use until the third module has been operating for some time.

---

### Exercise 7.4

With all of the discussion of the length of the phases of development of a computer system, what are they? The house building example in *Figure 7.1* provides a clue. Can you suggest what might be corresponding phases for an information system, particularly for a mechanized information system?

---

## Phases of Computer System Development

*Figure 7.4* lists the usual phases of development and operation of a mechanized information system. If a project is quite small, some of the phases might be indistinguishable from one another. This is because the amount of work and the time requirement may be small. The phases are most clearly identified by their products—the deliverables.

1. Prefeasibility
2. Feasibility
3. Definition
4. Design
5. Construction
6. Installation
7. Post-implementation
8. Support

***Figure 7.4.*** Development phases of computer systems

## Prefeasibility Phase

The prefeasibility phase (*Figure 7.5*) can be very brief, a moment of insight or inspiration, or it can be a long research process. Its primary deliverable is a concept of a new system function—some better way of conducting the business. Once the idea has been generated, it is necessary to lay out a work plan to explore the practicality of the idea and to make a corresponding cost estimate of the work to be done to evaluate the idea.

1. Concept of System Function
2. Work Plan of Next Phase
3. Cost Estimate of Next Phase

***Figure 7.5.*** Prefeasibility deliverables

## Feasibility Phase

In the feasibility phase (*Figure 7.6*), the first serious effort is made to assess the practicality of the concept for a new computer system. This is evaluated by two criteria, economic validity and practical workability. Can real people make the concept operate profitably in other than a laboratory environment? This is a phase in which one asks, "How much gold is there in those hills?", and "How can I mine it practically?"

1. Assessment of Technical Workability
2. Economic Evaluation of Project
3. Work Plan of Next Phase
4. Cost Estimate of Next Phase

***Figure 7.6.*** Feasibility deliverables

If the results of the feasibility study are positive, a work plan and cost estimate must be prepared for the next phase of development of the idea.

Note that in this phase the first rough estimate is developed of the economic value of the idea. This includes an estimate of the total investment which will be required to convert the idea into an operating system. It also includes an estimate of the payback from the effort. The payback is sometimes an increase in direct profit. Most often it is a reduction in operating expenses.

## Definition Phase

The primary output of the definition phase (*Figure 7.7*) is a description of the user requirements. This includes a description of the required services and is most often expressed in terms of data input and output formats, processing schedules for the delivery of output, and a broad design concept for the method of calculation of the output.

IBM calls this phase of a project the "external specifications" phase. It results in a description of the operation of the envisioned system from the user's viewpoint. This is done without significant concern about how the

1. User Requirements
2. Input and Output Formats
3. Processing Schedules
4. Broad Design Concept
5. Work Plan of Next Phase
6. Cost Estimate of Next Phase
7. Economic Evaluation of Project

***Figure 7.7.*** Definition deliverables

defined function is to be delivered. The system is described as a "black box" to perform specific tasks.

At the end of this phase, a work plan is developed for the next phase, and a cost estimate is made of the next phase. Since the project has progressed, it is also possible at this phase to make a more refined evaluation of the economic value of the expected system. At this phase, and at every succeeding phase, it is possible to make an ever more accurate judgement as to whether or not it is worthwhile to continue the effort.

## Design Phase

The design phase (*Figure 7.8*) results in the description of how the system will be built. It corresponds to the work of the architect in the house building project.

1. Database Layout
2. Processing Rules
3. Program Design
4. Testing Requirements
5. Work Plan of Next Phase
6. Cost Estimate of Next Phase
7. Economic Evaluation of Project

***Figure 7.8.*** Design deliverables

The database is designed to serve all of the envisioned data needs of the defined services. The critical logical steps in the development of system output are expressed in terms of processing rules, formulas, or algorithms. The structure of the major programs is established. These are the sequences of major logical steps which will direct the computer.

A set of test data and a testing plan are developed to verify that the final system product performs the required functions reliably.

IBM calls this phase of a project the "internal specifications" phase. It describes what happens inside the black box.

As in preceding phases, this one concludes with a work plan, a cost estimate of the next phase, and a refinement of the economic evaluation of the project. If the decision is to continue, work proceeds to the next, construction phase.

## Construction Phase

The component parts of a mechanized system take form in the construction phase (*Figure 7.9*). The programs are written and tested. Instructions are written for the user so that the programs can be given the input they need to perform their tasks. Instructions are also written for those people who operate the computer. These include how to load and back-up databases, how to respond to messages to load printers, and how to monitor the operation of other peripheral devices.

1. Programs
2. Operations Instructions
3. User Instructions
4. Completed Tests
5. Work Plan of Next Phase
6. Cost Estimate of Next Phase
7. Economic Evaluation of Project

***Figure 7.9.*** Construction deliverables

One last time, this phase also concludes with a work plan, a cost estimate of the next phase, and a refinement of the economic evaluation of the project. If the decision is to continue, work proceeds to the next, installation phase.

## Installation Phase

This phase (*Figure 7.10*) is sometimes called the implementation phase. It can occur repeatedly if the system is to be installed in a number of locations. Old files of data must be converted into the new database format required by the new system. The users and the computer operators are trained in the new operating procedures. Final tests are conducted by the users to verify from their viewpoint that the system reliably performs the expected functions.

1. Converted Data Files
2. Trained Users
3. Completed User Tests
4. Statement of User Acceptance
5. Economic Evaluation of Project

***Figure 7.10.*** Installation deliverables

If the system passes all checks, the user certifies in some fashion that the final product is acceptable. This might be in the form of a final payment of charges for a purchased system, or it might be as simple as a handshake for a small, internally developed system.

At the conclusion of this phase, the project is complete for all practical purposes. The total costs of implementation are known. This makes it possible to put one more polishing touch on the calculation of the expected value of the system.

## Post-implementation Phase

This phase is not really a part of the development process of an information system. It is a preparation for the next systems project. The purpose of the post-implementation phase is to review what has been done in order to improve the systems development process.

The primary tasks of this phase (*Figure 7.11*) are audits to verify the degree to which the new system performs the target functions as expected. The actual

1. Audit of System Performance
2. Audit of Development Costs
3. Audit of Operating Costs
4. Audit of System Value

***Figure 7.11.*** Post-implementation deliverables

costs of development are compared with the estimates to determine the causes of unexpected variances. The operating costs are calculated, including both user and data processing costs. These are compared with earlier estimates to compute actual return-on-investment.

For this exercise to be of value, the system should be in production for six to twelve months. This delay is necessary so that the operation of the system has settled down to a relatively mature and consistent process.

If the system is to be installed in a number of different facilities, the post-implementation phase has the possibility of immediate payback in terms of improved installation practices. Other benefits can be further improvements in the operation of the system, and ideas for more effective development of future systems.

## Support Phase

In the support phase (*Figure 7.12*), the system is adjusted as needed to adapt to changes in the environment, and to changes in the needs of the users. The "environment" includes the business and legal climate in which the company operates, and the technological world of computer and communications equipment. Both are changing today at an unprecedented rate.

1. Corrections
2. User Assistance
3. Feasibility of Expanded Function

***Figure 7.12.*** Support deliverables

Many of the changes to the system will be in the form of corrections. These are based upon maturity of experience in the use of the system by the user. These corrections are also based upon experience in the operation of the system by the data processor.

Many of the problems faced by users can be resolved by clarification of the procedures through which the process is managed. This requires assistance to the user by both the data processor and by a center of systems knowledge within the user organization itself.

As stated in the law in Chapter 6, "Mechanically available data generates new uses." This phase includes the evaluation of numerous potential extensions and expansions of the originally defined functions.

## Exercise 7.5

Of all of the responsibilities represented in the various phases of development of a mechanized system, which ones are the responsibility of the users, and which ones are the responsibility of the data processing or systems organization?

## Phase Responsibilities

The responsibilities which devolve upon any portion of the organization are a function of the expertise of that portion of the organization. Refer to *Figure 7.13*.

**Prefeasibility Phase.** The idea for a new system can come from any organization, but the Data Processing department has primary responsibility (and expertise) for developing a work plan for the exploration of the practicality and economic validity of the idea.

**Feasibility Phase.** The user organization has the primary responsibility for evaluating the economic worth of the proposed system. The Data Processing department is primarily responsible for determining the workability of the idea. The Data Processing department is also responsible for determining the work plan for further development of the idea, if the proposal is demonstrated to be worth exploring in detail.

**Definition Phase.** The users are the ones who are responsible for the systems by which they manage. Thus, they have the primary responsibility for defining the requirements of the new system. This includes a description of the functions which the system will perform. It also includes a description of the input and output media and formats. The user will normally require significant assistance from the data processor in completing these tasks, since the typical user doesn't work with this level of technology every day.

The data processor has the technical expertise to determine how to produce the desired function. Therefore, the data processor is responsible for determining the processing schedules for the computer and for determining the basic design of the system. This includes selection of the type of computer or computers, the design of the database, and the selection of the programming language and the database management software.

**Design Phase.** The design phase is primarily a data processing phase, because the emphasis is not so much on the function of the planned system, but on how to deliver the function through the use of a computer. At this phase, the data processors design the details of the database structure. They develop a detailed design of the logic of each program, and define the testing requirements to verify that the resulting programs will reliably perform their function.

As a part of the program design, the user refines the rules for the processing of the information. An example of such rules might be the method of determining lot sizes or safety stock in a requirements calculation.

As in previous phases, the data processor is responsible for the work plan for the next phase, and the user for reviewing the economic justification.

| PHASE | USER | ANALYST |
|---|---|---|
| Prefeasibility | J - Concept<br>J - Work Plan | J - Concept<br>P - Work Plan |
| Feasibility | P - Justification<br>J - Workability<br>J - Work Plan | J - Justification<br>P - Workability<br>P - Work Plan |
| Definition | P - Requirements<br>P - I/O Formats<br>J - Process Schedules<br><br>J - Work Plan<br>P - Justification | <br><br>P - Process Schedules<br>P - Design Concept<br>P - Work Plan<br>J - Justification |
| Design | P - Rules<br><br><br><br>J - Work Plan<br>P - Justification | J - Rules<br>P - Database Layout<br>P - Program Design<br>P - Test Requirements<br>P - Work Plan<br>J - Justification |
| Construction | <br><br>P - User Instructions<br>J - Testing<br>J - Work Plan<br>P - Justification | P - Programs<br>P - Operations Instructions<br>J - User Instructions<br>P - Testing<br>P - Work Plan<br>J - Justification |
| Implementation | J - Conversion<br>P - User Training<br>P - Testing<br>P - Acceptance | P - Conversion<br>J - User Training<br>J - Testing |
| Post-implementation | P - Performance<br><br>J - Operation Costs<br>P - Value Analysis | <br>P - Development Costs<br>J - Operation Costs<br>J - Value Analysis |
| Support | J - Corrections<br>P - User Assistance<br>J - Enhancements | J - Corrections<br>J - User Assistance<br>J - Enhancements |

***Figure 7.13.*** Phase responsibilities

This is the last phase where it would be reasonable to expect the systems project to be cancelled due to economic infeasibility. The major problems have been identified and resolved by this phase. In addition, the next phase will complete the major portion of the investment, and will deliver usable programs.

**Construction Phase.** In the construction phase, the data processor is responsible for delivering usable software. The user representative is responsible for delivering the materials required to train and support those who will be using the system.

The data processor completes and tests the programs to verify that the defined functions are reliably performed. The data processor also develops a set of instructions for those who will be operating the computer. This includes start up and shut down procedures, data backup and recovery procedures, and data security procedures.

The user representative develops user training materials and reference materials for user assistance at workstations. The user also assists in the testing to verify that the programs deliver the defined functions, and to verify that the screens and reports are truly usable.

As before, the data processor is responsible for developing the work plan for the next phase. The user is responsible for a final check of the economics. Here, the emphasis is on refining the estimate of operating costs, since this is the first time that a reasonable measure can be made of computer processing volumes and costs.

**Implementation Phase.** During the implementation phase, the data processor is responsible for converting all old data files to the new data formats required by the new system. The planning and programming for this had been done in the construction phase.

The user representative completes the training of all those who will be using the system. Their first use of the system completes the testing of the system with actual, converted data, and true volumes of data as will be experienced in normal processing. Finally, the chief user expresses acceptance of the new system by signing some sort of acceptance document. This formality is less necessary within a company than it is between a user and an outside contractor of computer software. The agreement signifies the transition from a period of free correction of system bugs to a period of payment for improvements.

The completion of the implementation phase is the end of the development cycle, but there are two more phases to the total life cycle of a mechanized system.

**Post-implementation Phase.** It is a good idea for the user and the data processor to review what they have accomplished six to twelve months after completion of the installation. At that time the user can speak from experience regarding the true performance and value of the system. Also at that time, the data processor can add up the total development costs and assist the user in summing the operating costs.

The purpose of this post-implementation phase is to improve the systems building process by identifying what has been done well, and by learning from the mistakes. Obviously, the exercise is of most value to the data processor, who will probably be developing other mechanized systems with all departments.

**Support Phase.** While the system is being used in production, there is need to provide ongoing support. The user organization has the primary responsibility to provide daily troubleshooting and counsel to those who push the buttons and read the reports. Both the user and the data processor share in the responsibility to correct latent bugs, to upgrade the system as required with environment changes, and to evaluate any new ideas for enhancement or addition to the functions of the system.

## Availability of Skills

Although the responsibilities are split in *Figure 7.13* on the basis of organizational roles, it is often the case that one department must make up for a lack of skills in another department. For example, although the user department has the primary responsibility to define the requirements and the input/output formats for a new system, it is a rare user department which has people trained in the necessary analytical techniques. For this reason, the Data Processing department often must assist or even lead the user in performing these tasks.

This role of leading the user to perform a new function in a new way has its dangers. The data processor can begin to dictate to the user, presuming to know more than the user about what is needed. Or, the user can abdicate responsibility to the data processor. To the extent either of these two extremes happens, the viability of the resulting system is jeopardized. The relationship between the two departments is also jeopardized.

One of the purposes of this text is to begin to prepare the user to bear full and active responsibility for those aspects of systems development which are necessarily user responsibilities. There is no inherent reason why a user cannot become as skilled as the data processor in systems definition, and even in most aspects of systems design.

---

## Exercise 7.6

Review the various phases of the development of a mechanized system, and try to determine which is the most critical phase—that is, the phase which must be done thoroughly and well if all subsequent phases are to be completed without the need to go back and pick up pieces.

---

## The Critical Phase

It doesn't take much evaluation to recognize that the most critical phase is the definition phase. A house cannot be built on sand, nor can a system be developed upon a vague set of specifications. Changes after the definition phase can have a profound effect upon the development schedules and costs.

A common, but unproved, rule of thumb states that it costs 10 times as much to make a change during the design phase as it does during the definition phase. It costs 100 times as much to make a change during the construction phase, and 1000 times as much after implementation.

If one were contracting with a software house for the development of a computer system, one would take great care to have the definition of the system spelled out completely and in sufficient detail so that a firm price could be quoted.

The second most critical phase is the first part of the design phase where the major decisions are made regarding the database design and the choice of computer and peripherals. The remainder of the work is merely following the master plan.

Probably the major danger in these two phases is the temptation to begin program development too early. After all, the user is always in a hurry, and the programmers are waiting for work to do. If management gives in to either of these two temptations, there will be a heavy price to pay.

## Purchase Alternative

Not all mechanized systems must be developed in-house. The development of software is a very costly process. If someone else has developed the necessary software and is willing to sell it at a reasonable cost, much investment of capital can be avoided, and a year or two of delay can be avoided.

So, where in the development process is it appropriate to consider the purchase of commercially available software?

The alternative of purchased software first becomes apparent during the feasibility phase. At this time, enough of a description of the desired functionality is available so that a search can be conducted for available software packages. It is only upon the completion of the definition phase that a choice of commercial software can be made intelligently. In fact, if several software packages are available, the definition can be developed with them in mind. This is a good way to verify the workability of the choices, and the degree to which internal operating preferences must be sacrificed.

---

## Exercise 7.7

During the description of the various phases of mechanized systems design, several potential mistakes were mentioned. Using these as a starting point, and reviewing your own experience, try to develop a list of the types of major mistakes which should be conscientiously avoided during the systems development cycle.

---

## Mistakes to Avoid

- When systems people develop systems *for* the user rather than *with* the user, the result is likely to be a system which is ill-used or which fails. If the system is used, it is likely that the user will feel a degree of bitterness toward the data processor who feels more knowledgeable about the user's business than the user.
- When users define systems, or even design systems without adequate systems training and experience, the results can be inadequate and an expensive consumption of staff and computer resources. This mistake is more prevalent in recent years, because computer manufacturers are now marketing directly to the end user. Such user-developed systems are often slow to be corrected, since the user is reluctant to admit an error to the data processor whom he or she originally ignored.
- Where very large projects have been undertaken without adequate attention to phasing and modular development, the development costs

tend to grow continuously. If such projects ever reach completion, the resulting systems are usually subject to early obsolescence.

- The consideration of alternative approaches is appropriate in the feasibility phase and in the definition phase. This is especially true if purchased alternatives are to be considered. It is obviously a mistake to fail to consider alternatives. If no alternative is considered, the resulting system is more than likely to provide some additional, marginal services which are not worth the cost to develop.
- The development of programs without a good, complete system definition and a sound basic design is a rather common mistake. It usually happens when there is a drive to complete the project early, or when there is a programming staff which needs to be kept busy. The result is often the rework of a number of programs and a disjointed program testing plan. The system will probably have a large number of latent bugs, and will probably be difficult to maintain.
- Systems have often been developed to serve a narrowly defined function in one department without due consideration for potential service to other departments, or possible negative impact on other departments. The temptation to reduce a systems project to a very narrow function is common, since the alternative often seems to be too large a project with no obvious sponsor.
- If the desired system is not thoroughly defined in terms of how the user can perform the function better, the result can be complex software. The software then serves only as a band-aid on yesterday's way of doing business. It takes dedicated users to really rethink their function in terms of the capability provided by new technology.

## CIM—Additive Data with a Vengeance

CIM obviously supports the concept that manufacturing data is additive by nature. In fact, CIM is based upon that premise.

The design of a new product on a graphics terminal makes use of existing electronic images of parts stored on a database. The electronic image of the designed product is used as a basis for computer applications to analyze stresses and product performance. The electronic image is the source of electronic part and assembly drawings which are extracted from it and supplemented with detailed information.

The electronic drawings are used by the processor as a basis for developing the process description, the tool design, the numeric control program, etc. Encoded features on the original drawing are used to guide the selection of process steps and tools. The process data is used to guide the control systems in the factory. The original engineering "drawings" are the source of the bill of material.

The master production schedule is the source of the material requirements in the material requirements planning (MRP) or the just-in-time (JIT) system. The output of the JIT system drives the procurement and production systems. The enterprise operates under the control of integrated systems, selectively aided by the computer.

## Summary

The systems of any business are interdependent, whether or not this fact is realized by the management of the various departments. If it is not realized, then the systems most likely won't operate with the degree of effectiveness which could be possible.

The development of new information systems is a management responsibility. It should involve the management from all departments which are impacted by any newly planned system.

The development of any new system, particularly a mechanized information system should be done in phases. The purpose of breaking a development project into phases is to enhance control of the project and to allocate the work to the different organizations which have the specific skills required for each phase.

Large projects should be broken into phases, and even into modules to shorten the delivery time of usable functions. Since a control system depends upon related systems for master data, status data, and history data, the modules can consist of these related data systems.

A good rule of thumb is to keep the length of a project at less than eighteen months and at less than six months for a phase. This avoids the potential for the final product to be obsolete before it is delivered.

The definition phase is the most critical phase where the work must be completed in a high quality manner in order to avoid significant rework in later phases. The second most critical phase is the early portion of the design phase when the database and the computing approach are determined.

The consideration of alternative approaches, particularly purchased software, is most appropriate in the feasibility phase and in the definition phase.

The user and the data processor each have specific roles to play in the systems development process. If either tries to usurp the responsibility of the other, the final product will suffer, as will the relationship between the departments.

CIM is an integrated set of systems which takes full advantage of the additive nature of data in a manufacturing enterprise.

# 8

# *Team Function and Composition*

## Introduction

There is a tendency for people to take on large systems projects without adequate recognition of the complexity of information flow within the business, and without adequate representation of the needs and ideas of affected functional areas. The purpose of this chapter is to give the reader an awareness of the need for teamwork and an organized approach to systems definition and installation efforts.

## Exercise 8.1

Consider that you are responsible for the development of a mechanized information system which will impact a number of different departments within the business. Would you want to put together any sort of team to assist in the development effort? Would you want representation from the different departments? Why?

## Need for a Systems Team

The more complex a systems project, the more unlikely it is that a single person in one department could make good decisions for people in other departments. In fact, the less likely it is that the people in other departments would accept the decisions, good or bad. The list in *Figure 8.1* shows the major reasons why a systems team is needed.

Since departments are likely to be reluctant to delegate authority for decisions affecting them, it is necessary to establish some sort of decision-

1. Decision-making Body
2. Thoughts of all Functions
3. Nobody Knows Everything
4. Cooperation

***Figure 8.1.*** Reasons for a systems team

making body with representation from each of the involved departments. Although all of the decisions won't be popular in all of the departments, each department will have to recognize that it has had its day in court. Many times a decision which appears unfavorable to a single department has a very significant advantage to other departments and to the business as a whole.

The information and material flow through a business can be difficult to map and to understand. New ideas of how to conduct aspects of the business can be difficult to think through. For these reasons, it is desirable to have a forum in which the thoughts of each functional area can be represented.

Nobody knows everything, especially the person who seems to think that he or she does know everything. A team of people from varied backgrounds help to supplement the experience and judgement of the systems designer.

Finally, no matter how well a system is defined, designed, and constructed, it won't operate well unless the people who have to work with it have "bought in" to the idea. The best way for people to take responsibility for a new system is to have them deeply involved in the definition and installation planning. The Japanese are well aware of this. They go to great lengths to allow affected personnel to discuss new systems before attempting to implement them. But, once the discussions have been completed, woe to the person who demonstrates a negative attitude toward the project.

## Exercise 8.2

What are the functions that a multidisciplinary systems development team should exercise? Write the functions in a list and compare it with *Figure 8.2*.

1. Resolution of Procedural Rules
2. Evaluation of Mutual Impact
3. Generation of Solutions
4. Project Justification
5. Progress Monitoring
6. Installation Planning
7. Communication and Buy-in
8. Significant Decisions
9. Resolution of Conflict

***Figure 8.2.*** Systems team functions

## Systems Team Functions

The major responsibilities of a systems team are listed in *Figure 8.2*. The total list for any specific project could be more detailed, depending upon the size of the project and the culture of the company.

An important function is the generation and resolution of ideas for procedural rules. Remember that procedures are the true systems of the business. The impact of new procedures can be far-ranging and subtle. It makes a big difference if materials are ordered daily, weekly, or monthly and if an assembly line runs one, two, or three shifts per day. It also makes a difference if the Assembly department, the Master Schedule department, the Marketing department, or the Sales department owns and is answerable for the inventory of finished product.

The team must evaluate the impact each department will have upon other departments when operating according to the proposed new rules. If Assembly operates on a three-shift basis, then how will Materials Distribution stock the material storage bins in the assembly area?

The motivation for development of a new information system is often the hope of overcoming a major business problem. The solution to the problem is usually much less apparent than the problem. A team effort is a good way to generate and evaluate potential solutions. This was demonstrated during World War II when the British used teams with interdisciplinary skills to solve strategic battlefield problems.

When a new system is put into place, it usually causes a significant change in the way different parts of the business perform their functions. It adds effort and expense to some, and reduces effort and expense for others. It takes input from all disciplines to evaluate the expected costs and benefits from the proposed changes so that the economic value of the planned investment can be evaluated.

As work progresses on the project, a team is needed to review progress. It can make sure that no significant portion of the work is falling behind to the detriment of the schedule for the whole project. A team can evaluate alternatives when a portion of critically needed work falls behind or proves to be infeasible. Of course, group pressure helps to motivate units of the organization to meet the agreed-upon schedule.

When the construction phase nears its completion, it takes mutual planning and agreement to identify and to schedule the various tasks which must be performed to complete the installation—data conversion, user training, system testing and checkout. The conversion of data usually results in a great amount of "grief." Grief is old data records of demonstrated inaccuracy or records with missing data. The team can set targets and plans for resolution of this grief.

As discussed before, it is vital that affected portions of the organization "buy in" to the concepts of the new system and to their expected change in responsibility. Team members from the various departments are the first people to make that buy-in, through agreements reached in team meetings. They then have the responsibility to take the agreements (and proposals leading to agreements) back to their respective departments for discussion and internal acceptance.

The operation of a major portion of the business is more complex than it appears on the surface. There is nobody who is so brilliant and incisive that he can propose radically new procedures without the need to check out the implications throughout the organization. For this, a team is needed. When a significant new procedure has been defined, it usually turns out that there is no single authority who has the insight to approve or disapprove it. It is probably too complex an issue to be explained to the chief executive officer. In effect, the team itself becomes the decision-making authority for most major decisions—because there is no other knowledgeable authority.

In the resolution of business problems, there is bound to be a great deal of interorganizational conflict. For most any significant issue, one portion of the organization must make a concession to another. These concessions don't come easily, especially if budgets are tight. Often the resolution of a conflict is not accomplished through the cold application of business logic, but through peer pressure.

---

## Exercise 8.3

What functional areas should be represented in a team effort for definition and installation of a multifunctional information systems effort? Test your thinking by listing the specific departments which you feel should be included on a team to develop a material requirements system as in *Figure 3.4*. What should be the qualifications of team members?

---

## Systems Team Composition

The departments which must be represented on a systems team are simply those departments likely to be affected by the proposed system. The team should also include representation from any department, such as Data Processing and possibly Accounting, which can contribute to the formulation of procedures and the identification of economic factors.

The primary qualifications of team members are listed in *Figure 8.3*. The team should consist of broadly experienced people who can generate new ideas and have the background to evaluate the possible results of proposed new procedures. The greater the breadth of experience of team members, the more likely they are to be open-minded about proposals which put new requirements on their own department. This is one area in which the Japanese have a great advantage, since they make a specific effort to expose new management employees to a number of different functional areas.

The team must include a representative of the Data Processing department, usually as the primary architect of new mechanized procedures. This person is the one most likely to be skilled in systems analysis and documentation techniques. The Data Processing representative is also the one who is most likely to have insight into the inner workings of a number of functional areas.

1. All Involved Departments
2. Broadly Experienced People
3. Data Processing Representative
4. Middle-level Managers
   - o Know the system
   - o Make decisions
   - o Able to compromise
   - o Influence within department

***Figure 8.3.*** Systems team membership

This person has probably developed mechanized systems in the past for numerous departments.

When a department has to assign a person to an extra task which might demand a lot of time, there is a temptation to assign the person who can most easily be spared. This is usually the wrong person. It is in the department's best interest to assign a top-level thinker.

The heads of departments are usually not the right people, since they often have a surface-level knowledge of the systems by which their organization operates. Budgetary and personnel requirements tend to occupy much of the department heads' time. This prevents them from staying current with procedural detail.

A staff person or a first level supervisor is also probably the wrong person to assign to the team. The lower the level of the person in the department, the less likely that the person has a good perspective on departmental procedures and the impact of procedures upon neighboring departments.

A middle-level manager usually has a good perspective on the systems of the department and on relations with neighboring departments. Such a manager also is likely to have the perspective and confidence to make decisions and compromises which will affect the department—and then have the internal respect to obtain concurrence with the decisions.

## Exercise 8.4

Every team must have a leader if it is to be effective. What do you think the qualifications should be for the leader of a systems team?

## Systems Team Leader

The primary requirement of a team leader is to be respected and accepted in the role of leader by the membership of the team. Without this, any other qualifications are wasted. Refer to *Figure 8.4*.

The leader should be reasonably highly placed in the organization, usually at least as high as the highest ranking team members. Rank brings a degree of respect which is sometimes not gained by other qualifications. Rank alone will not retain respect if the designated leader proves to be inadequate to the task.

1. Respected by Team
2. Highly Placed in the Organization
3. Knowledgeable of the Territory
4. Good Systems Comprehension
5. Good Leadership Skills
6. No "Axe to Grind"

***Figure 8.4.*** Systems team leader qualities

It would help if the leader were broadly knowledgeable of the territory to be covered by the envisioned system. The knowledge will stand the leader in good stead when there are strong differences of opinion among the team members. Most often, team members are better at finding deficiencies in one another's ideas than they are at generating solutions themselves.

The leader would have a distinct advantage if armed with good systems sense. Some people seem to be almost intuitively able to track cause and effect in the flow of information and materials through an organization. Data processing experience and participation in systems projects are the usual vehicles by which a person gains a feel for the detection and resolution of systems problems.

Of course, the leader should possess the usually recognized leadership skills, which are the ability to plan meetings and keep the discussions on track; delegate responsibility and hold subcommittees to the completion of their assigned tasks; keep discussions orderly without losing necessary input from the retiring members; and prevent the domineering members from railroading half-completed ideas. Team meetings are a forum for analytical thinking, not for selling political ideas.

One of the most important characteristics of a good leader is to not appear to have a preconceived bias about the system concepts under discussion. If the leader appears to have a private axe to grind, the membership will be polarized and unwilling to seek the necessary compromises.

## Systems Planning Meetings

Practical experience from a number of project teams suggests a number of guidelines which seem to lead to success in the resolution and implementation of new information systems. These are summarized in *Figure 8.5*.

A meeting is always more effective if it is announced in advance with a formal agenda. The agenda helps the team to focus their thoughts in advance. In addition, it puts a gentle pressure on subcommittees to complete their work, especially if they are scheduled to report at the planned meeting.

The conduct of the meeting should be according to a rather loose interpretation of Robert's rules of order. If the meetings are conducted too formally, then good ideas will be lost due to procedural confusion. If the meetings are conducted too loosely, then the more outspoken team members will dominate, and their ideas will be accepted without adequate examination.

1. An Agenda
2. Loose "Robert's Rules"
3. No Subcommittee Work
4. Schedule for Hot Issues
5. Frequency as Required
   - o Weekly during definition
   - o Monthly during design
   - o Monthly during construction
   - o Weekly during installation
   - o Monthly until maturity
6. Regular 1-2 Hour Schedule

***Figure 8.5.*** Systems planning meetings

There should be a vote on all key issues during meetings. Hopefully the discussion of the expected impact of proposed procedures will be so complete that the vote is usually unanimous. If the vote is very close on an issue, it is a good sign that the thought process has been incomplete. After all, the purpose is to develop sound new procedures, not to do the popular thing.

Subcommittees should report in advance of meetings with formal written conclusions. These conclusions should be explored and evaluated during the meetings. By no means should a subcommittee be allowed to use the occasion of a team meeting to do the subcommittee work.

Often an issue will come up in meetings repeatedly and will be used by one or more team members as a "worry" item to retard progress. It is usually phrased as an idea killer in the form of, "But what are you going to do about ...?" No matter how well selected the team members are, there is a good chance that the team will include one or more people who have a hang up on one or more topics.

If the worrisome topics are dismissed out-of-hand, the worrier is lost as an active team member, and is quickly convinced that the whole thing is a railroad in favor of somebody else's pet ideas. If the worrisome topics are discussed in depth in a team meeting, they will retard progress. They will be discussed again in the next meeting, and the next, and the next. There is an effective way to deal with such items. The leader appoints a responsible party or subcommittee to address the topic, and assigns a date when the resolution is due. The leader then refuses to allow discussion of the topic in team meetings until the due date. This technique is a way of resolving a troublesome issue. It also delays discussion of the issue until enough earlier work has been done so that the issue can be dealt with in perspective.

Since meetings tend to interfere with the daily operation of the business, the sooner a meeting schedule is established, the better. Experience suggests that weekly meetings are required to make progress during the definition phase. Monthly meetings seem to be appropriate during the design and construct phases. If more frequent meetings are required, it is usually a danger sign that the definition was not as completely thought out as it should have been.

During the latter part of the construct phase, it is probably necessary to have weekly meetings to plan the installation efforts. Progress monitoring and problem resolution efforts during the installation phase might dictate the need to return to weekly meetings. Upon completion of the installation, it is still prudent for the team to meet every month or two until most of the latent problems have been identified and solved, and the system reaches a degree of maturity.

The meetings should generally last from one to two hours. If a meeting lasts much more than an hour and a half, it is usually necessary to take a break for biological needs. The time break brings a break in the thought process. This costs valuable time.

The day and hour of the meetings should be established in advance and should be set aside on the calendars of all team members. If the schedule is regular, it is more likely to be honored.

## Functional Analysis

In Appendix C there is a description of a systems analysis approach which is called *Functional Analysis*. It is a new technique developed by the author over a number of years. It is a technique for directly linking the systems development effort to corporate goals and strategies. The technique is highly structured.

To-date, the functional analysis technique has been successfully used in a number of classroom projects with students and manufacturing employees of limited systems experience. It has been used with success on two real business projects. Although detailed techniques are still being worked out, the basic concepts seem sound.

## Joint Application Development

IBM has developed and documented a systems definition approach called JAD (Joint Application Development). As defined by IBM, the technique is detailed and dogmatic, but it is sound in principle. Streamlined versions of the technique have been widely used with significant success.

The key to JAD is that the user, although responsible for the definition phase of a systems development project, is usually not skilled in the tools required to define the requirements of a system. The JAD technique provides a way for the data processor to lead a team of users to an acceptable system definition.

The systems analyst interviews a cross section of users, sometimes through a systems team, and sometimes in small projects without a systems team. The systems analyst then generates a definition of the anticipated requirements of the system.

A team of users is gathered to review the proposed definition specifications. It is vital that the team members be broadly respected by their peers, since they will be making decisions for all.

The team meets with the systems analyst to review the specifications in detail. A walk-through is conducted. This is a presentation of all aspects of the operation of the system. It uses a written description of the processes and the input and output formats. In effect, it uses a simplified mock-up of the operation of the system. The purpose of the exercise is to give the users something tangible to critique. All questions and changes are recorded by a scribe. All decisions are by consensus.

The team meets for one to five consecutive days to complete the review of the definition specifications. The results of the review session are published promptly for a final reading and approval.

The results are usually excellent. The team of users exchange good thoughts on the workability of the ideas presented to them. There tends to be good acceptance of the results by others because of the credibility of the team members.

One final advantage remains to be mentioned. It is usually easier for line management to free key staff members from their normal responsibilities for several consecutive days than it is to free them for several hours a week over many weeks.

## Barriers to Communication

Since so much of the systems development effort depends upon good communication, it is worthwhile to explore some of the potential barriers.

People often have a tendency to be judgmental when listening to other people's ideas. Of course, the idea behind a systems team is to evaluate ideas. But a sound evaluation is possible only if the idea is first understood. The team leader must restrain expressions of criticism of new ideas until the ideas have been thoroughly presented.

Sometimes business problems generate strong feelings among team members. Unsolved problems and tight budgets tend to make people tense, and quick to express frustration and hostility. Every attempt must be made by the leader to help people set aside their strong feelings while ideas are explored. A common technique is for the leader to review the thoughts expressed in an impassioned outburst. An example might be, "Let me repeat the substance of what I think you said." This repetition of the essence of the thoughts without the emotion can have two effects. It tells the speaker that he or she was really heard. It also summarizes the key points without the confusion caused by the emotion. When a person sees that he has been heard and understood, he usually restrains the tendency to overemphasize his point.

The communication among team members is aided if each tries to see the other department's needs through the eyes of the other department. Sometimes this can be enhanced by having team members play roles as members of other departments when working out the possible effects of proposed procedures.

Both the Functional Analysis and the Joint Application Development techniques are designed to reduce the emotion and to enhance the communication among peers.

## System Challenges of CIM

Computer integrated manufacturing (CIM) is a new way of running the manufacturing business. It causes a radical change, gradually implemented, in the use of computers and in the organization of the data required to manage activities and to measure results. It poses serious questions as to what data will be required to serve what purposes, what the quality of the data must be, and what the timeliness of the data must be. Even though relational databases are more flexible than other data management techniques, they have their limits. And we learned in Chapter 6 that data cannot be stored away for years before it is used. Its quality is certain to be inadequate to the need.

This leads to the inescapable conclusion that CIM must be carefully planned in advance by a team approach. It is necessary to define the type of production processes which can be put into place. This must be used as a base to rethink what product can most effectively be manufactured. It doesn't mean a different kind of product, but a product with a different architecture, such as fewer, more simply installed options.

It is then necessary to determine the rate at which production capabilities will be changed, and the rate at which product configuration will be changed to use these capabilities. The physical changes will determine the rate of new software and database development. But be careful! The old world will be around for a long time. Systems, both manual and mechanized, will have to handle both the old and the new methods of production.

## CIM as a Production Strategy

If CIM technology is merely grafted on the old way of doing business, it probably will yield minimal benefits, if any. The benefits come from rethinking strategies and procedures (systems), and then applying the computer selectively to make the new ideas possible. If the application of the computer is not done according to a master plan, the result is sure to be a loss of flexibility to adapt to future change in systems or environment.

The first step seems to be the definition of new production methods. How many cells are needed? Should cells be directed toward like parts or toward all components of subassemblies? To what extent should subassembly be performed in production cells? Once the production methods have been defined, the method of managing material can be rethought. This will affect the production processes. Manufacturing processes are very dependent upon material delivery and storage capabilities.

The method of scheduling production must be rethought. Does the master schedule drive the procurement and manufacture of production materials? Or, does the master schedule drive the rate of assembly, and the assembly schedule drive the procurement and manufacture of production materials? Is the assembly schedule based on customer orders? All is dependent upon whether the basic strategy is one of build-to-stock or one of build-to-order.

Should low volume options be deleted from the sales catalog? Will the loss of sales reduce profit more than the savings from increased manufacturing efficiency? Should the high volume options become standard? Would costs be increased more than the profit from the expected increase in sales? Should stock products be assembled? Should there be a price incentive for the customer to accept stock products? What merchandising strategies should be put in place to match the defined product line?

These are all difficult questions. They must be reasonably answered before a company ventures too far into CIM. Otherwise, any CIM progress can easily be negated by changes in the environment or the marketplace. The only way to answer such questions is by the use of a systems planning and implementation team. CIM is a system as well as a strategy—a very integrated system.

## CIM as an Information Systems Strategy

Reasonable answers to these questions are required before an information systems strategy can be formulated. All questions don't need to be answered, but some sort of basic strategy and structure must be put in place to guide efforts in the migration toward CIM.

Depending upon the direction of CIM, the data needs can be very different. For example, it makes a great deal of difference if production materials are to be provided to a regular schedule of standard product or to a last minute schedule of customer orders. It also makes a difference if materials are ordered by the production processes as needed or are delivered at a preset rate.

If the CIM environment requires fast response to unexpected stimuli, then there is a need for an omnipresent computer system which can balance the burden with the resources and can give directive orders. If the production schedule can be laid out in advance, and if exceptions are the exception and not the rule, then computer control systems can be reduced in number and complexity. The more there is a need to rely on the computer, the greater the potential loss of flexibility.

This is not to say that the use of the computer is an error. It does mean that needless use of the computer is an error. Systems should be simple wherever possible.

If production is well-organized and disciplined, the need for a computer is minimized. In a just-in-time (JIT) environment the parts carry information with them. The appearance of a part in a storage location can convey a wealth of information without the need for a fast response computer to display an order. The appearance of part A in a rack next to a machine can tell the operator of the machine that it is now time to produce part B and to assemble it to A, place the subassembly in the output rack, and then look into the input queue for the next physical message.

No matter how simple the production planning and execution processes, the design of new products is still a complex, labor-intensive task. There are endless opportunities here for specific economies—so long as the computer applications are built to a master plan.

Computer graphics systems have become very sophisticated. There is a danger that the fascination with graphics technology can cause management to inject it into new systems out of proportion to the need for graphics capability. In the old paper systems, the Design Engineering department produced change notices for the use of people who didn't need access to drawings. The same principle applies to the distribution of computer-generated graphics images.

## Evolution of CIM Information Systems

There are many reasons why CIM will be a long, evolutionary process. The technologies, the finances, the people, and the experience are not all available in adequate quantity.

The computer can be used to design product, but it can't recall a drawing which was manually drawn. The full benefits of the software cannot be obtained until a large population of electronic drawings has been produced.

The design of tooling by computer has a similar dependency upon the development of a library of standard images and tooling components.

JIT cannot be implemented practically until material requirements planning (MRP) disciplines have been established. Accurate inventory records and inventory transaction disciplines have to be put into place before MRP will work.

Group technology is a basis for CIM. Many manual and computer functions will be based upon coding systems describing key characteristics of parts, materials, machines, tools, and gages. These code structures must be defined and the characteristics of the items must be encoded. This is labor-intensive activity. It must be completed before the code values can be used to refine the design of products and processes.

## The CIM Planning Team

The CIM planning team has a large challenge before it. CIM is a broad, all-encompassing concept. Obviously, all aspects of CIM cannot be planned before implementation begins. The associated computer technologies are still immature in many areas. Adequate planning must be done to set a reliable direction so that development efforts will not quickly become obsolete. This planning includes basic business and departmental strategies, computer and communications architecture and conventions, the definition of classification and coding structures, and a priority system and sound project planning disciplines.

Nobody can do the job alone. CIM planning and implementation requires a team approach. The team needs to include representatives of the Manufacturing, Design Engineering, Assembly, Material Planning and Purchasing, Material Distribution, Accounting, Data Processing, Marketing, and Master Scheduling departments.

There will be a need to make significant compromises between departments. Each department will be more directly dependent upon its neighbors. Some will do more work than they do today so that others can work more effectively. Examples are legion:

- Tooling must be described in standard terms of capacity and capability so that Design Engineering can design cost-effective product.
- The product designer must adhere to specific drawing conventions so

that the draftsman (or the appropriate CIM counterpart) can easily separate the graphics images into part and subassembly images.

- The draftsman must draw and encode parts features (keyways, holes, surfaces, etc.) so that they can be readily interpreted by the processor (human or computer).
- The draftsman must document the product design to specific drawing rules so that the tool designer and the parts programmer can readily use the image of the part profile as a starting point for their work.
- The draftsman must separate the bill of material of the product under specific disciplines so that it is readily accessible to downstream functions.
- The tool designer must draw the tool so that the image of both the part and the tool are distinguishable. This is to aid the parts programmer in determining what material to remove and what material to avoid contact with.

This list could be quite long. The point should be clear—teamwork is of the essence, both in the planning and in the execution of CIM.

The job is never done. Each change in product or process has the possibility of causing significant rework to computer programs. The more automated the processes, the more that change must be avoided or planned in advance. Changes will tend to be batched. This all takes teamwork and coordination.

## Summary

Large systems projects require the formation of an interdepartmental team to develop the definition of the system, and to monitor the installation. The team should include membership from all affected departments.

The function of the systems team is to resolve complex problems, to make compromises between departments, and to ensure that the member departments honor the decisions of the team.

The team members should be from middle management, with a perspective on the business operation, willingness and ability to compromise and make decisions, and the creativity to find solutions to common problems.

The team leader should be skilled in leadership and, hopefully, in systems analysis techniques. But most of all, the leader should be generally respected and trusted not to have a personal axe to grind relative to the proposed system.

Team meetings should be conducted with discipline, but not with undue formality. The members must think through complex issues and not just vote on the apparent popularity of ideas. The meeting should be conducted with enough regularity to ensure that steady progress is made.

Two systems analysis techniques have been used with some success for team efforts. One is the *Functional Analysis* technique described in Appendix C. The other is IBM's *Joint Application Development* technique.

CIM requires the use of a systems team more than any previous systems effort. CIM affects almost every part of the organization. Since CIM is evolutionary, the definition and planning activities of a systems team will be ongoing.

# 9

# *Case: Assembly Line*

## Introduction

There is a tendency to assume that people will behave as they *should* behave when providing input to an information system or when using the output of the system in their daily activities. The opposite is often the case, and has resulted in some significant systems failures. People are subject to many outside pressures which can motivate them to work contrary to the purposes of a system, and contrary to the best interests of neighboring functions in the business. The purpose of this chapter is to make the reader aware of this and to give some clue as to steps which might be taken to reduce the results of mission conflict between functional areas.

## The Assembly Line

The assembly line is a mass production technique for final stage manufacture of products. The concept of an assembly line was introduced by Henry Ford in the early part of the century. It revolutionized the assembly process, and radically reduced the production cost of the automobile.

Products are physically assembled on a slowly moving conveyor. The assembly materials are stored in bins or racks next to the conveyor. The assemblers stand on the conveyor or climb onto the product to perform the assembly tasks. They leave the conveyor from time to time to obtain parts from the storage areas which line the path of the conveyor.

Each assembler has specific tasks to perform and does these tasks within a restricted length of floor space through which the conveyor passes. The tasks must be completed within this designated zone for two reasons. The necessary tools, such as an air hammer, are available only in the zone and have limited power supply reach (air hose or electric cord). The work must be completed by the time the unit of product leaves the zone, or else the assembler will be late starting on the next unit of product which has already entered the zone.

---

### Exercise 9.1

Can you identify some of the conditions which must be present for an assembly line to operate properly? The conditions are not necessarily obvious unless the reader has had experience in the assembly process.

---

## Assembly Line Requirements

Individual assemblers must know what parts to install on a unit of product and how to install them. This involves some degree of training based upon a description (documentation) of the processes. A mechanism is necessary for providing information to the assembler about what parts to install on the unit of product entering the zone.

The assembler must not be overloaded with work, or else some units of product will leave the zone incomplete. This would prevent the installation of other parts. Some procedure must be in place to ensure that the assembler has a reasonable work load. However, each assembler must be occupied for the majority of the day so that the number of assemblers—and the cost of assembly—can be held to a minimum.

The assembly materials must be available in adequate supply. If not, the line will have to be stopped, otherwise incomplete product would be produced. There must be some sort of information service to drive the delivery of material to the storage bins along the line.

## Build-to-stock Assembly

The traditional assembly line process was one of build-to-stock. In the early days all of the automobiles which Henry Ford produced from a single assembly line were the same model and the same color. The customer was offered no options.

In later years, some degree of product variety was produced on an assembly line. The majority of the options were added to the product after it had been completed on the assembly line. The final product was moved to an attachment bay where the necessary optional materials were marshalled as called for by the customer's order. The installation of the options was done by very experienced and versatile assemblers, using engineering drawings as reference material.

If customer orders were in short supply, the excess finished units of product were stored in a holding area. When customer orders arrived at a faster rate than the assembly line could satisfy, units of finished product were retrieved from the storage area and were delivered to the attachment bays to be fitted out as appropriate.

## The Product

In the case to be evaluated in this chapter, the build-to-stock assembly line produced a limited variety of product, three or four models. There was a limited variety of options which could be added to finished product, usually without the need to remove any standard material from the final product.

## The Process

The assembly line was operated only one shift each day. The quantity of units which was assembled per day was low, four to ten units, depending upon the general level of customer demand. Special options were "pinned on" to the final product in an attachment bay. The options were only installed in response to a specific customer order. The assemblers were personally instructed in their tasks by the foreman, and performed the same set of tasks for a month at a time, with little variation between months. Production materials were purchased or manufactured in monthly lots and were usually stored at the assembly line in adequate quantity to last for one to four weeks.

## Build-to-stock Assembly Systems

The major systems which supported build-to-stock assembly are shown in *Figure 9.1*. The systems were well suited to the assembly process. There was only a limited amount of computer support for the systems.

## Design Product

The design engineer developed the definition of the product and represented it in the form of engineering drawings and engineering notices. Both of these documents contained the bill of material of the product. The bill was manually copied from the engineering drawing to the notice. Then, a distribution copy of the notice was typed and checked against the drawing for accuracy.

A copy of the engineering drawing was distributed to anyone who needed detailed specifications of the product. The drawing was the authoritative source of all product specifications.

The engineering notice was distributed to those who needed basic product information, but not the complete specifications. It was of primary importance to those who were concerned with the availability of materials and the scheduled dates for introduction of new or changed product.

The engineering drawing served as a primary source of information for those people who designed and installed production processes. The engineering notice served as a primary source of information for those people who planned and procured production materials.

## Material Procurement

The Materials Planning people marked up the engineering notice to add any supplemental data they required. They then entered the bill of material into a file to be used for computation of material needs. For example, if a shim or a spacer was noted by Engineering as "use as required," an estimate of average usage per product had to be developed by Materials Planning.

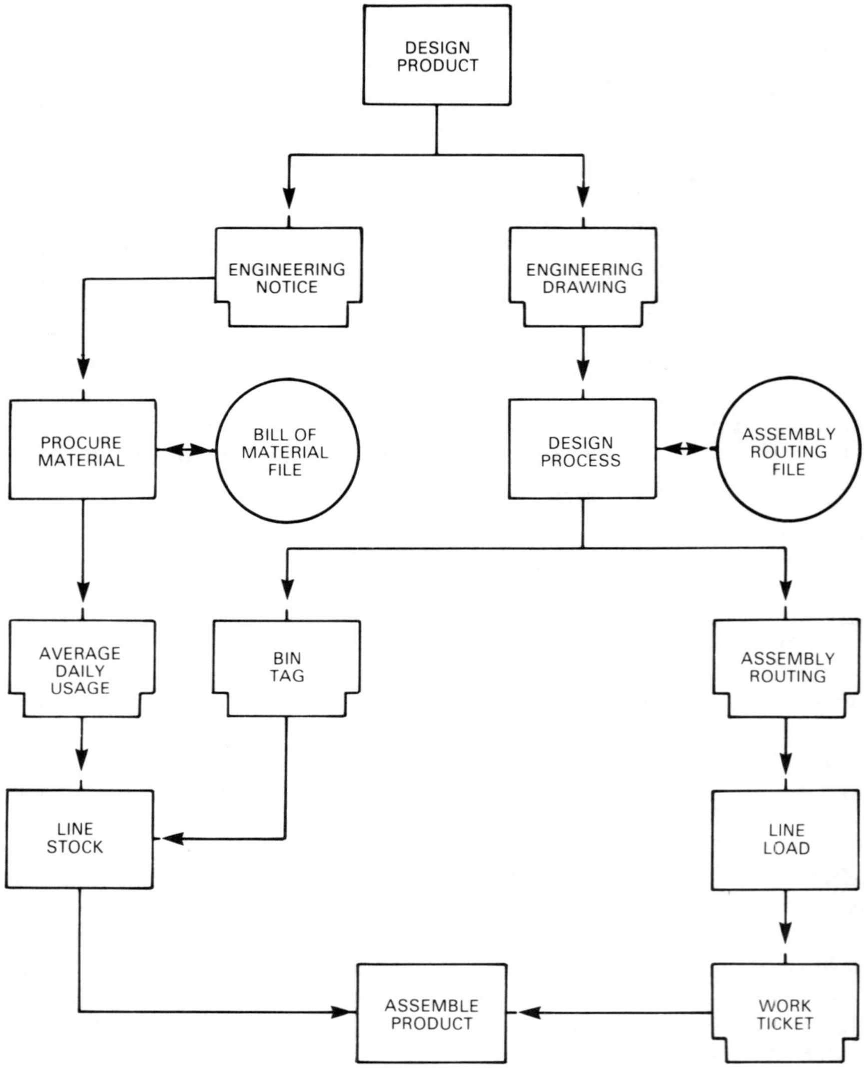


***Figure 9.1.*** Product assembly systems

While the engineering bill of material contained the bill for the whole product, including components of purchased assemblies, the Materials Planning bill of material contained only those components of the product which were purchased or manufactured by the plant. The bill contained no breakdown of a purchased assembly.

The bill of material was updated weekly. The material requirements calculation took place twice a month. The first time, at the end of the month, the monthly lot sizes of material needs were calculated. The second time, in the middle of the month, adjustments to the orders were made for any unexpected event. This might be a loss of material, the scrapping of a lot of material, or the sale of an unexpectedly large amount of material to customers as spare parts.

## Line Stock

Many smaller materials were delivered directly to the assembly line in the monthly quantity as purchased or produced. Other more bulky materials were delivered each night as needed in a process called *line stocking*.

The need was determined by line checkers. They walked the line, looked into bins, and estimated the number of parts in each bin. If the quantity seemed low, the checker would estimate future needs from the bin tag. The bin tag was fastened to the front of each bin and showed the average daily usage of the part on each model. The checker would multiply this quantity by the scheduled assembly rate of each model to determine the amount of material to order from a storage area.

## Design Process

The assembly processor determined the method and sequence of assembly of the product on the assembly line. Often it was found to be more efficient to assemble components in a sequence different from that implied by the engineering drawings. For example, part of the drive mechanism of a bicycle is assembled into the rear wheel, and part is assembled into the frame. For this reason, the assembly bill of material would differ in structure from the engineering bill of material, which described the drive mechanism as a single assembly.

The components of the product which were permanently fastened together, as by welding, were considered as manufactured parts under the control of a production routing. These parts would not appear on the assembly bill of material. Only the resulting assembly would appear on the assembly bill of material, since it was the item delivered to the assembly line. This constituted another difference between the assembly bill of material and the engineering bill of material.

The assembly process was documented in an assembly routing. This data was maintained by a simple computer system as a sort of word processing file. The file was updated monthly. The file included standard times, descriptions of assembly tasks, and tools for each assembly task.

The output of the computer processing was a printed assembly routing and a bin tag for each part to be stored in the assembly area. The routing was maintained in a manual file, and copies were distributed as needed. The bin tag was delivered to the assembly area and fastened to the front of the bin selected by the processor as the most convenient for part storage for the assembler.

## Line Load

Great effort was made to minimize the number of assemblers required on the line. For this reason, the assembly scheduler distributed the assembly tasks carefully among the assemblers in various zones of the line. This task was called *line loading*.

Line loading was done monthly by a cut and paste method wherein the assembly routing was physically cut into pieces representing individual assembly tasks. These were then pasted onto blank sheets of paper to compose work tickets. A work ticket contained the list of tasks assigned to a specific assembler.

The standard time for each task for a specific model of final product was multiplied by the number of units of the product scheduled to be built per day. The total of all of the extended times represented the workload of the assembler. The line load function typically resulted in a workload of 97% of the assembler's available time.

Since the line load task was very tedious, it was performed only once a month. The assembly schedule changed very little from month to month, so the task was primarily one of modification of the work tickets from the previous month.

## Product Assembly

The assembler was never given the work ticket to read. He was instructed in his tasks by the foreman. Time was not allocated for reading the work ticket.

The assembler didn't need to read. He could tell what parts to put on a unit of product by recognizing the shape of the product which was approaching his zone on the assembly line.

Line inspectors checked the quality of the completed product by comparing it to the specifications in the engineering drawings.

## Product Changes

In recent years, the variety of models produced on a single assembly line increased to ten or more (*Figure 9.2*).

The variety of options offered on any given model increased by an order of magnitude. Some options were frequently ordered. Others were ordered only two to four times a year. The typical customer order called for far more options than in past years.

The combination of a large variety of models and a large variety of options resulted in an environment in which it was highly unlikely for two similar orders to move down the assembly line together. Each unit of product tended to be unique.

The rate of production increased, especially in smaller products. The assembly rate on different assembly lines varied from four units per day to more than fifty units per day.

**PRODUCT CHANGES**

1. More Models
2. Higher Production Volumes
3. More Options
4. More Options Per Order
5. Integral Options

**PROCESS CHANGES**

1. Line Installation of Options
2. Line Life Lengthened
3. More Items Stored at Line

***Figure 9.2.*** Product and process changes

## Process Changes

Some options were of the type which required them to be an integral part of the product as opposed to being add-ons. This fact, coupled with a 50% labor efficiency in the attachment bay, led to incorporating the installation of options on the assembly line.

Essentially, the assembly system changed from build-to-stock (and add options to customer order) to a system of build-to-order (and install options on the assembly line).

The time a unit of product was resident on the assembly line increased for larger products. Some products spent as much as three to five days moving from the beginning to the end of the assembly line.

The installation of options on the assembly line radically increased the variety of parts which had to be stored at the line. Space constraints forced a reduction of the quantity of material on the line. Most components were limited to a one-day to three-day supply.

## Exercise 9.2

Do you see any deficiencies in the traditional systems supporting the assembly process? After all, the changes in the environment and the change to a build-to-order process certainly add some new and different requirements to the systems which provide information and material to support the assembly process. List the problems you perceive. Also make note of what sort of solution you think might be appropriate.

**Problem 1.** The physical appearance of the product as it comes down the assembly line no longer tells the assembler what parts must be installed. In addition, there is a greater variety of optional components to install. How can the worker be instructed to do the job? How can one know what tasks to perform on any specific unit of product which comes down the line?

**Problem 2**. The line load process is much more complicated with the introduction of the installation of options on the assembly line. Units of product can vary widely in terms of the amount of installation labor required. The line load of one month is unlikely to be a good start for the line load of the next month. Since customers change orders for options at the last minute, a detailed monthly line load is impractical.

**Problem 3**. The stocking of the bins on the basis of average daily usage has no meaning for options, since the quantity called for by one day's orders can vary widely from another day's orders. How can line stocking requirements be determined?

**Problem 4**. When a customer order is not available, the common practice has been to build a stock order. The stock unit of product is stored until customer orders are in excess of the assembly rate. With options being installed on the assembly line as integral parts of the product, the question arises as to what configuration of stock product should be built. If the wrong options are installed on the stock unit, it must either be reconfigured by removal of the unneeded options, or it must remain in storage until a compatible customer order comes along. Are stock orders really practical in the new environment? How can they be properly configured to maximize the possibility that they will match a future customer order?

**Problem 5**. Like the production routing, the assembly routing has not been kept current with actual assembly methods on the shop floor. For example, many parts were moved by assemblers to bins which were more conveniently located. Any system for stocking and loading the line must have reliable information to support it. This is particularly true if the supporting systems use computer processing. The volume and variety of parts on the new assembly line obviously suggest the possible use of a computer.

**Problem 6**. Since the assembly line no longer has room to store a month's supply of parts, the question arises as to why parts are procured and produced in monthly quantities. Could the investment in production materials be reduced by the purchase and production of component parts in smaller lots?

**Problem 7**. The processor develops a bill of material which differs from the engineering bill. There is a significant possibility of error in this. When an error occurs, material will not be ordered for delivery to the line, or the wrong quantity will be ordered. How can this be avoided?

***Solution 1***. The customer order is the key to what parts must be installed on the product. One company tried the approach of exploding the customer order against the assembly routing file to prepare a detailed work ticket for each scheduled unit of product. This did not work well. The detailed list took too much time to read. Nor was it easy to handle, since it was quite large.

Another company tried a similar approach to prepare a brief list of the most significant optional parts called for by each customer order (*Figure 9.3*). The key parts were flagged on the assembly routing file. As it turned out, there are really relatively few key parts. For example, if an engine has four different oil pan options, the only real difference among the options is in the oil pans themselves. Most all of the other parts are obvious choices (gasket, bolts,

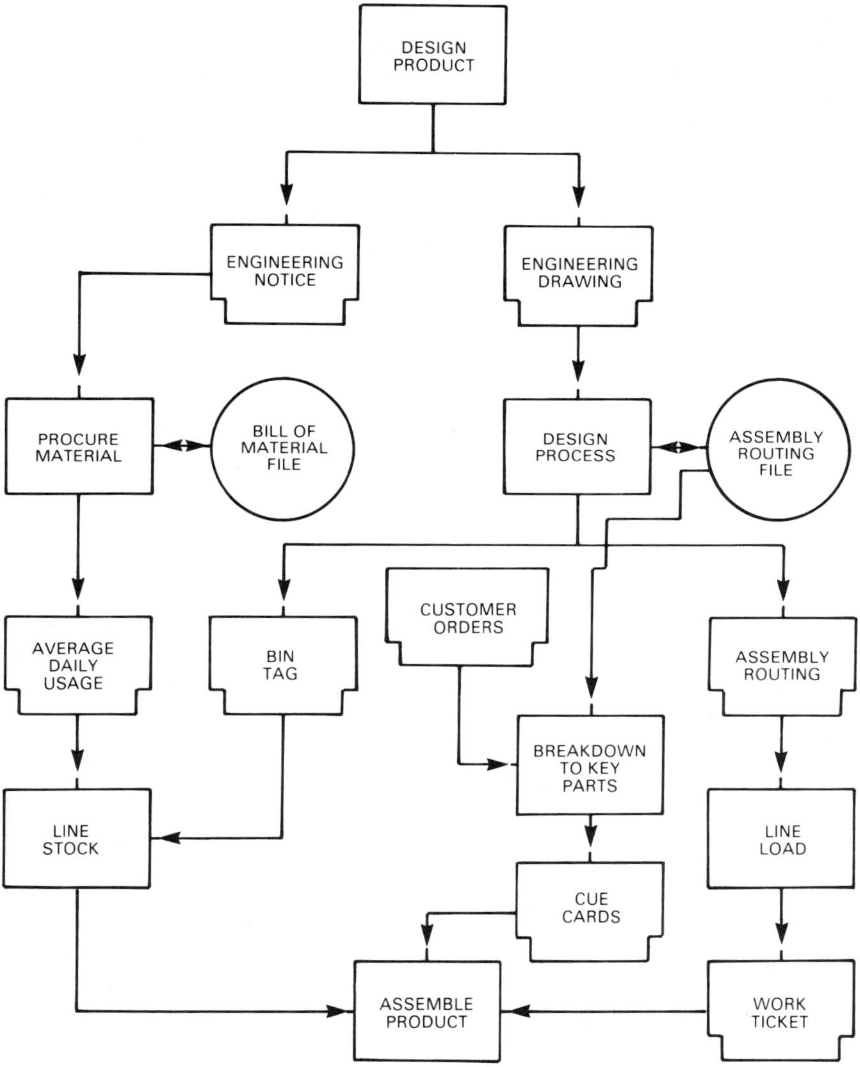


***Figure 9.3.*** Cue cards

washers, nuts) once the correct oil pan has been chosen. The list of key parts is called a *cue card* and is attached to the unit of product in a mylar packet so that it is readily available to the assembler.

***Solution 2.*** The line load function must be done no less often than weekly in the new environment in order to keep up with order changes and to accommodate an order board which is not full for a month into the future.

The obvious answer is a mechanized system for line load. There are two varieties of line load systems which have been tried by various companies.

The first type of line load system (*Figure 9.4*) performs a detailed task breakdown of each customer order. This is very costly and requires detailed and accurate maintenance of assembly line data, such as zone limits and constraints on the use of tooling. It has met with only limited success. It requires exceptional discipline in the maintenance of accurate reference data

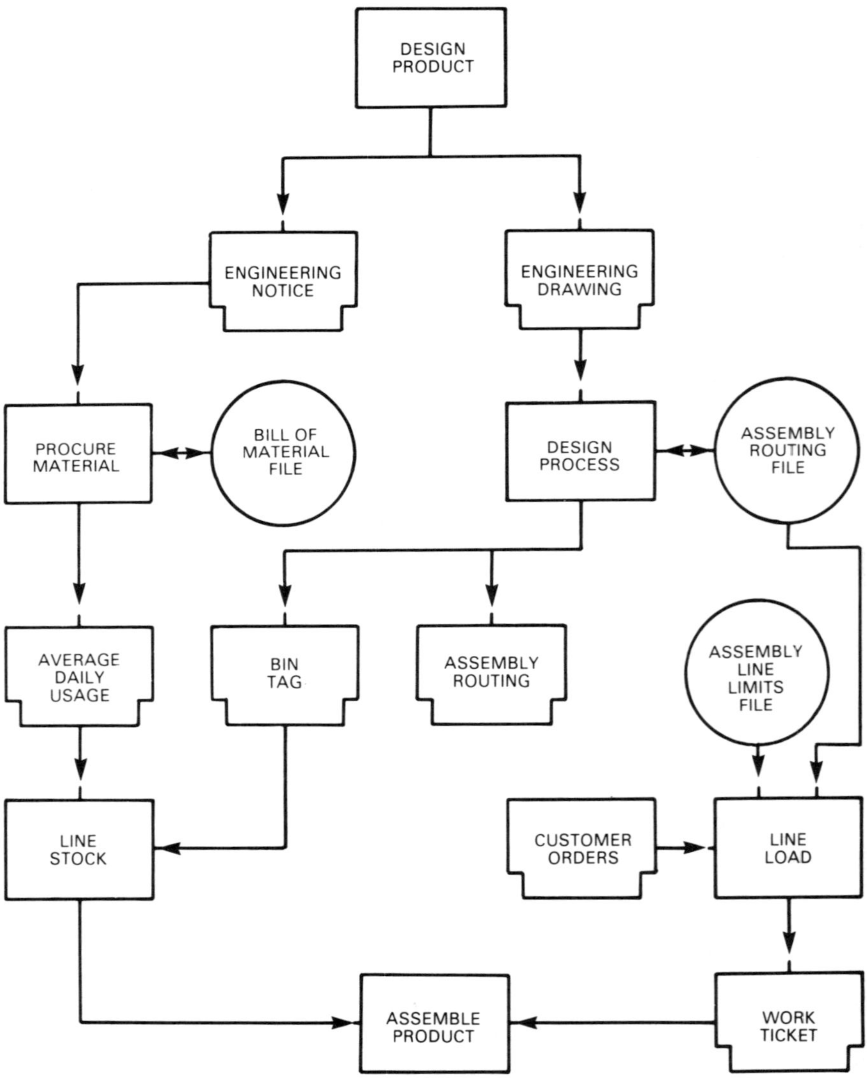


***Figure 9.4.*** Assembly line load

in the assembly routing file and in the file describing assembly line limitations. In addition, it has the disadvantage of constantly changing the task mix of the assembler. This requires the assembler to be much more experienced and versatile.

An apparently more practical system is a mechanized line load assist (*Figure 9.5*) which uses a file of approximate standard times for a typical unit of product of each model. The human scheduler partitions the work into

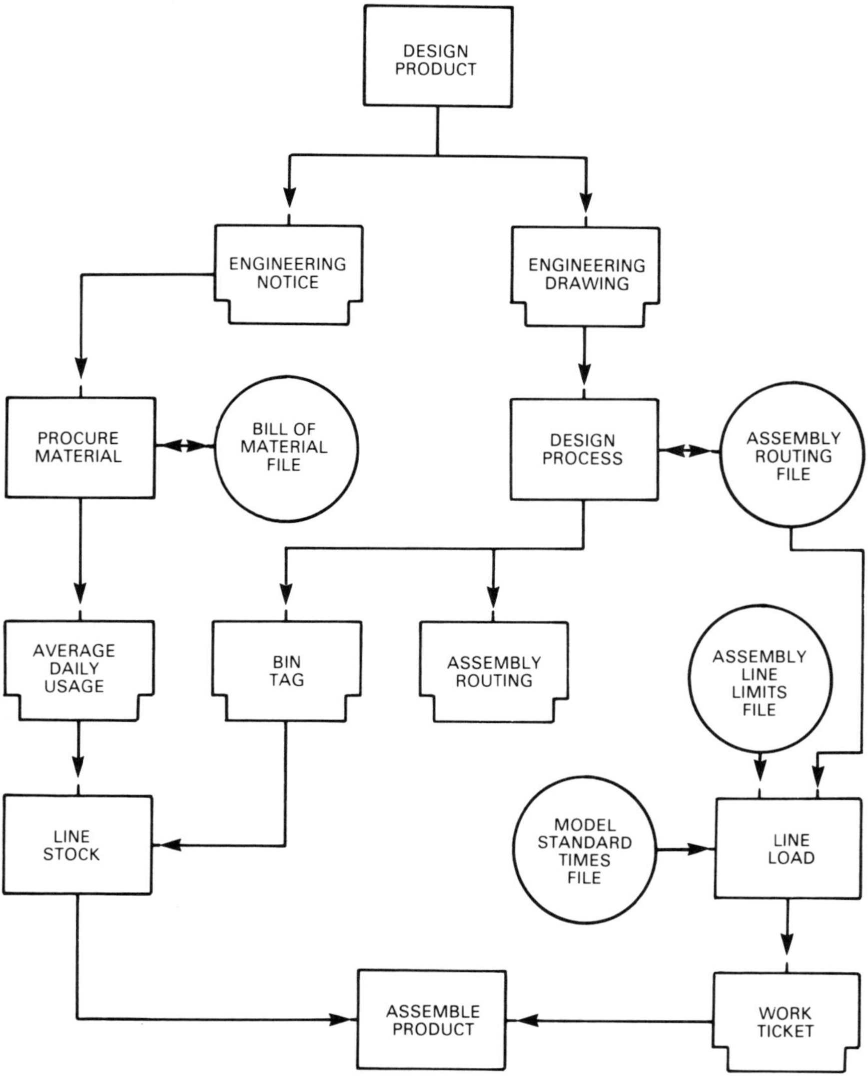


***Figure 9.5.*** Assembly line load assist

rough work tickets. In doing this, he works with a word processor type of image on a terminal. The computer adds up the burden per scheduler and displays the resulting work loads. This allows the scheduler to then move tasks around to improve the work load balance. This system does not take into account the options called for by specific orders. To this extent, it is limited and can result in unexpected peaks and valleys in the work load on the line.

***Solution 3***. For stocking the bins there are again two possible solutions. The first is for the assembly line to call for bin replenishment when the quantity of parts in a bin has been reduced to a predetermined level. This has not worked well, because of the response time for replenishment. It is also difficult for a heavily loaded assembler to keep an eye on the level of material in each bin. And, if the assembler or the Material Handling department fail to be prompt and accurate in filling the bins, the result is incomplete product or a stopped assembly line.

The second approach (*Figure 9.6*) is much more complicated, but works well in practice. It is based upon a computer system which maintains a record of the quantity of parts in each bin. The quantity is increased with each delivery of material and decreased by a breakdown of the product assembled each day. A breakdown of scheduled product provides a picture of the demand for material in the bins. By comparing the bin inventory to future demand, the system can place orders for bin replenishment each day during a shift when the assembly line is not operating. Where record disciplines are reliable, the system automatically places replenishment orders. Where record disciplines are less precise, the system recommends order quantities to line checkers who verify bin quantities before placing the orders.

***Solution 4***. One possible answer to the stock order problem is to build no stock products. This has generally been rejected because of the economic advantages of a stable assembly work force which results from a stable assembly schedule. Without stock orders, the work load on the assembly line would surge up and down with fluctuations in the volume of customer orders.

The other alternative (*Figure 9.7*) is to determine "safe" configurations of product with options which are commonly in demand and are unlikely to result in product reconfiguration—removal of components to install other components. This history of past customer orders is the guide to the selection of safe configurations. The assembly routing file is also needed in order to distinguish which options must be line installed, and which can easily be added after receipt of a customer order.

***Solution 5***. In order to support the above types of applications, the assembly routing file had to be upgraded to a database system. It was expanded to include assembly process descriptions, flags on key parts within options, preferred material delivery quantities, "stock options," and a catalog of parts assignments to bins. The new system contains many checks and balances to warn the processor when data of questionable validity has been entered. Since it cannot identify all erroneous data, the responsibility for data accuracy ultimately falls on the shoulders of the processor. The major source

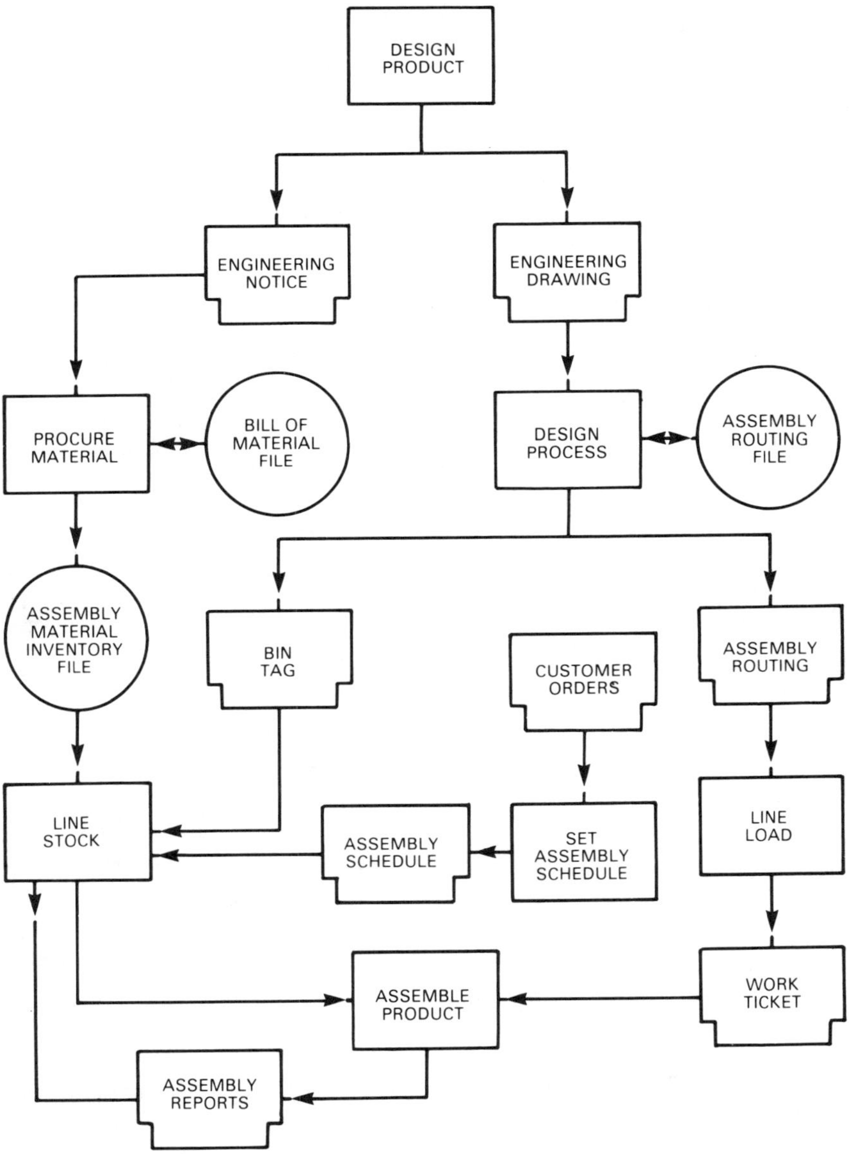


***Figure 9.6.*** Assembly material control

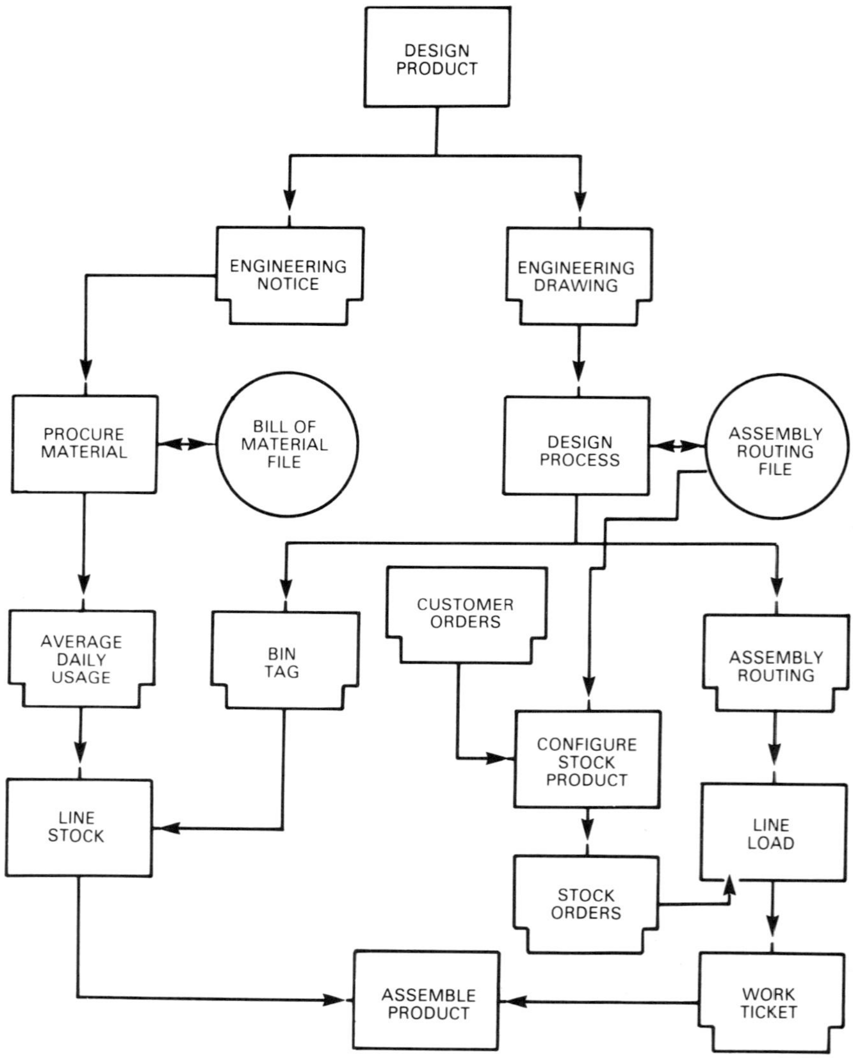


***Figure 9.7.*** Stock product configuration

of potential error is in the manual processing task of rearranging the engineering bill of material into an assembly sequence by assembly line zone.

***Solution 6***. The line stock or assembly material control system (*Figure 9.6*) maintains a record of future material requirements based upon scheduled orders. As long as the order board is reasonably full for a horizon beyond the material procurement lead time, the system can be used to order material from suppliers. This has been done with good success in several locations. It reduces the inventory of material in the assembly facility. However, if the supplying facility cannot produce quickly upon demand, then it must stock a supply of finished parts in anticipation of orders. This is merely a shift of inventory from the user to the supplier.

***Solution 7***. A computer system had to be developed to periodically compare the assembly database to the procurement database in order to detect inconsistencies in the bill of material. Another more complex system (*Figure 9.8*) is possible to maintain control over both databases under the

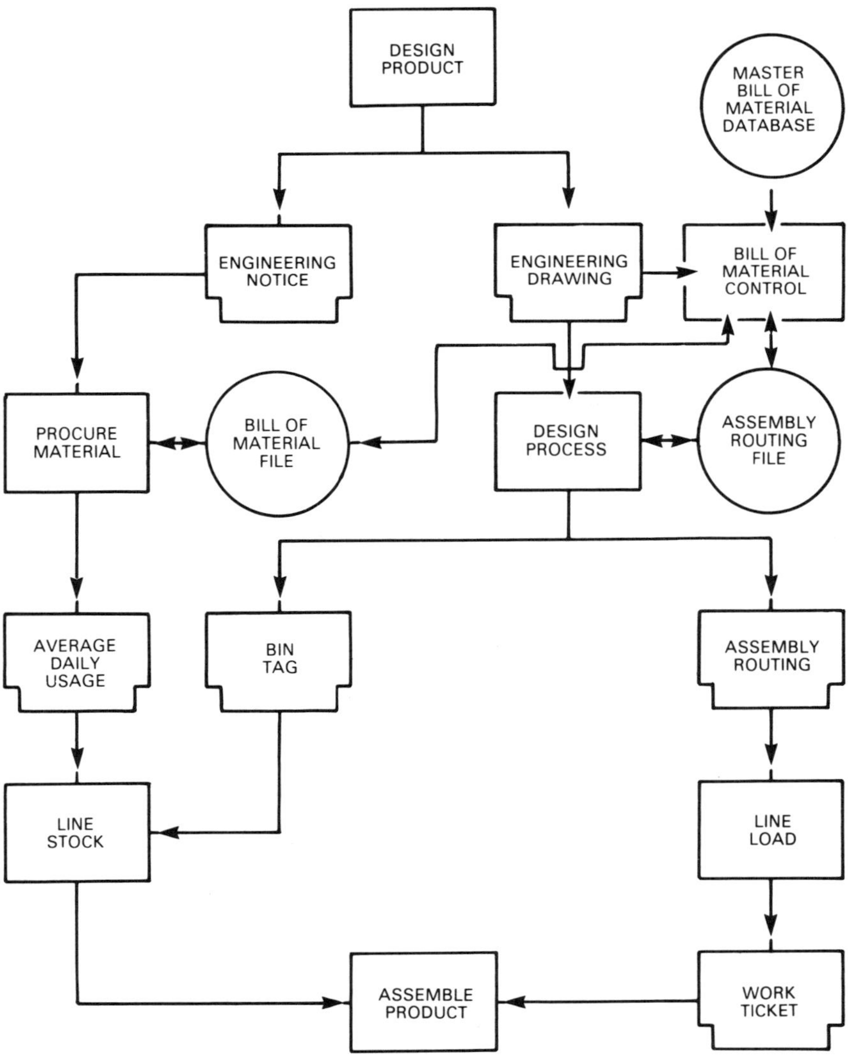


***Figure 9.8.*** Bill of material control

umbrella of the engineering bill of material. It is, after all, the authoritative source of all product bills of material. The final answer is to maintain a single bill of material database wherein each organization can view the product in whatever fashion is appropriate to the accomplishment of the organization's mission. This is discussed in more depth in Chapter 17.

## Exercise 9.3

Do you see any areas where the new methods of assembly and the new computer systems might result in conflicts of interest among different organizational units? Remember that people tend to try to make their own jobs easier, sometimes at the expense of someone else. List the potential conflicts you perceive to be possible.

## Conflicts of Interest

The pressures on people to perform their tasks can motivate them to do things which have a negative impact upon their neighbors. The following is a partial list of the possible conflicts of interest within the assembly area in this new world of build-to-order.

- The assembler has a tendency to be casual about those parts which have low value, and therefore isn't inclined to pick up dropped parts or to report damaged parts. This can result in a bin inventory record showing more parts than are really available for assembly. The Material Handling people can thus be put under pressure to respond to emergency orders for material which ought to be in the bins.
- The assembly processor is under pressure to document the assembly process more completely and accurately. This requires greater effort, with no obvious benefit to the processor. It is difficult for this one part of the organization to accept the need to increase its work load so that assembly and materials people can reduce theirs.
- The supplying facility doesn't necessarily like the idea of having to stock materials in order to reply to short dated orders from the assembly facility. The economic management of materials motivates toward the production of materials in economic quantities, and the shipment of full lots of material.
- If the inspection and testing of final product discloses damaged or nonconforming parts, they must be replaced. The natural tendency is to quickly replace the parts from the most convenient source. This is usually the assembly line bins.

  If one bin is short of parts, it is most convenient to supply it from another bin containing the same part. Another alternative is to substitute a similar part. This is easily done with such items as bolts and grease fittings.

  When such acts take place under time pressure (a 97% assembler load) there is little motivation to report the exceptions to the materials systems. This results in material records discrepancies, material shortages, and emergency orders for restocking bins.

- If a customer order becomes hot, or if some critical component is lacking, there is a tendency to vary from the established assembly sequence. This is a source of potential material shortage in the bins.
- If a unit of stock product needs to be reconfigured, there is again a tendency not to report the parts which are removed. Often such parts are not examined for recovery, but are merely scrapped. If they are returned to inventory, they might not be returned to the proper bins. This is especially true about parts which are stored in several different areas of the assembly line. This is one more source of record error.

**LAW**

**We Do as We are Measured.**

People tend to respond to the expectations implied in the primary measurements by which their performance is evaluated.

The thrust of this law is that people tend to respond to the expectations implied in the primary measurements by which their performance is evaluated. Often the measures of performance are directed toward the mission of the department without consideration of the mission of dependent departments.

For example, if Manufacturing is measured by the production of parts at a pace close to standard times, the timely delivery of parts to Assembly could suffer.

---

### Exercise 9.4

Can you think of examples of the above law from your own experience? How about the driver who drives past a fellow motorist with a flat tire because it is more important to get to the football game on time?

---

**LAW**

**A System Which can be Manipulated will be.**

Weak employees, like weak or "clever" managers, will tend to cheat the system.

The thrust of this law is that weak employees, like weak or "clever" managers, will tend to cheat the system. If it is easier to fake performance than it is to perform, then the weak employee will cheat the system. A wag once said that it is often easier to heat the thermometer than it is to heat the room.

An example is the machinist who has a good day of production and then does not report all of the work. He squirrels some of the parts away. When he has a bad day, he brings out the stored parts and reports them as just produced.

---

### Exercise 9.5

Can you also think of examples of this law from your own experience? What about the driver who drives at 62 miles an hour in a 55 mph zone, because he knows that the state police have their radar units set to detect speeds in excess of 65?

---

## Assembly System in a Transitional Factory

The case study in this chapter is an example of a manufacturing enterprise in transition to CIM and to JIT. The mechanized applications are generally patches on existing systems until refined systems can be defined and implemented. The computer applications are a means of adapting batch manufacture of components to a JIT assembly of final product to customer order.

The necessary systems components in this transitional manufacturing enterprise are:

1. A reliable bill of material reflecting the assembly sequence and lead time
2. A comparison of the assembly bill of material to the engineering bill of material to ensure that no components have inadvertently been added or deleted
3. Accurate assembly bin inventory records based upon reliable reports of material delivery, scrap, material movement between bins, and completion of assembly of final product
4. Computer-generated restock orders for assembly bins
5. Simplified cue cards to tell assemblers the unique option components to install on each unit of final product
6. Training of individual assemblers to expert levels for a limited variety of standard components and options
7. A mechanized line load assist to allocate assembly tasks within the task families taught to the assemblers
8. A mechanized line load assist to produce a reasonable (a bit less than 97%) burden for the average assembler.

## Assembly System in a Home Appliance Factory

The method of assembly of a product has a very significant influence on the systems by which supporting activities are managed. A few examples will illustrate the point.

A manufacturer of large home appliances operates with a build-to-stock strategy. A variety of final product is offered, but without options. The products are sold to retailers from a warehouse. The Sales department "owns" the inventory of final product and is measured on the inventory as well as on sales volumes. This tends to make sales projections more realistic.

The product is assembled on a moving assembly line in batches of identical product. The assembly of a single batch might last for as much as a week. The only variance in the product is the color of the exterior. The color of a unit is established by the color of the control panel. The cover panels are selected to match it.

Materials are delivered to the assembly line in prepackaged quantities, in the same packages in which they are received from suppliers. This eliminates any need to pick and count assembly materials. The only time material is counted is when a broken package is returned from the assembly line to storage. This happens at the time the assembly of a new batch of product begins.

There is not enough room at the assembly line to store many panels. These are delivered on an overhead conveyor. The assembler selects panels from the conveyor and stacks two of each type next to the assembly line. As panels are used from his store, the assembler replaces them from the conveyor. The warehouse then reloads the empty conveyor position with the equivalent replacement.

The assemblers are instructed by the foreman who walks the line with the first unit of a batch. The rate of movement of the line is slow at first until the assemblers become thoroughly familiar with their tasks.

This is an example of simple manual systems based upon simple strategies for assembly and management of materials.

## Assembly System in an Electric Hand Tool Factory

In this case, the product is assembled in batches like the home appliances. Assembly is done at a long table. As each assembler finishes his task, he places the finished module in a space between him and the next assembler. The assembler takes input from the left and places output to the right. There are no options and no color variations in the product.

Materials are stored in a locked warehouse until ordered by the assembly line. The parts are purchased in prepackaged quantities. There is no counting of material unless a package is broken or the unused remainder of a package is returned to storage at the end of assembly of a batch of product.

This is another example of simple systems from simple product and production strategies.

## Assembly System in a Computer Backplane Factory

A computer backplane is a large panel filled with wires to connect various circuits within the computer. Physically, a backplane is very much like a solid aluminum door with a rectangular matrix of thousands of holes. In large mainframe computers, the backplane is very much customized to unique customer specifications. It is unusual for several backplanes to be identical. The basic "door" is standard. The arrangement of wires on the backplane is customized.

The assembler sits at an assembly station with the backplane and about six boxes, each filled with wire assemblies of different lengths. The assembler completes the whole backplane at the single station.

A computer terminal tells the assembler each assembly step for the specific backplane. Each step consists of selecting a wire assembly of a specific length and plugging its ends into two backplane holes, identified by coordinates. The computer passes a current through the circuit to verify that the wire assembly is connecting the correct holes. If not, a warning is displayed until the assembler corrects the error. If the wire assembly has been correctly placed, the terminal displays the next assembly step.

The inventory of wire assemblies is assigned to the foreman of the assembly area. He is measured on material loss and scrap.

Although the product is assembled to customer order, the component part variety is very limited. The systems are simple. Even though a fast response computer system is required, its function is simple.

## Assembly System in a Japanese Auto Factory

In a specific Japanese auto factory, the assembly systems are driven by a simple marketing strategy. There are limited varieties of models and colors. They are manufactured in a scheduled mix aimed at satisfying the forecasted demands of the marketplace. The only options are air conditioning and radio. These are provided as kits for the dealer to install. The master schedule is set somewhat below market demand in order to ensure that all units will be sold and that customers will accept a color other than their preferred color—or will wait until the preferred one happens to be delivered to the dealer. The loss in sales is compensated for by economy in the production process.

The level of production is maintained at a stable rate. This allows suppliers to preplan their work and to deliver materials in modest quantities close to the time the material is needed. It also allows the production force to be stable and to operate at a stable, highly burdened rate.

The in-process inventory is very small, since the production rate is stable and the variety of product is small and preset.

An interesting convention exists between a parts cell and an assembly cell. They are separated by a rack which has slots to hold specific parts. The assembler selects parts from the rack to produce a subassembly. The empty slot in the rack is a signal to the parts cell that it must produce one of the specific part. Refer to *Figures 9.9* and *9.10*. In *Figure 9.9*, the rack is placed between the supplying parts cell and the assembly cell.

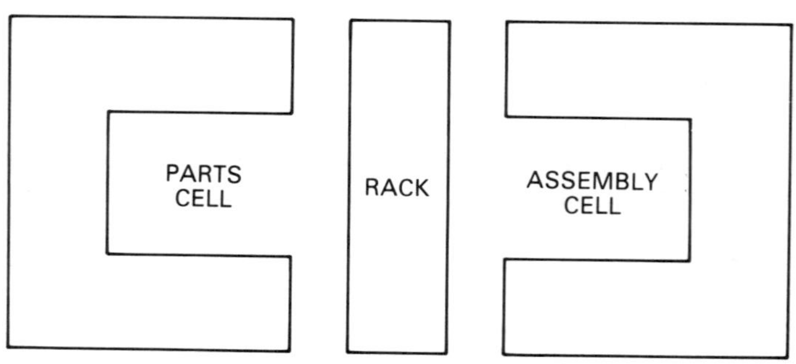


***Figure 9.9.*** Material storage rack between cells

In *Figure 9.10* the parts are pictured in the rack. Each slot in the rack has a tag marking the part which is to be stored in that place. With a quick glance at the rack, the operator of the supplying cell can tell which parts should be produced next. The parts missing from the rack are F73, G44, and A11. The operator will probably make G44 next, since there are two empty slots.

The factory uses computer systems to plan the master schedule and to establish burden rates for factory workstations. The daily operation of the production process is so simple and stable that there is little need for computer assistance.

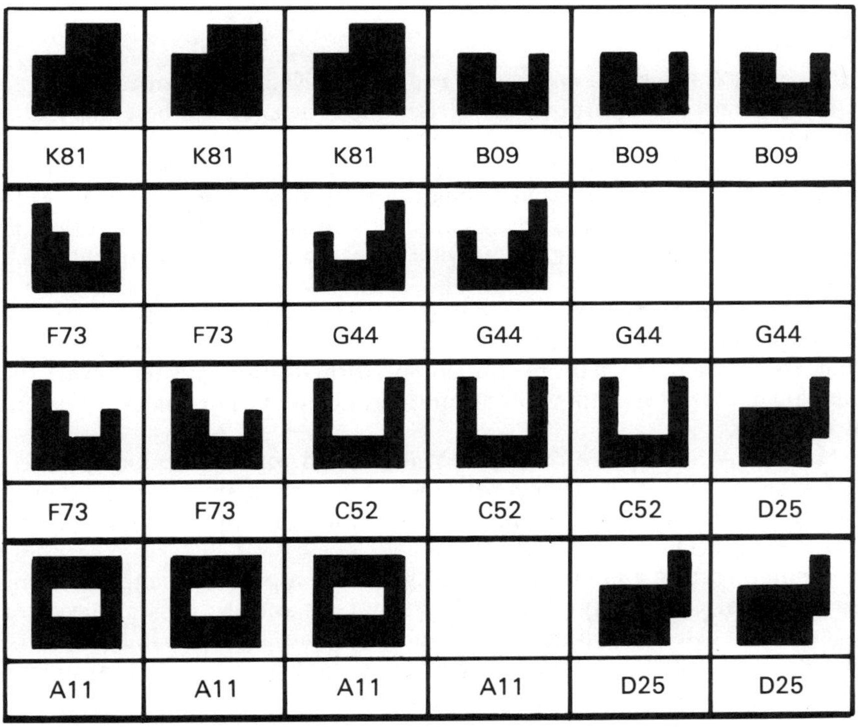


***Figure 9.10.*** Parts in an intracell storage rack

## Assembly to Customer Order Under JIT

The critical factor which will determine the operating strategy of a CIM facility in the future is lead time. It makes a world of difference if material procurement plus production lead time is more or less than the lead time from receipt of a customer order to the promised time of delivery of the final product. If procurement lead time is long, then material has to be provided in anticipation of customer orders. If procurement time is short, then procurement can be driven by the contents of customer orders.

In the first case, the operation of the factory is driven by a forecast of sales. In the second, it is driven by the assembly schedule.

If there are many options, then the forecast-driven factory will have to stock much material. If there are few options the material inventory can be reduced. In any event, the assembly schedule-driven factory can minimize in-process inventories.

The variety of options can cause significant assembly scheduling complexity in either type of factory. If possible, the schedule should be physically visible as it is in the storage rack between cells.

A key strategy, if possible, is staged assembly of modules, pulled by the assembly schedule of final product.

## Summary

People are subject to many outside pressures which can motivate them to work contrary to the purposes of a system and contrary to the best interests of neighboring functions within the business.

Analysis of assembly line functions illustrates that information systems and materials systems are quite similar. Each provides specific resources to operating units within the business. Each is subject to the motivation and dedication of real people to provide what is needed with quality and promptness.

**LAW—We Do as We are Measured.** People tend to respond to the expectations implied in the primary measurements by which their performance is evaluated. Often the measures of performance are directed toward the mission of the department without consideration of the mission of dependent departments.

**LAW—A System Which can be Manipulated will be.** Weak employees, like weak or "clever" managers will tend to cheat the system. If it is easier to fake performance than it is to perform, then the weak employee will take the easier route around the system.

Manufacturing and assembly strategies have a profound impact on the simplicity or complexity of information systems and the possible need for computer assistance in the production process. Key factors are the method of scheduling production (forecast-driven or assembly schedule-driven) and the variety of options.

# 10

# *Project Estimation*

## Introduction

There is a tendency to make project work estimates on too broad of a basis with the assumption that the development of mechanized information systems is more of an art than a science. In fact, many of the involved tasks can be estimated and controlled with some degree of accuracy. The purpose of this chapter is to give the reader some useful techniques which can be applied by users and by data processors.

## Estimating Steps

The best known way to estimate the staff time requirements for a phase of an information system development project is a three step exercise. The steps are illustrated in *Figure 10.1*.

The first step is to itemize the specific deliverables which are to be the final product of the phase. A deliverable is either a document or a piece of software or hardware, depending upon the phase. The easiest way to visualize a deliverable is to imagine that the phase of the project has been contracted to an outside firm. That firm is not expected to carry the work beyond the specific phase which has been contracted. The deliverables are those things which the outside firm must hand over at the completion of the contract so that the next phase can be contracted with someone else. The key point here is that the documentation of the results of the phase, the deliverables, must be complete. The major deliverables of each phase are listed in *Figures 7.5* through *7.12*.

1. List the Deliverables
2. List the Tasks
3. Estimate Time Requirements

***Figure 10.1.*** Estimating steps

The second step is to list the sequence of tasks which must be performed to accomplish each deliverable. Preferably, the tasks are listed in such detail that the longest tasks take no more than two to four weeks. It is also of value to develop a dependency sequence of the tasks in order to assist in the allocation of resources, and in the estimation of intermediate target dates and a phase completion date.

The final step is to estimate the resources required for each task. The most critical resource in an information system development project is staff time. It is easier to estimate resource requirements after the design phase. It is also easier to estimate resource requirements if the work of the earlier phases has been well done. A significant portion of this chapter is dedicated to a description of detailed staff estimation techniques.

## Exercise 10.1

Why is it of value to estimate and forecast resource requirements? This might seem like a foolish question, but there is ample evidence that many managers are reluctant to make advance estimates for staff work. Write down your thoughts.

## Reasons for Estimating

Although there are many valid reasons for estimating the anticipated staff time for a phase of a project, there are three primary reasons (*Figure 10.2*).

The first reason for estimating staff requirements is to use the information as a basis for estimating the cost of the development work. Sound development work is not based upon good feelings alone. Nor is it based upon return on investment alone. It is based upon management conviction that the effort is in the best interest of the organization, checkpointed by means of an economic evaluation.

The second reason is to estimate a completion date for the phase itself, and to estimate a coarse completion date for the project as a whole. The staff time estimates are applied to the sequenced tasks to determine a completion date for the phase, and possibly to determine intermediate checkpoints.

1. To Forecast Costs
2. To Estimate Completion Date
3. To Schedule Resources

***Figure 10.2.*** Reasons for estimating

Where there is competition for the time of critical resources, the estimates and the dependency sequence of tasks are necessary in order to plan in advance how to allocate these resources. This also helps to refine the phase completion date.

## Exercise 10.2

Should estimates be padded for safety, or should they be made so as to force progress at a fast pace? Write down the relative advantages and disadvantages you see for estimates which are optimistic, realistic, and pessimistic.

## Biases in Estimating

The possible impacts of the three biases (optimistic, realistic, and pessimistic) in estimating are illustrated in *Figure 10.3*. There are advantages and disadvantages to each.

| OPTIMISTIC |
|---|
| + Pressure on Staff to Perform<br>- Late Projects<br>- Shortcuts |
| **REALISTIC** |
| + A Basis for Scheduling Resources<br>+ A Basis for Performance Evaluation<br>- No Buffer for Problems |
| **PESSIMISTIC** |
| + Ensures Meeting Target Date<br>- No Pressure to Work Hard |

***Figure 10.3.*** Biases in estimating

If the estimate of staff requirements is optimistic, it surely tends to put pressure on the staff to complete the work with dispatch. But, it can backfire in terms of staff apathy and late projects, because the staff can develop the feeling of being used as a pawn. In order to meet tight target dates, staff can be tempted to cut corners in the work effort. This has the potential of lengthening later phases because of the need to complete the missing work.

If the estimate of staff requirements is realistic, it provides a sound basis for scheduling resources and for evaluating the performance of the staff. However, it allows no buffer for dealing with unexpected delays and difficulties. This is a particular problem in early phases of a project. It is also a problem in later phases if new technology is being employed.

If the estimate of staff requirements is pessimistic, it gives some degree of assurance that the target date for completion will be met. However, it puts no pressure on the staff for efficient performance of their tasks. Given more than adequate time, the staff can find it easy to waste time. This would add unnecessarily to the cost of the effort.

## Value of Realistic Estimates

In the experience of the author, realistic estimates are the best policy in the long range. They give a sound basis from which to make intelligent decisions. After all, a specific, identified pad of time can be added for contingencies without invalidating the original estimates.

A good general rule is to make realistic task estimates so that all project work comes reasonably close to the original phase estimate. Then it is to be expected that the majority of the tasks would be completed within some modest degree of error on either side of the target.

---

## Exercise 10.3

Reviewing the project phases in Chapter 7, what impression do you have of the possibility of overlapping the work of one phase with another? That is, can work on a later phase be started before work on an earlier phase is completed? There is often pressure to do this, since the user is customarily impatient for results, and since programming staff is often available before the systems analysis work is complete.

---

## Completion of Phases

A good general rule is to avoid overlap of the work between phases. There is always the danger of having to redo work on a subsequent phase because of some new complication discovered during the completion of an earlier phase. This is particularly true between the definition phase and the design phase. It is an exercise in discovery. The definition of a system is like removing the rocks from the bottom of a river. Until a large rock has been removed, there is no way to know how many small rocks might be hidden beneath it.

However, there can be some overlap of phases if necessary, particularly for phases after definition is complete. But a few conditions must be met. They are illustrated in *Figure 10.4*.

If the work plan for the subsequent phase has been completed, it usually means that some work can begin. If there were any expected surprises, the work plan could not have been completed.

If there is a shortage of work for key skills, as mentioned above for programmers, some work can be begun. However, care must be taken to

1. Work Plan for Next Phase is Complete
2. Shortage of Work for Key Skills
3. No Risk of Wasting Effort

***Figure 10.4.*** When to overlap phases

begin work only in areas where there is little possibility of change from completion of work on the previous phase.

Above all, work should only be done in areas where there is minimal risk of wasting effort for lack of completion of work in the previous phase.

## Traditional Estimation Error

Historically, information system development projects had a reputation for requiring twice as much time as was estimated. The data processing community had a poor reputation for project completion. The reputation was generally well deserved.

As the techniques for estimating and controlling projects have become more refined in recent years, the underlying causes of the originally poor estimates have become clear. Like many "discoveries," they should almost have been obvious from the start. The factors are summarized in *Figure 10.5*.

1. People Overestimate Ability 20%
2. People Overestimate Availability 20%
3. Testing Slows Progress 20%

80% x 80% x 80% = 50%

***Figure 10.5.*** Estimation error

As it turns out, most people tend to overestimate their ability. Another way of saying this is that they tend to underestimate the difficulties they will experience in a task. The amount of error in the typical estimate is 20%. It can be stated in two ways. A task will tend to take about 20% more staff time than originally estimated. The work effort required to complete a task will tend to be about 120% of the original estimate. Or, it can be stated that personal performance tends to be at a level 80% that of the estimate.

When people estimate the calendar time to complete a task, they often forget that they are not normally able to dedicate themselves full time to the defined task. They spend about 20% of their time in meetings, in training sessions, on vacation, on sick leave, etc. So, only about 80% of their time is available for the task in question.

Finally, in the later stages of testing and validating the results of the work, particularly in testing programs, the work tends to prolong. It is not so much dependent upon the amount of staff time invested as it is dependent upon the passage of time—time to gather the necessary people for meetings, time to wait for a computer test to be run, etc. In approximate arithmetic terms, the performance seems to be about 80%.

The total impact of the three factors can be phrased in rough arithmetic. The three 80% factors equal about 50% total performance when multiplied together. This is an explanation in principle of the early experience that information system projects seemed to take twice as long as estimated.

Once identified, these errors can be avoided in the future. All three errors can be avoided once we are aware of them. The next chapter offers a project tracking technique which deals with the first type of error. It proves to people that they underestimate what it takes to complete tasks—and that they overestimate progress once they have begun the tasks. Once the amount of error is demonstrated, future estimates can be made with greater accuracy.

The second type of error can be avoided by using such factors as a four-day effective work week or a 17-day effective work month. The third error can be compensated for by adding a pad to the calendar for the checkout activities at the end of phases, especially those activities which involve computer programs.

## Staff Experience Level

The lead analyst on a project team is usually the one who makes the work estimates. Such a person is usually a high performer and tends to estimate the amount of his or her own time which would be required to complete a given task. Then, out of respect for the fact that the typical team member is less skilled, the estimates are increased by a factor.

To aid in such factoring of estimates, guidelines are set up (*Figure 10.6*). These are based upon experience over numerous projects, and performance records of many staff members. If estimates are based upon the "average" programmer or analyst, the estimates should be multiplied by the appropriate factor from the figure. A top staff person performs at least twice as effectively as the average staff person. A staff person with about two years of experience takes twice as long as the typical experienced analyst. The novice takes four times as long to complete a task.

| | |
|---|---|
| 1. Top Analyst Programmer | x 0.5 |
| 2. Experienced Analyst | x 1.0 |
| 3. 2 Years Experience | x 2.0 |
| 4. New Programmer | x 4.0 |

***Figure 10.6.*** Staff experience factor

Of course, there are exceptions to this rule, just as there are for any rule. But it is a good starting point for task estimates and for selecting the person to be assigned to a specific task.

## Functional Knowledge Level

Different aspects of experience and skill levels are illustrated in *Figure 10.7*. While *Figure 10.6* refers to personal maturity in systems disciplines, *Figure 10.7* refers to experience the systems person has in the functional area of the business for which the information system is being developed.

| | KNOWLEDGE REQUIRED | | |
|---|---|---|---|
| JOB KNOWLEDGE | MUCH | SOME | NONE |
| Detailed | 1.00 | 1.00 | 1.00 |
| Good in General | 1.25 | 1.00 | 1.00 |
| Fair in General | 1.50 | 1.25 | 1.00 |
| Related Subjects | 1.75 | 1.25 | 1.25 |
| No Knowledge | 2.00 | 1.50 | 1.25 |

***Figure 10.7.*** Functional knowledge factor

The figure has two dimensions. On the vertical axis it refers to the level of knowledge the analyst has in the functional area. On the horizontal axis it refers to the level of knowledge of the functional area which is believed to be necessary to perform the task adequately.

## Rule of Thumb for Estimating Task Time

The basic estimate of staff time requirements for a task should be based upon what is expected of the average staff person. Tracking individual performance over a period of time can give a good basis for such estimation. This will be shown in Chapter 11.

The basic estimate is then multiplied by the appropriate factors from *Figure 10.6* and *10.7* to give a refined task estimate for a specific employee.

For example, consider a task which has been estimated at 10 staff days for an average staff person. The task is to be assigned to a programmer with two years of experience. Knowledge of the functional area is considered to be very important. The programmer has only a fair knowledge of the functional area. The final estimate is then 10 x 2.0 x 1.5 = 30 staff days.

Although the results of the above calculation might seem surprising, it is the author's experience that the performance of different staff people varies widely. At times it varies as much as eight to one.

### Exercise 10.4

To check out your understanding of the above concepts, calculate the final estimate of staff time to complete a task estimated as 10 staff days for an average staff person. The task is to be assigned to an experienced analyst who has good general knowledge of the user area of the business, but isn't familiar with it in detail. The task requires a significant amount of knowledge of the user area.

### Exercise 10.5

Can you define what you think is meant by *risk*? What types of risk do you think exist for information system development projects? List some of them.

## Risk—A Dictionary Definition

Webster defines risk as a hazard or a dangerous chance. In practice, risk is the possibility of failing to accomplish an objective. The failure might be partial or it might be complete.

## Risk—A Systems Definition

An information systems project is subject to a number of types of risks, (*Figure 10.8*). It is possible that the project might not be completed. The user might lose interest in the project, particularly if it takes too long. A more knowledgeable economic evaluation in a later phase might negate the return-on-investment expectations of an earlier phase.

1. Failure to Complete the Project
2. Development Cost Overrun
3. Failure of the System
   - o To perform as defined
   - o To perform within cost targets
   - o To accomplish objectives
4. Failure of User Acceptance

***Figure 10.8.*** Types of project failure

The actual development costs might prove to be significantly greater than the original estimates. This is a particular danger if only coarse work estimates have been made.

The system might be completed and put into operation, but then fail to live up to expectations. It might not do what it was intended to do—an error in definition, or design, or construction. It might perform the expected functions, but be exceptionally costly to operate. It might perform the desired function at the expected operating cost, but still be a failure. The theory of what it should do could have been in error. An example is the detailed assembly line load system in Chapter 9.

The user might provide the input, but for his/her own reasons fail to use the output. The previous chapters on case studies contained several examples of how this might happen.

## Exercise 10.6

What factors can you identify which tend to cause risk of project failure of one type or another? Make a list of them.

## Risk Factors

*Figure 10.9* lists a number of the most likely risk factors which apply to an information system project.

1. Project Size
   - o Large staff
   - o More than 18-month duration
   - o Multiple organizations
   - o Remote organizations
   - o Dependency on other projects
2. User Involvement
   - o Disinterest or apathy
   - o Limited available skills
   - o Pressure for a fast answer
   - o Lack of a decision maker
3. New Technology
   - o New hardware or software
   - o Weak supplier
   - o Complex logic
   - o No pilot system
4. Staff Capability
   - o Limited experience
   - o Possible turnover

***Figure 10.9.*** Risk factors

If a project is of a very large size, there is increased likelihood that it will last significantly longer than the 18-month guideline. Every additional month increases the possibility of premature system obsolescence.

If the project requires cooperation and compromise from a number of departments, the risk is increased. If some of the involved departments are not physically located near the development team, there is an increased risk due to the difficulties of communication.

If a project is dependent upon the successful completion of other projects, the risk is increased by any risk affecting the other projects. This factor applies when a large project is broken into modules. It also applies when a project is dependent upon the success of research into new equipment, software, or computational techniques.

A committed and capable user is critically important to development projects. If the user is disinterested, or apathetic, or even hostile, the project is almost certainly doomed to failure when the resulting system is placed in production.

If the user lacks the necessary skills, or if there is unusual pressure for a fast development effort, there is a danger of the system failing in some degree, due to inadequate analysis of true needs.

If there are many difficult decisions to be made, but no accepted decision maker, then the systems staff will be forced to make decisions by default. When this happens, there is no way to be certain that the right decisions are being made, or that the users will accept the results of the decisions when the system is implemented.

The introduction of new technology brings its own set of risk factors. New hardware and software are never without defects or bugs. In addition, there are always operating peculiarities to be discovered and adapted to with experience.

If the supplier of the new technology is weak, then the likelihood of unexpected bugs is amplified. There are a surprising number of new products which suppliers have been forced to remove from the marketplace after they have been subjected to production workloads.

If the new computer programs involve complex logic or algorithms, there is a significant risk of unexpected results under unanticipated conditions. If there was no opportunity to develop and exercise a pilot of the new system, then there is the possibility of unpleasant surprises for the user—and for the system builder.

Of course, there is a significant dependency upon the skill level of the systems staff. If they have only limited experience, then they are likely to leave holes in the logic of the new system. They are also likely to be naive as to what might be expected from a user.

The longer the project lasts, the more likely that it will be prolonged by turnover of systems staff. Every time a key staff member is lost, an investment must be made in bringing the replacement up to speed. In this process some continuity might be lost.

---

### Exercise 10.7

Do you see the possibility that any of the above risk factors might be accommodated by addition of some sort of time and cost pad in the work estimates of a phase of a project?

---

## Padding Estimates for Risk

Three factors seem to lend themselves to selective padding of task estimates (*Figure 10.10*). When a new technology is involved, allowance should be made for piloting it and working out the obvious bugs. In addition, time should be allocated for modifying plans when it becomes apparent that there are operating limitations under load. The amount of pad depends upon past experience with other new technology. The real exposure is the temptation to be overly optimistic about the quality of the new technology.

Staff capability can vary by a factor of up to eight to one, as illustrated earlier in this chapter. When in doubt, the best practice is to expect that the requirements of the work effort will be more complex and more demanding of staff skills than you might want to wish. With turnover, experienced staff is usually replaced by less experienced staff.

1. New Technology
2. Staff Capability
3. Staff Turnover

***Figure 10.10.*** Padding factors

Also, staff turnover adds new work in the form of updating and educating the replacement. Even if the lost employee maintained excellent documentation, it takes time for that material to work its way from the paper to the mind of the new staff person. On the average, six staff months of effort are lost by such a turnover.

## Summary

Successful systems work is highly dependent upon good task estimates. The first step in estimating a phase of a project is to identify the deliverables. Tasks for the deliverables are listed and sequenced. Then time estimates are made for the tasks.

Time estimates should be as realistic as possible, with allowances made for specific risk factors. Such factors include new technology, staff capability, and staff turnover. Realistic estimates are of great value in setting reliable target dates and in setting measurement standards for staff performance.

Several factors tend to cause projects to take up to twice as long as expected. People tend to overestimate their capabilities and the amount of time they have available for the project. Work tends to depend upon the passage of time and not the number of available resources when a phase nears completion.

There are reliable numeric techniques for making reasonably accurate staff time estimates.

There are a number of risk factors which can cause a project to fail even if the development work is completed. The best way to avoid failure is to deal realistically with the identified risks.

# 11

# *Project Tracking*

## Introduction

There is a tendency to assume that all is going well on a project unless someone reports difficulties. There is also a tendency for people to think that they are making more progress than they actually are. The purpose of this chapter is to expose the reader to a simple, manual, project tracking technique which brings to the fore any project stoppage—before the project is so far along that there is nothing that can be done to adjust plans and estimates.

## Exercise 11.1

Do you think that there is any value in trying to closely track progress on a large project? What reasons do you think there are which justify the effort?

## Value of Project Tracking

It is naive to believe that a large endeavor will stay on track without some sort of close managerial attention. The larger the project, the more necessary it is to employ some sort of project tracking system. The primary reasons for project tracking are summarized in *Figure 11.1*.

By keeping track of the work effort expended and the progress made on individual tasks, a manager can refine the estimates where they prove to be in error. Then, based upon the improved estimates, he/she can reallocate the work over available resources, and determine a likely completion date.

1. Refined Work Plans and Estimates
2. Tangible Measure of Progress
3. Projected Completion Date
4. Accurate Future Task Estimates
5. Upper Management Reporting

***Figure 11.1.*** Value of project tracking

A good project tracking system provides a measured and believable picture to the project manager of the rate of progress toward the completion of the project.

By comparing progress and work effort by task and in total, the project manager can make an educated estimate of the likelihood of meeting predetermined target dates. He/she also has a means of reliably predicting new target dates if necessary.

If a manager keeps records of the performance of the organization and of individual staff members on previous projects, he/she has a basis for improving future estimates. As stated in Chapter 10, accurate estimates are important in allocating resources and in planning target dates.

A good project tracking system provides a credible mechanism for measuring and reporting progress to upper management.

## Costs of Project Tracking

It takes time from the project work to estimate progress and to report how staff time has been spent. Most project team members tend to begrudge spending the time to report work effort. It seems to them that it interferes with progress.

In addition, an accurate tracking and reporting mechanism makes it very difficult for staff to hide problems or lack of progress. It also makes poor time estimates very obvious. People don't like their failings to come to the attention of their bosses.

Both of these deterrents can be handled by a wise and supportive manager who uses the tracking technique as an aid in improving estimation and planning capabilities. If the manager ever uses the technique as a club, the quality of the staff work will suffer.

## A Simple Project Tracking Technique

The remainder of this chapter describes a simple, manual project tracking technique which has been proven to be of value in numerous projects. It is not magic. It must be used with intelligence. It is not the only available technique, but, it is simple, proven, and...free.

The work effort should be broken into small tasks, hopefully from 5 to 15 or 20 days. Each task should, if possible, have a clearly-defined end point, such as the completion and acceptance of a deliverable (program, user manual, database layout, etc.).

The time to complete each task is estimated at the beginning of the project, or at least at the beginning of the point in time when it is decided to employ project tracking. These estimates can be adjusted if necessary after experience on the project has shown any of them to be significantly in error.

The progress on each task is reported weekly in the form of two factors. One is an estimate of the percentage of completion of the task. The other is the number of staff days actually expended upon the task. From these, the progress of the project as a whole can be measured, the estimates can be adjusted where necessary, and the completion schedule can be forecasted with ever-increasing accuracy.

## The Reporting Form

An example of the reporting form is shown in *Figure 11.2*. It is left blank in case the reader would like to make a copy of it to try it out on a project.

The project name, the target date for completion of the project, and the date of preparation of the form are entered at the top. The percentage overall performance of the project team is also recorded at the top of the form when progress is reported each week.

The tasks are listed in the body of the form and are sequentially numbered in the left-hand column. The heading "IN" heads a column under which are placed the initials of the person who is assigned to a task. The next column contains the target date for each task. The next column is for reporting the date on which a task has been completed.

The column labeled "EST" contains the number of staff days estimated to be necessary to complete the task. The total of all the estimates is placed in the box at the top of the "EST" label.

An example of a completed form for the start of a project is shown in *Figure 11.3*. The total estimated time for the project is 145 staff days, the total of the estimated staff days for each task. This estimated staff day is the base unit of measure against which progress and performance will be measured.

In the example, the report was filled out on August 10, 1986. The target date is December 1, 1986 for completion of the project to develop and install a small information system called ABC.

## Progress Report

*Figure 11.4* is a progress report about half way through the project. These progress reports have been developed weekly.

Three tasks have been completed. Their completion dates are shown, and they have been shown as 100% complete under the column labeled "%." The number of units of work completed (the number of estimated days) is 100% multiplied by the estimated days. The result is shown in the column labeled "COMP" for completed days of accomplishment. The actual staff days spent on the completed tasks are entered in the column labeled "ACT." Task 3 was estimated at 20 staff days, but took 26 actual staff days to complete.

For tasks which are not yet completed, the responsible staff person estimates the degree of completion and reports the number of staff days actually expended to-date. For task number 1, analyst TR estimated that the task of developing test materials is 80% complete and that he spent 16 staff days of

PROJECT:
DATE:
TARGET: PERFORMANCE:

| NO. | TASK | IN | TARGET | COMPLETE | EST | % | COMP | ACT. | R |
|---|---|---|---|---|---|---|---|---|---|
| | | | | | | | | | |
| | | | | | | | | | |
| | | | | | | | | | |
| | | | | | | | | | |
| | | | | | | | | | |
| | | | | | | | | | |
| | | | | | | | | | |
| | | | | | | | | | |
| | | | | | | | | | |
| | | | | | | | | | |
| | | | | | | | | | |
| | | | | | | | | | |
| | | | | | | | | | |
| | | | | | | | | | |
| | | | | | | | | | |
| | | | | | | | | | |
| | | | | | | | | | |
| | | | | | | | | | |
| | | | | | | | | | |
| | | | | | | | | | |
| | | | | | | | | | |

***Figure 11.2.*** The scorekeeping form

PROJECT: INFORMATION SYSTEM ABC
DATE: 8/10/86
TARGET: 12/ 1/86 PERFORMANCE:

| NO. | TASK | IN | TARGET | COMPLETE | EST | % | COMP | ACT. | R |
|---|---|---|---|---|---|---|---|---|---|
| | | | | | 145 | | | | |
| 1 | DEVELOP TEST | TR | 11/ 1/86 | | 15 | | | | |
| 2 | CONVERSION | DV | 10/15/86 | | 5 | | | | |
| 3 | PROGRAM A | TR | 10/15/86 | | 20 | | | | |
| 4 | PROGRAM B | TR | 11/15/86 | | 15 | | | | |
| 5 | PROGRAM C | DV | 11/ 1/86 | | 25 | | | | |
| 6 | DEV. TRAIN. | PJ | 10/ 1/86 | | 20 | | | | |
| 7 | SYSTEM TEST | FW | 10/20/86 | | 10 | | | | |
| 8 | OPER. DOC'N. | PJ | 10/25/86 | | 5 | | | | |
| 9 | INSTALL PLAN | PJ | 09/25/86 | | 5 | | | | |
| 10 | COORDINATION | FW | 12/ 1/86 | | 5 | | | | |
| 11 | UNPLANNED | | 12/ 1/86 | | 20 | | | | |
| | | | | | | | | | |
| | | | | | | | | | |
| | | | | | | | | | |
| | | | | | | | | | |
| | | | | | | | | | |
| | | | | | | | | | |
| | | | | | | | | | |
| | | | | | | | | | |
| | | | | | | | | | |
| | | | | | | | | | |

***Figure 11.3.*** The filled-in scorekeeping form

| PROJECT: INFORMATION SYSTEM ABC<br>DATE: 10/20/86<br>TARGET: 12/ 1/86 PERFORMANCE: 81% | | | | | 150 | 71 | 96 | 118 | |
|---|---|---|---|---|---|---|---|---|---|
| NO. | TASK | IN | TARGET | COMPLETE | EST | % | COMP | ACT. | R |
| 1 | DEVELOP TEST | TR | 11/ 1/86 | | 15 | 80 | 12 | 16 | |
| 2 | CONVERSION | DV | 10/15/86 | 10/15/86 | 5 | 100 | 5 | 14 | |
| 3 | PROGRAM A | TR | 10/15/86 | 10/12/86 | 20 | 100 | 20 | 26 | |
| 4 | PROGRAM B | TR | 11/15/86 | 10/20/86 | 15 | 100 | 15 | 18 | |
| 5 | PROGRAM C | DV | 11/ 1/86 | | 25 | 60 | 15 | 17 | |
| 6 | DEV. TRAIN. | PJ | 10/ 1/86 | | 20 | 50 | 10 | 8 | |
| 7 | SYSTEM TEST | FW | 10/20/86 | | 10 | | | 1 | |
| 8 | OPER. DOC'N. | PJ | 10/25/86 | | 5 | 80 | 4 | 4 | |
| 9 | INSTALL PLAN | PJ | 09/25/86 | | 5 | 100 | 5 | 4 | |
| 10 | COORDINATION | FW | 12/ 1/86 | | 10 | | 4 | 4 | A |
| 11 | UNPLANNED | | 12/ 1/86 | | 20 | | 6 | 6 | B |
| | | | | | | | | | |
| | | | | | | | | | |
| | | | | | | | | | |
| | | | | | | | | | |
| | | | | | | | | | |
| | | | | | | | | | |
| | | | | | | | | | |
| | | | | | | | | | |
| | | | | | | | | | |

A—5 DAYS ADDED DUE TO UNDERESTIMATION
B—PRESENTATIONS

***Figure 11.4.*** Progress reporting

work bringing it to that point. The amount of actual accomplishment from those 16 days of work is 80% of the originally estimated 15 staff days, or 12 staff days of accomplishment.

Coordination effort was estimated at 10 staff days. Although four staff days have been spent on the effort, it is almost impossible to estimate percent completion, since there is no deliverable. If necessary, the original estimate can be revised at any time.

The unplanned work was estimated at 20 staff days. This is a contingency pad. To-date, six staff days have been expended. As for coordination, no estimate of percent completion is appropriate, since there is no single defined deliverable.

The completed work is summed and entered in the box above the label "COMP." The actual investment in staff time for the tasks is summed up and entered in the box above the label "ACT." At the date of the report, 118 staff days have been expended to accomplish an effect of 96 of the originally estimated staff days.

Dividing 96 by 150 (the total estimate) yields the information that the project is 71% complete. This is entered above the box labeled "%."

Dividing 96 by 118 (the total staff day expenditure) yields the information that the work effort has been only 81% effective. This is entered to the right of the label "PERFORMANCE:" to show that the staff is accomplishing at a level 81% of the original estimate—about what most staff groups do until use of a project tracking technique shows them how to improve their estimating ability.

Although the above paragraph refers to the "original" estimate, this report actually was based upon a revised estimate. The revision is shown at the bottom of the form and keyed to the associated task in the column labeled "R." It is wise to allow updating the estimates in order to avoid staff embarrassment. After all, the exercise is for the purpose of tracking the project and improving staff estimates.

---

## Exercise 11.2

1. Which incomplete tasks in *Figure 11.4* require more work than originally estimated?
2. Which incomplete tasks in *Figure 11.4* require less work than originally estimated?
3. Which incomplete tasks in *Figure 11.4* are behind schedule?

---

## More Progress Reporting

*Figure 11.5* shows the report submitted the week after the report in *Figure 11.4*. Each of four team members has completed another four staff days of work. The estimate of accomplishment is the equivalent of 15 staff days of work (111-96). The performance has improved slightly from 81 to 83%. Actually, the performance was quite good, since the 83% represents cumulative performance from the beginning of the project.

| PROJECT: INFORMATION SYSTEM ABC<br>DATE: 10/27/86<br>TARGET: 12/ 1/86 PERFORMANCE: 83% | | | | | 150 | 74 | 111 | 134 | |
|---|---|---|---|---|---|---|---|---|---|
| NO. | TASK | IN | TARGET | COMPLETE | EST | % | COMP | ACT. | R |
| 1 | DEVELOP TEST | TR | 11/ 1/86 | | 15 | 90 | 14 | 20 | |
| 2 | CONVERSION | DV | 10/15/86 | 10/15/86 | 5 | 100 | 5 | 14 | |
| 3 | PROGRAM A | TR | 10/15/86 | 10/12/86 | 20 | 100 | 20 | 26 | |
| 4 | PROGRAM B | TR | 11/15/86 | 10/20/86 | 15 | 100 | 15 | 18 | |
| 5 | PROGRAM C | DV | 11/ 1/86 | | 25 | 80 | 20 | 21 | |
| 6 | DEV. TRAIN. | PJ | 10/ 1/86 | | 20 | 70 | 14 | 12 | |
| 7 | SYSTEM TEST | FW | 10/20/86 | | 10 | 20 | 2 | 3 | |
| 8 | OPER. DOC'N. | PJ | 10/25/86 | | 5 | 80 | 4 | 4 | |
| 9 | INSTALL PLAN | PJ | 09/25/86 | | 5 | 100 | 5 | 4 | |
| 10 | COORDINATION | FW | 12/ 1/86 | | 10 | | 6 | 6 | A |
| 11 | UNPLANNED | | 12/ 1/86 | | 20 | | 6 | 6 | B |
| | | | | | | | | | |
| | | | | | | | | | |
| | | | | | | | | | |
| | | | | | | | | | |
| | | | | | | | | | |
| | | | | | | | | | |
| | | | | | | | | | |
| | | | | | | | | | |
| | | | | | | | | | |

A—5 DAYS ADDED DUE TO UNDERESTIMATION
B—PRESENTATIONS

***Figure 11.5.*** Further progress

## Exercise 11.3

1. In *Figure 11.5*, what was the performance of the team for the work accomplished during the week of 10/20/86 to 10/27/86?
2. In *Figure 11.5*, how many staff days do you think will be required to complete task number 1?
3. In *Figure 11. 5*, how many staff days do you think will be required to complete task number 5?
4. In *Figure 11.5*, how many staff days do you think will be required to complete task number 6?

## Work Progress Tracking

The graph in *Figure 11.6* is a simple and effective way of tracking the progress of the project and of projecting the completion date. The horizontal axis represents the calendar weeks from the beginning of the project to the originally established target date. The weekly progress reports are plotted as asterisks. If the work progressed reliably at a steady rate of progress, the plot of asterisks would follow the line of dots from the origin of the graph to the + in the upper right-hand corner.

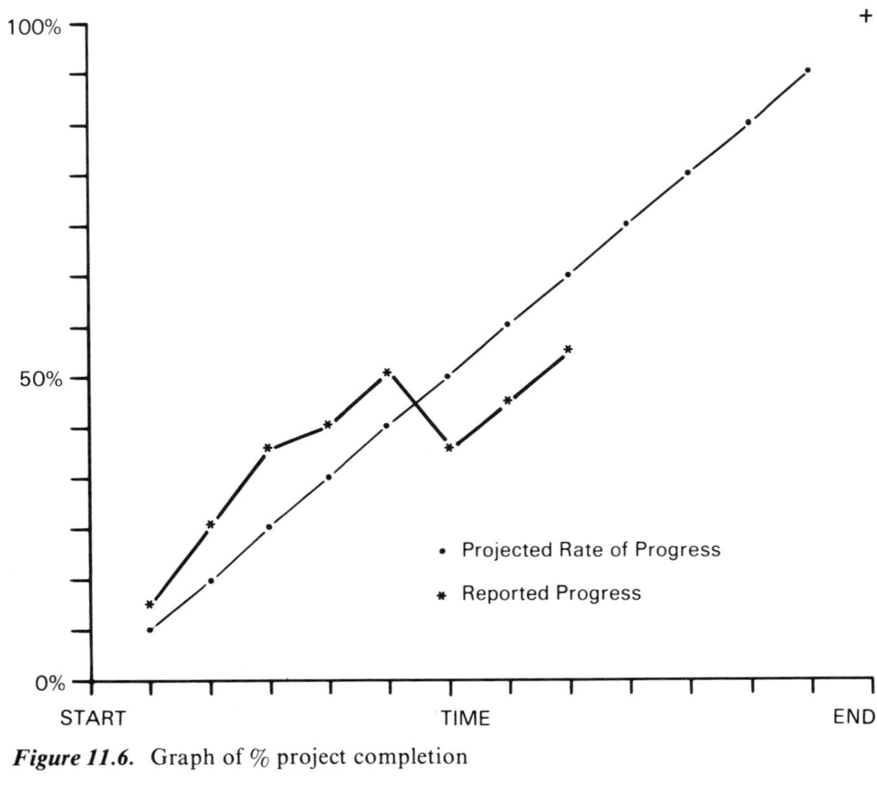


***Figure 11.6.*** Graph of % project completion

In the early weeks, the rate of progress seemed to be ahead of schedule. Then the rate seemed to slow down a bit in week number four. This is a normal pattern. People tend to overestimate the amount of work they have completed. As tasks near completion, the earlier overestimation of progress becomes apparent.

For a long task, the first week's estimate could be 40% complete. The second week the report could be 70%. The third week the report could be 90%. The fourth week it could be 95% with the explanation that some unexpected complications had arisen. The fifth week could be 98% with the statement that just a few little things remain to be cleaned up. The sixth week would probably bring a sheepish admission that the original estimates had been ureasonably optimistic and that the task was really only about 70% complete at this point in time.

This moment of truth is very important. Rather than being frustrated at the disappointing news, the project manager should ask the staff person to use the exercise as a learning experience, revise the estimate for all incomplete tasks, and strive for more accuracy in the future. From this point on, the project will probably proceed on a more reliable basis.

In the graph in *Figure 11.6* the moment of truth is shown as happening between week five and week six. If a project tracking mechanism like this is not used, the moment of truth will occur toward the end of the total project, not toward the end of early tasks. This would normally be expected to yield disappointing and unpleasant results.

## Estimating Completion Date

From the reports of progress in weeks six through eight, it would appear that the project will be completed about a week late. This is not so. The dependency of tasks should be reviewed to determine if any of the late tasks have a significant effect on subsequent tasks.

In Chapter 10, it was pointed out that a project could have a 20% delay in the later stages of completion due to testing and checkout activity, which are not as much dependent upon direct staff effort as they are upon completion of sequential tasks. For this reason, it is best to expect that later reports of progress will begin to drift to the right on the graph. The project will probably be completed three weeks later than originally estimated.

Staff productivity in the later stages need not decline if other work is assigned to fill in the time spent waiting for the results of tests by the computer and by users.

## Work Performance Tracking

The graph in *Figure 11.7* is another way of tracking the progress of the project. It illustrates the performance of the staff against the original estimates. In the early weeks, the performance is typically reported in the 120% range. Then, after the moment of truth, the performance drops.

From this point the rate of performance can be either 80 or 100%. It will be 80% if the original task estimates are not adjusted. In the author's experience, it is usually better for staff morale to reestimate the tasks so that performance

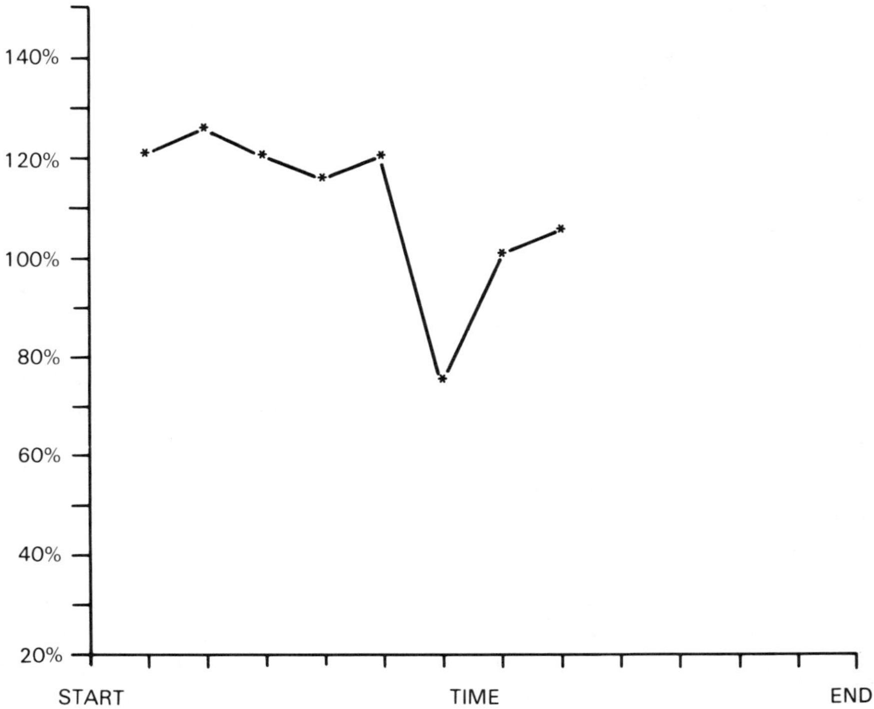


*Figure 11.7.* Graph of % performance

will be about 100%. This is consistent with the goal that project task estimation should be based upon realism.

In the case shown in *Figure 11.7*, the tasks were reestimated between weeks six and seven.

## Value of Project Tracking

The time spent by staff in reporting project progress is a small price to pay for the two benefits obtained. The project manager obtains an early and accurate perspective on the expected completion date and cost of the project. The staff learns a valuable lesson on the how and why of accurate estimating and progress reporting.

When progress on task completion is 80% of the original estimate, at least one of two possible causes can be identified. The original estimate could have been too optimistic, or the actual work effort could be deficient. Most people want to do a good job. For this reason it is usually better to assume that the estimates are the problem, rather than the work effort. If staff effort is assumed to be the cause, then the staff is in a position of being criticized for sloth rather than inexperience. Pressure to improve work performance could result in slovenly work to make apparent progress.

## Summary

A good project tracking system provides a measured and believable picture to the project manager of the rate of progress toward the completion of a project.

By comparing progress and work effort by task and in total, the project manager can make an educated estimate of the likelihood of meeting predetermined target dates. The manager also has a means of reliably predicting new target dates, if necessary.

The work effort should be broken into small tasks, hopefully from 5 to 15 or 20 days. Each task should, if possible, have a clearly defined end point, such as the completion and acceptance of a deliverable (a program, a user manual, a database layout, etc.).

The time to complete each task is estimated at the beginning of the project, or at least at the beginning of the point in time when it is decided to employ project tracking. These estimates can be adjusted, if necessary, after experience on the project has shown any of them to be significantly in error.

This chapter demonstrates a simple and effective technique for tracking the progress of a project and for learning how to make better task and project completion date estimates.

A graph is a simple and effective way of tracking the progress of the work effort and of projecting the completion date.

The time spent by staff in reporting project progress is a small price to pay for the two benefits obtained. The project manager obtains an early and accurate perspective on the expected completion date and cost of the project. The staff learns a valuable lesson on the how and why of accurate estimating and progress reporting.

# 12

# *Case: Product Options*

## Introduction

Manufacturing companies have great difficulty in handling attachments, options, customization, or any form of variation in the standard product to satisfy the desires of individual customers. It is difficult to balance the pressures for responsiveness to the customer and the pressures to limit component inventories. It is especially difficult if the various departments act for only their own best interests. This chapter contains a case study of product options. The purpose is to illustrate how deeply interdependent the various functional areas of a company are upon one another. They must work together to accomplish effective response to the marketplace.

## Planning for Options

The process of planning and controlling the inventory of options is very complex. The typical systems and information flow for planning option inventories are shown in *Figure 12.1*. It illustrates a typical older system of planning for options in a build-to-stock industry.

Procurement and manufacture of production materials is in monthly lots. For this reason it is necessary to make a forecast of the expected volume of each option which might be ordered by customers. If the inventory of option material is inadequate, the result is lost sales or delayed delivery of customer orders. If the resulting inventory is excessive, there is a high material carrying cost in terms of borrowed money, storage space usage, and loss of material due to deterioration, damage, or loss.

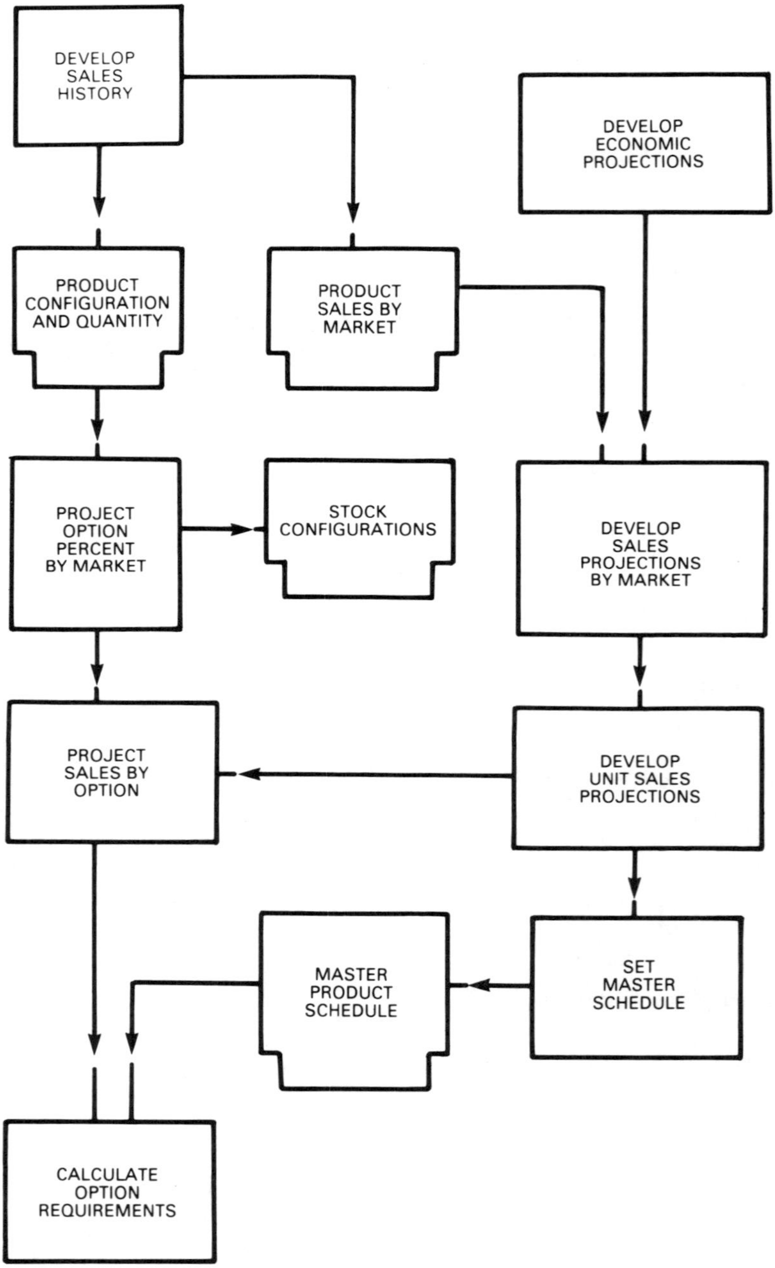


***Figure 12.1.*** Planning for options

The production materials which compose the option inventory are not stored in kits as completed options. They are procured, manufactured, and stored as individual piece parts and subassemblies. Many parts are components of both finished standard products and of options. The option materials are marshalled and delivered to an attachment bay as appropriate to modify a finished product to customer order.

In this case study, the manufacturing company is a build-to-stock manufacturer which has found the marketplace to be forcing it to build-to-order much of the time. However, the systems were designed around the concept of build-to-stock.

## Develop Sales History

A mechanized system maintained a history of the sales of final product to customers. The history file contains such data as the date each unit of final product was built, the date it was sold to a customer, the list of options installed on the product, the type of work to which the customer intended to apply the product, the type of market in which the customer competed, and the general geographic area in which the customer located his/her place of business. The term *market* refers to the type of industry in which the customer works—railroad, farming, mining, lumbering, for example.

With the record of each unit of product there is an associated model code. The model code indicates the specific type of product. Example products in an auto manufacturing company could be compact cars, station wagons, or pickup trucks. Different products tend to be used in different applications.

Every month a set of statistical programs are processed against the history file. They produce a report of the historic distribution of demand for the product in the marketplace. Two types of reports are prepared.

The first report is a list of the most commonly ordered options for each product for each different type of market. The report shows the frequency of use of each option on each type of product in each type of market. In the auto analogy, the report might say that a clock was ordered for 95% of the luxury cars sold to private owners, but was ordered for only 60% of the luxury cars sold to auto rental agencies. The report shows this percent of option use in each past year, by month.

The second report is a summary of the percent of each model sold in each type of market in each year in the past. This report is also by month. The first report is a set of tables of monthly demand by product over the various markets. The second report is a set of tables of the percent of each option ordered by month on each of the various products.

## Develop Economic Projections

A computer system processes a linear programming model to develop a projection of expected total dollar sales for several years into the future. The economic model considers the historic relationship of product sales to such factors as gross national product, single dwelling housing starts, and value of mine production.

Given a projection, however fallible, of the expected growth or shrinkage of the various markets, the model makes a statistical projection of the monthly total dollar sales of product. This projection is made by market—the expected dollar sales to lumbering, or the expected dollar sales to mining.

## Develop Sales Projections by Market

A third computer system develops a projection of product sales by market for each model of product. The projection is rather simple to compute, given the output of the two previous systems—product unit sales history by market, and dollar sales projections by market. The result of the computation is a dollar sales projection by model by market. The projection is made in terms of the number of dollars worth of each product expected to be sold each month for two years in the future.

## Develop Unit Sales Projections

The result of the sales projection by market is then translated into a projection of total product unit sales for each model of product. This computation is also done by computer. It uses the current price of each model of product as added input. (This is not illustrated in *Figure 12.1.*) This projection, like the others, is by month for two years into the future.

The final product is sold through independent dealerships who each maintain an inventory of final product. The inventory is for display and to satisfy short-dated customer orders. Another system maintains a record of the final product inventory within the dealerships. This inventory is taken into account when making unit sales projections.

## Set Master Schedule

The projection of monthly unit sales by model is reviewed by the head of the company. It is adjusted moderately where subjective business judgement suggests that past history might be a poor indicator of future trends. The resulting projection becomes not just a refined projection, but also a master schedule for the production of final products.

The master schedule is more than the results of a refined forecast. It is an order to the Assembly department, to the Manufacturing department, and to the Materials Planning and Purchasing department. It dictates the quantity of material which will be purchased by month, the quantity of parts and subassemblies which will be manufactured, and the number of units of final product which will be assembled. This quantity is set, no matter what the level of customer orders might prove to be.

Of course, the farther the schedule is set into the future, the more fallible the projection. For this reason, the master schedule is an order for production for only the first several months. That is, it is an order for the procurement and production of material within the lead time of the processes of procurement and production. Outside that horizon, it is not an order, but a projection based upon the best intelligence available. Beyond the lead time horizon, the master schedule is a forecast for planning purposes.

Usually the process of developing the master schedule in one month results in a different projection of expected sales volumes from that of the previous month. Based upon this new projection, quantities could be changed in months beyond the material lead times. This period, usually three months, is known as the *freeze period*.

## Project Option Percent by Market

The historic percent of sale of each option on each product is used in a computer system to make a projection of probable future sales. This is calculated as a percent of use on future sales of final product. The computation technique uses a time series analysis which takes seasonability of demand into account. The computational technique is quite sophisticated, but the variability in the historic data is such that the projection contains an appreciable amount of potential error.

At the same time that this computation is performed, an analysis is made of the historic data to determine several stock configurations of each final product. Such a configuration consists of a final product and a selection of commonly used options.

This selection of stock configurations results in different configurations for different types of markets. This concept of a stock configuration is quite important. The master schedule is based upon a build-to-stock concept. Product will be built to customer order if the order is in hand. But for lack of a customer order, the product will be assembled to a stock order so that the total authorized assembly rate is honored.

Since the product is built-to-stock, it is important to have on-hand units of product which can readily be adapted to satisfy a given customer order. This adaptation is done by installing options to the stock unit in an attachment bay. More than that, it is very expensive if a unit of stock product contains an option which is not desired by the customer. The removal of such an option causes material scrap and wasted labor. It also has the potential of causing leaks in liquid compartments of the vehicle.

## Project Sales by Option

The projection of option percents by model is matched against the unit sales projections by model. It is a relatively simple computation to translate the results into a quantity projection of expected sales of each option on each product. The total quantity of each option is then summed by month into a sales projection for each individual type of option.

Consider a specific clock used as an option on two different models of final product. It is projected to be sold on 20% of model A and 30% of model B. In a given month, sales of 50 and 100 units are projected for models A and B respectively. Thus, the projected demand for the clock is 40 (20% of 50 and 30% of 100).

## Calculate Option Requirements

The calculated projection of option sales is matched against the master product schedule as a final check on the accuracy of the forecast. On occasion, the projection is changed by the head of the company, as is the projection of final product sales.

The master product schedule is a specific order for the assembly of a number of units of final product. The master option schedule is an order to have on-hand a given quantity of finished option material in anticipation of customer orders.

Because any projection is subject to error, a safety stock of option material is kept on-hand. If the safety stock falls to a low point or accumulates to an excessive quantity, an adjustment is made. The first month of projection beyond the freeze period is adjusted up or down to bring the safety stock within reason.

All of these systems are mechanized due to the volume of record keeping and the need for accurate and speedy computation. These systems are all based upon simple files, since the systems were developed before computer technology provided for databases.

## Providing Options

The above sequence of activities is dedicated to the purpose of planning for the stocking of production option materials in advance of their use to satisfy customer orders. There is another sequence of systems which is dedicated to the physical provision of option inventories. The relationship between the two sequences of systems is shown in *Figure 12.2*.

## Rackup Requirements

The master option schedule is a directive to procure and produce a specific schedule of option material quantities. The directive is not absolute. The Materials Planning and Purchasing department personnel are free to modify the schedule as long as the modification does not result in lost customer orders due to option shortages.

The Materials people are measured on the basis of material availability. They are also measured on the basis of the total value of production materials in inventory. In order to satisfy the second measure, they sometimes reduce the quantity of some option materials below the authorized level, gambling that there will not be a high level of customer demand for them.

Since there is a safety stock of option materials, and since some options use common materials, this selective reduction of the schedule is not as much of a risk as might first appear. The process of adjusting the master option schedule is called the *rackup*. It is done mainly by a clerk who operates under broad management guidelines.

## Rackup Example

As an example of the rackup process, consider a farm tractor which can be purchased with any of three optional cabs. The first, an open cab, is called the *standard option*—the option normally installed on the tractor unless the customer orders a different option. The second and third optional cabs are an air-conditioned cab and a cold-weather cab.

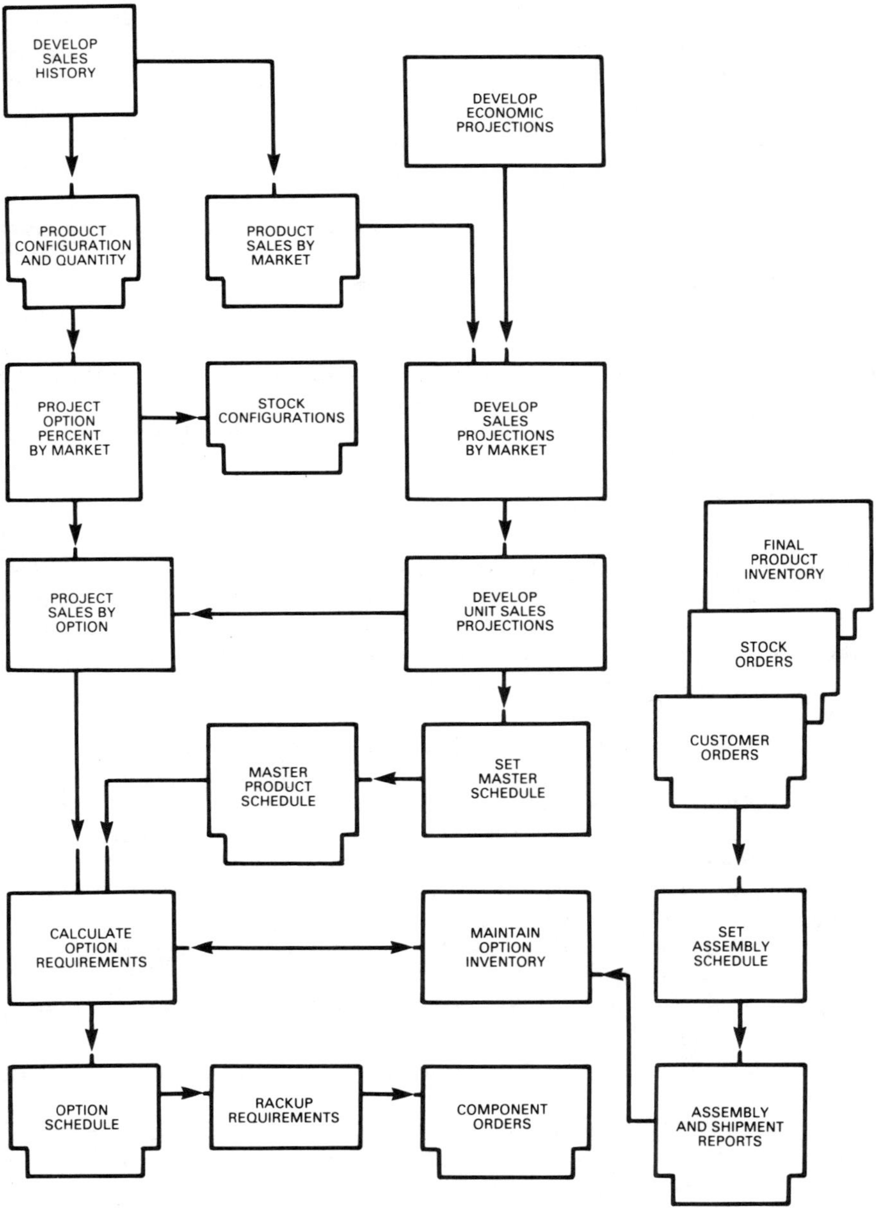


***Figure 12.2.*** Providing options

The master product schedule calls for assembly of 100 farm tractors next month. Historic sales rates result in a projection that of the 100 tractors, 50 will be ordered with open cabs, 30 with air-conditioned cabs, and 20 with cold-weather cabs. Because there is fluctuation in the pattern of customer orders, a safety stock is provided in the schedule for each type of cab—15 for the open cab, 10 for the air-conditioned cab, and 8 for the cold-weather cab. In total, the inventory at the beginning of the month is to include the components for 65 open cabs, 40 air-conditioned cabs, and 28 cold-weather cabs. This is a total of 133 cabs, 33% more than could possibly be sold. For this reason, the Materials people could safely make some careful reductions in the schedule.

The final racked quantities of the options are passed on to the material requirements system. This system explodes the quantities for the option rackup, together with the quantities from the master product schedule to calculate the total required component quantities. From this, orders are prepared for the purchase and manufacture of parts and subassemblies. These materials are to be available for use the first day of the month of product assembly—a full month of materials.

## Set Assembly Schedule

Each month, a final product assembly schedule is set. It receives a lot of weekly and daily adjustments, however, as customer orders change and as last minute customer orders are received. The quantity of each model is dictated by the master product schedule. But the assembly schedule is set to alternate the different models on the assembly line for efficient distribution of labor—a high burden product being followed by a low burden product. In addition, specific customer orders and stock orders are slotted for specific days in order to honor customer delivery dates and to maintain the inventory of stock product.

The options to be installed on each scheduled unit of final product are set by the customer order or the stock order. Most such options are installed in the attachment bay, but some are internal to the product and are installed on the assembly line. If a customer order arrives after the month's assembly schedule has been set, it could replace a similar stock order in the schedule. This avoids the need to bring a stock unit in from the storage area and the need to take a completed stock unit back to the storage area.

When customer orders arrive in excess of the assembly schedule, a review is made of a manual stock unit inventory record to see if an appropriate stock unit exists in inventory. That is, a search is made for a stock unit with compatible options.

Since a safety stock of option material is maintained, there is no review of the option inventory to ensure that the necessary option materials are available. It is expected that they will be.

## Option Inventory

Every day, reports are made of the assembly of product, which options have been installed, and which units of product have been shipped to the dealers in response to customer orders. These reports are used daily to track production against the master product schedule.

A theoretical inventory record is maintained of the inventory of options. It is theoretical for a number of reasons. For accounting and tax purposes, an option is not considered as part of a final product until the product has been shipped. Weeks could elapse from the time of assembly of an option on a product to the time it is shipped. Months could pass from the time of assembly of options on a stock unit to the time of attachment of options to a customer order, and then to the shipment of the product.

Also, since the options exist as individual parts and subassemblies in tubs and bins, they do not really exist as finished options. Finally, the attachment inventory is not reduced for consumed options until the end of each month. As a result, the option inventory is not a record of option availability, but a starting point from which the option inventory could be calculated—with questionable validity.

The addition of options into the option inventory comes from the master option schedule. Each month the authorized quantity of each option is accumulated against the option inventory at the same time that the consumed options are subtracted from the inventory. The rackup function exists as a tolerated exception to the preferred system, so it is the rackup quantity and not the master option schedule quantity which is added to the option inventory.

In summary, the inventory of an option is a theoretical quantity of the option. It consists of the total scheduled (rackup) quantity of the option from the time the option was first released for production, less the total quantity of options installed on final products which have been shipped to dealerships. The options on units of product not yet shipped are considered to be in the option inventory.

## Product Changes

As shown in *Figure 9.2*, the number of models of final products has increased significantly. There is a greater number of total units of final product which are assembled each day. There is a greater variety of available options; and a greater number of them are included in a typical customer order. Many of the new options are designed so that they must be assembled into the final product on the assembly line. They cannot be added to the final product in an attachment bay.

## Process Changes

There are also a number of very significant process changes, shown in *Figure 9.2*. Most options are installed in the final product on the assembly line simply for the increased efficiency of assembly labor. The length of time that a product is physically present on the assembly line has lengthened to a period of up to five days. This is a result of the increased assembly line burden from the installation of options. The variety of options has caused a marked increase in the variety of assembly materials stored in bins along the assembly line. Many of the bins hold only a few days of material due to space constraints.

In essence, the assembly process has changed from assemble-to-stock to a process of assemble-to-order, but the supporting systems are still based upon assemble-to-stock practices.

## Exercise 12.1

Do you perceive any specific problems which might be caused by this evolution to assemble-to-order practices? Certainly the assemble-to-stock systems cannot all be appropriate for such a dramatic change. Make a list of your observations before you read farther.

**Problem 1.** The projection of product sales from a sales history is subject to error when the demand for product exceeds the production capacity. Production capacity places an upper limit on the sale of product. At such times, more units could have been sold if the capacity were available. What was the true demand for product? One cannot make reliable projections of the future based upon flawed observations of the past.

**Problem 2.** How can one reliably and quickly determine if a stock unit of product can be readily adapted to a specific customer order? If the number and variety of stock product is large, the screening of customer orders can be difficult and error-prone. Which stock orders can be used without the need to retrofit? Which is the specific unit which will require the least labor in the attachment bay?

**Problem 3.** If the quantity of stock units is very large, there is the possibility that a customer will refuse to accept a product whose serial number suggests that it was originally produced many months in the past. It is missing the latest engineering changes—probably implemented for better performance, better operating economy, and better safety. After all, nobody really wants last year's model unless there is a significant price incentive. How can the inventory of stock products be monitored and controlled so that the oldest units tend to be used first?

**Problem 4.** Does option inventory really exist? There doesn't seem to be much sense in considering an option as available when it might already be installed on a unit of unshipped product. There is a possibility that incoming customer orders can call for more of a type of option than is available in inventory. This would cause the assembly of an incomplete unit of product. How can one be sure that the option is available, especially if a rackup function reduces the quantity of options in inventory?

**Problem 5.** The options don't really exist as options; they exist as piece parts. How does one take into account availability of components which are common to several options?

**Problem 6.** Many options have common components. When the options are authorized with safety stock, the common components can be procured or produced in excessive amounts. Consider the tractor cab example. If the frame of the three optional cabs is a common item, then the safety stock would include 133 frames when only 100 could possibly be used in a month of assembly. How can one avoid an inflated inventory of material which is unneeded, and indeed, cannot be used?

**Problem 7.** Some options are mutually incompatible. If you install option A, then you can't install option B. You can't install an air conditioner in an open cab. At least, you don't do it if you are sensible. There are other option interdependences. If you install A and B, then you must also install C. In an automobile, one must accept hydraulic steering if one wants hydraulic brakes. How does one determine whether a customer order is calling for a valid combination of options?

***Solution 1.*** When orders are in excess of production capacity, some sales are lost. An estimate can be made of the volume of sales lost by failure to respond to the delivery dates requested by customers. This is very subjective, but it is likely to result in less error than failing to adjust the sales record.

***Solution 2.*** A computer application could be developed to screen customer orders against stock products (*Figure 12.3*). A file of stock orders could be maintained with a list of the options installed on each. It would also be of help if a supplemental master file were maintained to keep a record of each option, showing the burden to install it, the burden to remove it (retrofit), and indicating whether the option is an add-on or must be built-in.

***Solution 3.*** The solution to this problem is more one of a change in company strategy than it is one of information system techniques. The problem would be reduced if a policy were established limiting the amount of stock product which could be stored. If stock inventory becomes too large, the carrying cost of the inventory is greater than the potential revenue loss from lost sales for lack of product. Stock inventory and lost sales should be kept in balance by economic evaluations on a regular basis.

The above system for maintaining an inventory of stock products would be of assistance. It would also assist in monitoring the age of stock units.

This solution illustrates a point made in Chapter 4. Computer systems should not be used as band-aids for business problems. Very often a more effective solution can be found by rethinking the function in question.

***Solution 4.*** This is another information problem which can be avoided or reduced by a change in company strategy. Any option which is installed on a unit of product could be considered unavailable for other use. That is, it is allocated to an order.

The original convention of retaining the option in production stores inventory rather than in finished product inventory was based upon accounting and tax principles. This was a case of allowing supporting practices to overshadow the primary function of good materials management.

The installed option could be flagged as unavailable and still be considered as part of finished product inventory. This would require a change to the option inventory system.

Once the option inventory is made more realistic, the same inventory can be used to screen customer orders for option availability (*Figure 12.4*). An option in inventory could be available, allocated to an order, installed on a

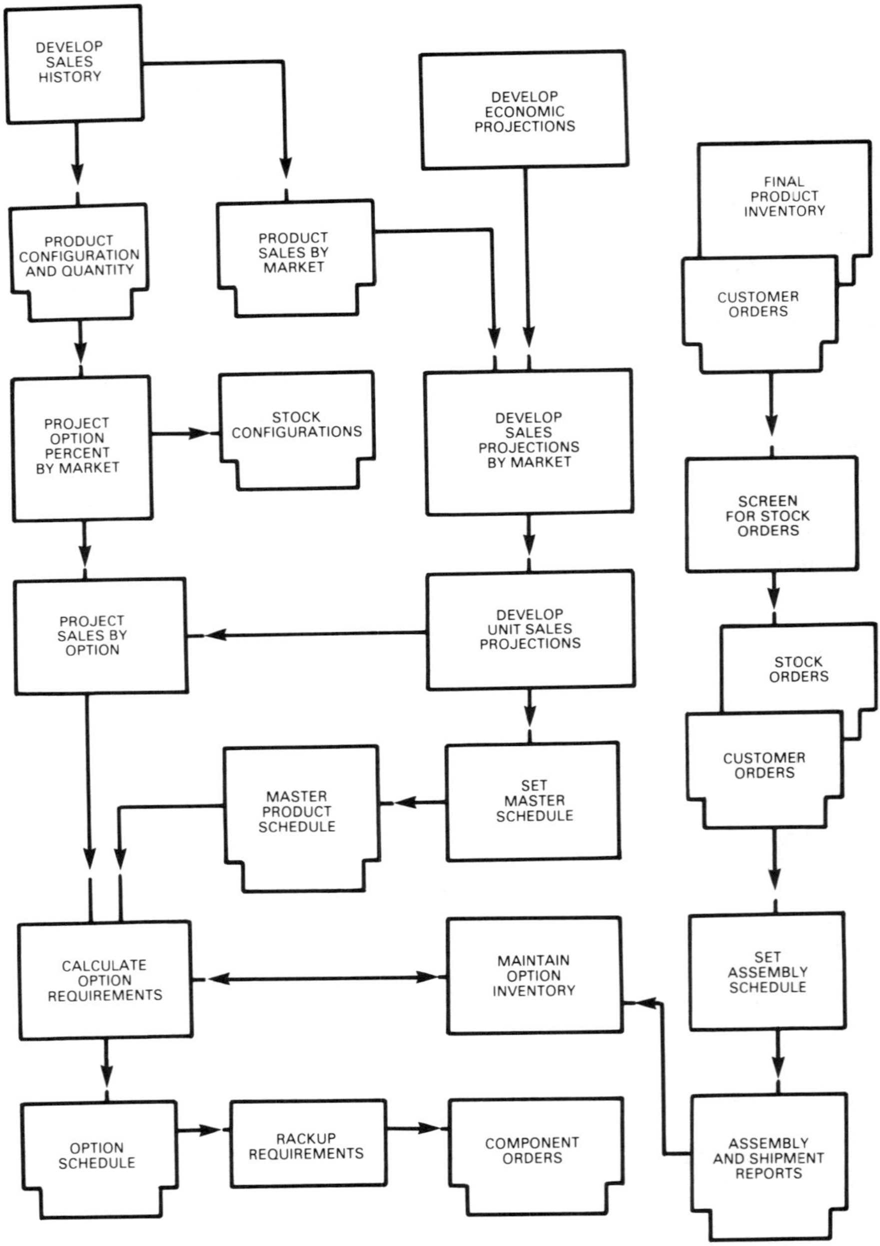


***Figure 12.3.*** Screening for stock orders

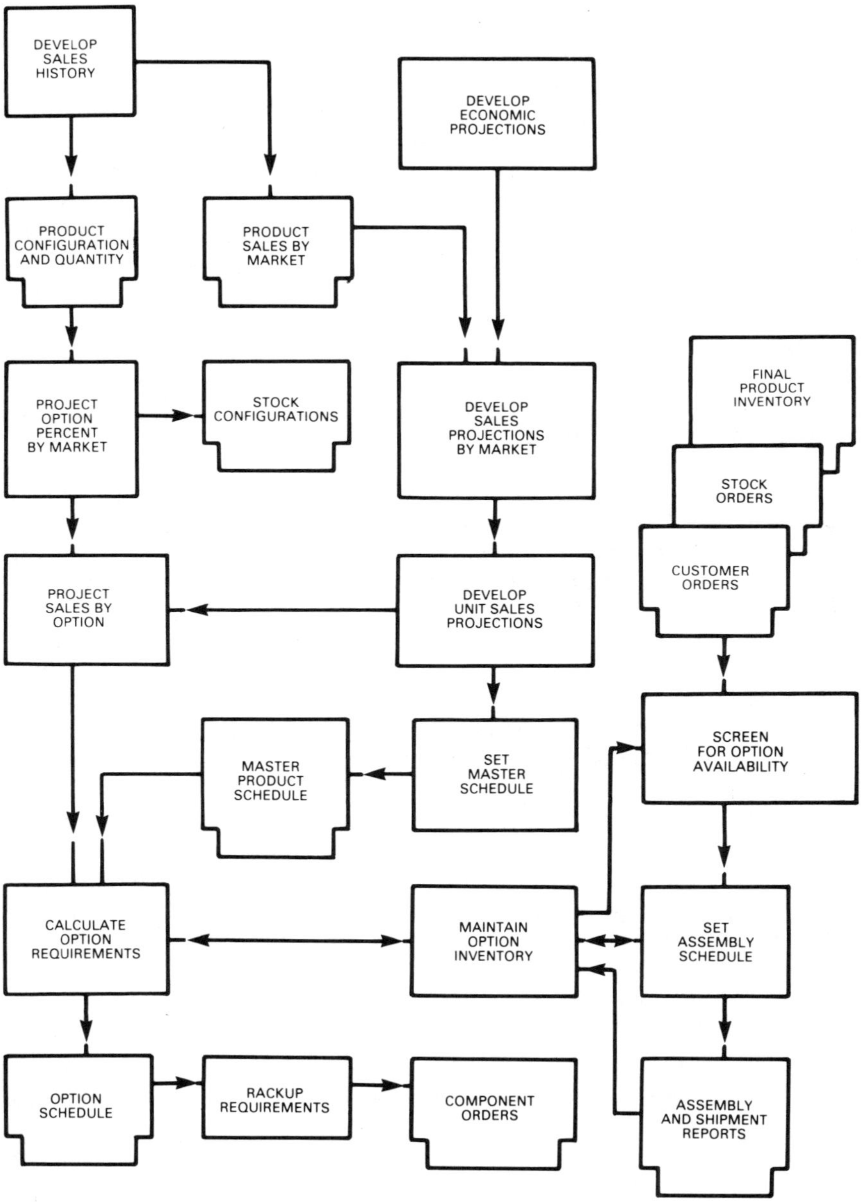


***Figure 12.4.*** Screening for option availability

unit of product, or shipped. If a customer order calls for an option which is not available, the assembly of the product must be postponed until the option can become available—unless the option is one which can be added in an attachment bay.

***Solution 5.*** Key components of options could be the control in the screening of orders. For each option this could be a single component which has no usage other than on a specific option. Preferably, it would be one of the more expensive components, or one with a long lead time. An example is the air conditioner as the key component of the air-conditioned tractor cab. It would be assumed that the smaller and more widely used components will likely be available. Although this solution is not a complete solution, it is a significant step forward from the past practice which assumed that all components were available.

***Solution 6.*** A computer system (*Figure 12.5*) could be developed to evaluate common material and compare its total authorized quantity to the total authorized quantity of the final products on which it can be used. The procurement quantity could then be limited to the authorized quantity of final product or even to a percentage of that quantity.

Safety stock is based upon statistical computation of the variance in customer demand. The variance of demand for the total of several items is the sum of the variances of the individual items. Based upon intelligent use of statistics, the inventory of option material can be minimized without additional exposure to stock outs.

***Solution 7.*** The computer application which screens for option availability (*Figure 12.4*) could be changed to make it also screen for option compatibility. It would require, however, the development of a file of option dependencies. The file would contain records linking options which are mutually incompatible, and showing those options which require the installation of other options.

## Exercise 12.2

Can you identify any business policies or strategies (a policy is an operational statement reflecting a strategy) which have affected the operation of the business as illustrated in the above case? Consider *Figure 12.1* and the accompanying description. After all, the concept of build-to-stock is itself a strategy.

## Key Strategies

Some of the more important strategies which have influenced the management of options are:

- Assemble exactly as many units of product as the master product schedule authorizes, whether or not there is a customer order.
- Assemble stock orders to fill in the gaps where there are insufficient customer orders.

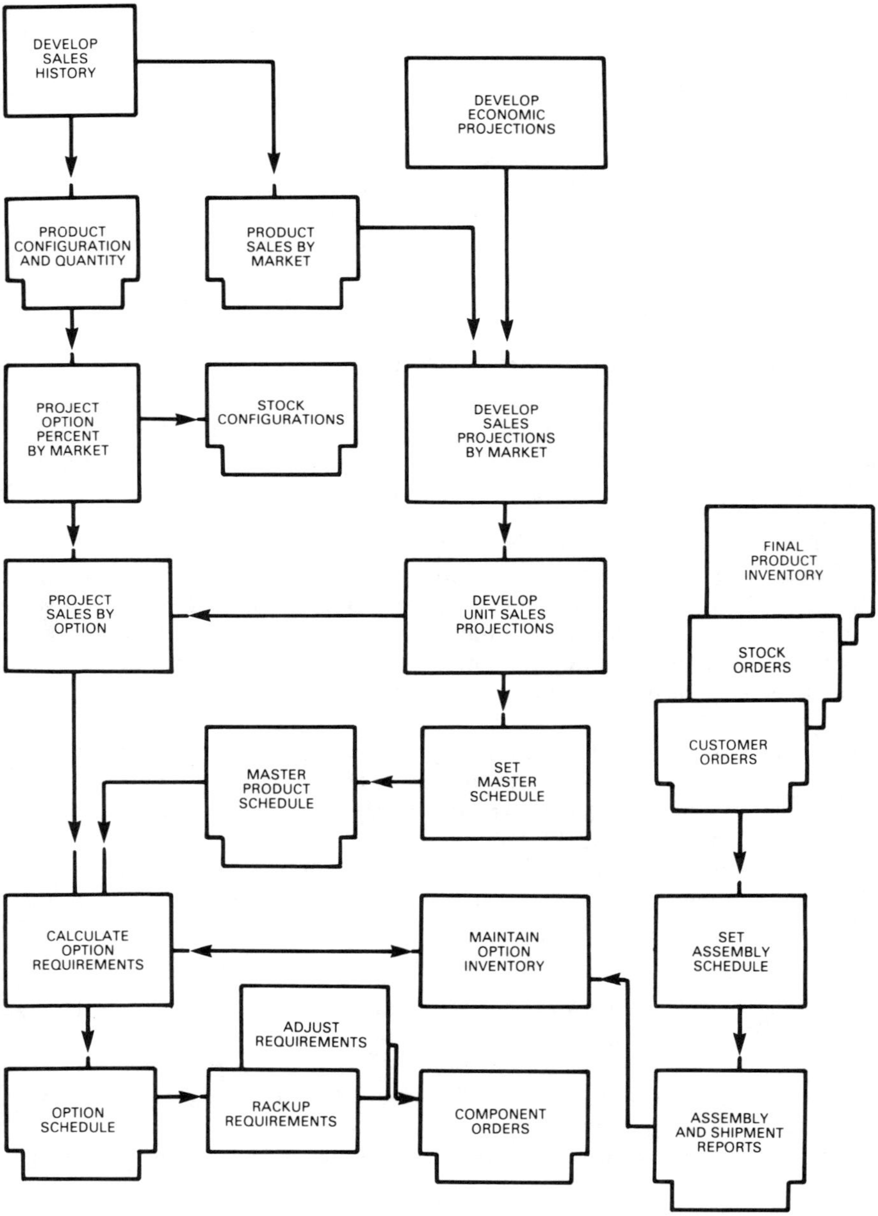


***Figure 12.5.*** Adjusting requirements for common components

- Configure stock orders around the most frequently ordered combinations of options.
- Accept customer orders for any type of option, even if it is seldom ordered.

---

## Exercise 12.3

Compare these four strategies to those which seem to be in effect in the Japanese auto industry. If you examine the practices of Toyota and Honda, you should be able to identify a number of totally different product strategies. Do they have a significant impact on the simplicity and cost effectiveness of the manufacturing and assembly process? Would so many computer applications be needed in such a business?

---

### Japanese Manufacture of Automobiles

It seems that the Japanese auto manufacturers are content to make good profits without the drive to obtain every possible sale. They limit the production of automobiles so that the market demand is always in excess of product availability. This enables the factory to set a steady rate of production well in advance.

The variety of options is strictly limited to just a handful. A limited number of options are available to the customer as standard content of different models of final product. The rest are available as add-ons which must be installed by the dealer, not by the factory. Most of the desirable features which American manufacturers offer as options are built into the standard Japanese automobile as standard components. This radically reduces the cost of the "luxury" items.

There is virtually no exception to the standard method of manufacture and assembly. All is done at a steady pace. The materials don't need to be procured a month in advance. The suppliers just need to deliver the materials at a steady, predetermined rate.

This analysis could continue at great length, but the point is made. Good business strategies avoid the need to use computers to accommodate for poor business strategies.

### Summary

A number of generic statements can be made about managing through information systems in light of the analysis of this case.

Computer systems are a reflection of the operating procedures of an enterprise. Computer systems are often an effort to overcome or to reduce problems in the operating procedures.

Operating procedures are the true systems by which the business is managed.

Strategies can either simplify or complicate the operation of the business and the operation of the information systems which serve the business.

Strategies which simplify the business are best, so long as they don't hurt profitability. For example, in the case describing the management of product options, one could ask whether it might not be more profitable to eliminate the low usage options. There would be a certain loss of business, but inventories would be reduced, and assembly operations would be simplified. The result might be better profit margins.

Problems and errors in information systems most often stem from causes other than merely input errors. They are also caused by failure in feedback of operations results, by inappropriate measurements of personal and departmental efficiency, and by basic company and departmental strategies.

# 13

# *Application Testing*

## Introduction

Computers are unforgiving of errors in data input and of errors in program logic. They are very literal. A wag once complained that his computer kept doing what he told it to do and not what he wanted it to do. Errors in program logic can be very difficult and time-consuming to correct, especially when operation of the business is hampered by the error. The purpose of this chapter is to develop an awareness of the degree to which testing of computer systems is appropriate, and the relative responsibilities of users and systems staff for that testing.

## Exercise 13.1

Why do computer systems need to be tested? Write down the reasons which are apparent to you.

## Purposes of Testing

The primary purpose of testing anything is to verify that it performs its intended functions properly and reliably. This simple image can be expanded into more detail appropriate to computer systems (*Figure 13.1*).

Testing is necessary to exercise all functions of a system in order to attempt to eliminate all possible errors or bugs. The more functions imbedded in the programs, the more important the testing—and the more difficult. It is not at all uncommon for bugs to appear months, or even years after testing has been

1. To Eliminate Error
2. To Measure Processing Performance
3. To Avoid Impact on Other Systems
4. To Instill Confidence in Users
5. To Minimize the Need for Rework
6. To Train Involved People

***Figure 13.1.*** Purposes of testing

completed. This doesn't negate the value of testing. On the contrary, it reinforces the need for intelligent and thorough testing.

It is possible to estimate the processing time of new programs, and the response time which might be expected of on-line transactions. There is no way to be certain of the performance of the programs until they are exercised under real-life conditions. Performance of software can be critical. Output is of no value if it is produced later than needed or at an exorbitant cost.

As described in Chapter 3, systems provide data to other systems. The output of a source system (master data, feedback, status) cannot be fully tested until it is processed mechanically by a using system (control, status, analysis). Any thorough test of a new system must include linking it to associated source and using systems.

Users are often leery about the use of a new computer system. It is often a traumatic change from past practices. One way to develop user confidence in a new system, and in one's ability to use it, is to have the user help in testing it.

Since computer programs are difficult to change, it is important to identify and repair any deficiencies as early as possible. This requires testing before the system is placed into production. Once a system is in production, changes often involve rework of the contents of the database as well as changes in program logic.

Just as testing of a system develops user confidence, it is a good method of training the user. In addition, a novice user will often make input errors not anticipated by the programmers. It is hard for a programmer to test for conditions which weren't anticipated. Early testing of the system by the user helps fill the void.

## Exercise 13.2

What aspects of a computer system do you think need to be tested? There are probably more aspects than you think, when testing is taken in its broadest meaning. It might help to refer to Chapter 7.

## What Needs to be Tested

There are tests which are appropriate at each phase of the development and operation of a mechanized system. The earlier that deficiencies are identified, the more easily they are corrected.

## Prefeasibility Phase

In the prefeasibility phase it is appropriate to examine the basic concept of the new system to see if it has validity (*Figure 13.2*). This examination is usually no more than a logical testing of the idea among knowledgeable people. The user has prime responsibility for this test.

The development of the work plan and of a cost estimate of the next phase of the proposed development are other rough ways of testing the economic feasibility of the proposal.

1. The System Concept
2. Work Plan and Cost Estimate

***Figure 13.2.*** Prefeasibility phase

## Feasibility Phase

If the proposed system is dependent upon a new technology or on a novel mathematical algorithm, it is important to test the concept for workability before a full system is built around it (*Figure 13.3*). The responsibility for this is the user's, but he or she might need to have some computer logic developed to perform the test.

1. Technical Workability
2. Economic Justification
3. Work Plan and Cost Estimate

***Figure 13.3.*** Feasibility phase

The economic justification is also the user's responsibility. The systems person probably has to take the lead in estimating the development and operating costs, but the user is responsible for estimating the value of the new system. The value is usually phrased in terms of avoided costs or increased profits.

The development of the work plan and the development of a cost estimate of the next phase of the proposed development are other checks of the economic feasibility of the proposal.

## Definition Phase

In the definition phase (*Figure 13.4*), the user is responsible for developing a set of user requirements for the proposed system. As stated in Chapter 7, the aid of the data processor will probably be required. The requirements should be tested by a joint application development (JAD) team effort or by a

1. User Requirements
2. Input/Output Formats and Schedules
3. Broad Design Concept
4. Work Plan and Cost Estimate

***Figure 13.4.*** Definition phase

walk-through with a group of knowledgeable users who haven't been involved in the development of the requirements.

The JAD team or walk-through are other ways of testing the utility and completeness of the input and output formats and the processing schedules.

The data processor is responsible for testing his or her broad design concept for the new system. This is done by conducting one's own walk-through with an audience of experienced and imaginative data processors who are challenged to look for omissions and for possible improvements.

The development of the work plan and the development of a cost estimate of the next phase of the proposed development are two checks of the economic feasibility of the proposal.

## Design Phase

The data processor tests his or her detailed system architecture in this phase in the same manner as was done in the definition phase (*Figure 13.5*). The user is of great assistance in this test, since he/she is the one who can verify whether the system architecture is consistent with the definition of system requirements.

1. System Architecture
2. Processing Rules
3. Testing Requirements
4. Work Plan and Cost Estimate

***Figure 13.5.*** Design phase

The processing rules are reviewed in program walk-through sessions with the programmer and one or two other experienced data processors.

The testing requirements are developed by the systems analyst. They are then reviewed in the same program and system walk-through sessions. The purpose is to determine if they are missing any significant conditions. The user assists in both the development and evaluation of the test requirements.

One more time, the development of the work plan and a cost estimate of the next phase of the proposed development are a check of the economic feasibility of the proposal.

## Construction Phase

During the construct phase (*Figure 13.6*) the programmer conducts a reverse walk-through when the programs have been written. The programmer reviews the programs with the analyst who originally assigned them. The analyst reviews the test data again to be certain that it includes comprehensive examples of unusual situations and erroneous input data.

1. Programs
2. Operations Instructions
3. User Instructions and Manuals
4. Work Plan and Cost Estimate

***Figure 13.6.*** Construction phase

The instructions for operating the computer are given to the operators to review. The operators check to see if the instructions are complete, understandable, and comply with the computer center standards. The instructions are checked to see if they adequately handle back-up and recovery conditions for any foreseen type of processing failure.

The instructions and reference manuals are also given to a select group of experienced users to see if they are adequate. They are checked for clarity and completeness. The best way of checking the instructions is to use them to operate the system during tests.

And yet one last time, the development of the work plan and the development cost estimate of the next phase of the proposed development are a check of the economic feasibility of the proposal.

## Implementation Phase

During the implementation phase (*Figure 13.7*), the conversion of files and databases is checked out to ensure that there are no deficiencies. It is best if this is done early to provide time to correct any grief which might result. There is usually a large amount of grief, since new systems tend to place greater demands on data than did the previous generation of systems. The responsibility here is joint between the user and the data processor.

The user representative is responsible for verifying that all of the users have

1. Converted Files and Databases
2. Trained Users
3. Usability
4. Parallel

***Figure 13.7.*** Implementation phase

been thoroughly trained in working with the system. This is often done by running them through test data with exception conditions.

During this check-out of the users, and during a parallel operation of the new system with the old one (if practical), the usability of the new system is verified. During this period every attempt should be made by the users to make the system malfunction. This is a protection against an unforeseen malfunction during production operation of the system.

## Post-implementation Phase

Testing of the post-implementation phase (*Figure 13.8*) is a joint responsibility of the user and the data processor. It is too late to make much improvement to the new system, but things can be learned to aid in the development of other systems.

1. Development and Operating Costs
2. Value of System
3. Performance of System

***Figure 13.8.*** Post-implementation phase

The development and operating costs of the new system are measured and are compared to earlier estimates. The purpose is to improve estimating accuracy in the future.

The value of the system is determined by the user based upon six to twelve months of production operation. The user verifies the degree to which the earlier expectations have been met and also verifies that the system is being used to its fullest potential.

Finally, the user measures and reports to the data processor the degree to which the system performs in accordance with earlier estimates. Performance measures are such things as length of time for batch processes, response time for on-line transactions, and the percent of the work day that the system is available for use.

## Support Phase

During the support phase (*Figure 13.9*), the user and the data processor examine any problems which come up in the operation of the system. The problems are reviewed against the original specifications to see if corrections are needed or if they represent new demands on the system.

1. Corrections
2. Feasibility of Expanded Functions

***Figure 13.9.*** Support phase

If the use of the system results in ideas for new functions (and it will), these ideas are tested by the user and data processor for validity. In effect, a new prefeasibility phase has begun.

## Exercise 13.3

With all of the formality in testing and retesting during the development of a new mechanized information system, it would seem that there should probably be some sort of formal certification of the completed product. What do you think? What form should it take?

## System Certification

There should be some point in time where development ends and production operation begins. If not, the development staff will constantly be badgered to customize the system to suit private needs. Eventually the system will not comply with the original user specifications. There is no value in disciplined development techniques if the discipline is lost when the system is used in production (*Figure 13.10*).

1. Training is Complete
2. System is Operating Correctly
3. Operating Instructions are Adequate
4. Controls and Security are Adequate

***Figure 13.10.*** System certification

The user should certify when training is complete and the system is operating in agreement with the definition.

The people who operate the computer should certify that the controls and back-up/recovery procedures are adequate.

Auditing should certify that data access security measures are appropriate to the value of the data as a business resource.

The formality of these certifications can vary with the organization. However, if the system is developed by an outside firm, the certification should be presented in writing to forestall serious misunderstanding and potential litigation.

## Summary

Computerized information systems can be critical to the successful operation of the business. They are also very difficult to change if they are inadequate. For these reasons, it is vital that new systems be thoroughly tested to ensure that they operate correctly and reliably.

Incomplete work in any phase of development of a system can result in significant waste and rework in later phases. For this reason, there is need for testing of the deliverables at each phase of development. Some of the testing responsibilities belong to the user and some to the data processor.

Also at each phase of development of a system, the economic justification of the system should be reverified, based upon the increase in detailed knowledge of the expected development and operating costs. Since systems can be complex, it is difficult to make accurate cost and benefit estimates early in the development cycle.

The resulting system should be certified by the user, the computer operations staff, and the auditor as being fit for use. This is the end of the development activity and the beginning of the support activity.

# 14

# *Security*

## Introduction

There are contradictory pressures regarding the subject of data security. The provision of good data security measures is expensive. And the implementation of security procedures interferes with the user's free access to data. For these reasons, there is a tendency to shortcut security.

Since the user can't see the data inside the computer, he is motivated to request more data security than that which is requested for paper files. Since there are strict laws regarding the protection of corporate assets, including data, there is a tendency for the auditor to recommend strict security measures. Sometimes these go beyond the value of the data or the possible risk of loss of data.

The purpose of this chapter is to develop a reasonable balance between the contradictory pressures, and to make the user more aware of his or her responsibility for security.

## Security—A Definition

Security is the protection of vital assets from loss, damage, or misuse. In recent years management has come to recognize that data about the business is a vital corporate asset. The security of that asset is of significant concern, since traditional security procedures aren't always appropriate for mechanized data.

## Exercise 14.1

What are the data related assets of the business? There are more than you might think. Remember that mechanized data and the contents of data storage devices are not visible.

## Vital Assets to Secure

Traditional paper records of the business have been the subject of standard security disciplines for many years. They will not be addressed here. The subject of concern is computer data and related assets. These assets are listed in *Figure 14.1*.

1. Files and Databases
2. Programs
3. Computer, Peripherals, Lines
4. Training Material and Procedures
5. System Documentation

***Figure 14.1.*** Vital assets to secure

The most obvious form of mechanized data is that which is stored in files and databases. It might be stored on any of the input/output media listed in *Figure 2.3*. The data might be in master files or in transaction files.

The programs which direct the processing of data are also corporate assets. This is particularly true if the programs are internally developed with proprietary processing rules and techniques.

The computer equipment is a vital asset, since it is very expensive. Another reason for it to be considered a vital asset is that it must be available for portions of the business to operate. If the computer equipment in an airline doesn't work, there are no flight reservations. No tickets are printed. The computer becomes the only tool by which some aspects of the business are operated.

Computer equipment includes more than the computer itself. The terminals are necessary, as are the printers, the storage devices, and the communications lines and modems.

The users need training manuals and reference materials. The computer operators need operations manuals and catalogs which tell the contents of the stored data files. Manual procedures are also vital.

The program development staff maintains a significant amount of system documentation. Some of it is on paper, and some of it is stored in mechanical form. If this material is lost, the mechanized system will continue to operate, but it will become difficult or impossible to make system changes when necessary. For this reason, system documentation is also a vital asset.

## Exercise 14.2

What are the risks to which each of these assets might be exposed? The risks are different, because the physical nature of the assets are different. Remember that there are three types of exposure—loss of the asset, damage to the asset, and misuse of the asset.

## Risks to Files and Databases

The risks associated with files and databases are shown in *Figure 14.2.*

1. Loss—Physical Destruction
2. Loss—Overwrite
3. Damage—Program Error
4. Damage—Erroneous Input
5. Misuse—Copies to Others
6. Misuse—Fraud

***Figure 14.2.*** File and database risks

The data could be lost through physical damage or destruction of the storage device. A tape or disk could be burned or scratched. Or, the device could be stolen or physically lost.

On occasion, the read/write head of a disk file will contact the surface of the disk, scratching it. This "head crash" results in effective loss of the data. Only some of the data is physically lost. But what specific data?

The data could be lost even though the storage medium remains undamaged. New data could be written on a master file, overlaying the original data. A data file could be lost in the process of cleaning the storage device. A long-standing concern of computer centers is the possible exposure of a magnetic medium to a powerful magnet.

The most likely of these risks is the accidental overwriting of a master file with new data. This is not an uncommon occurrence. It happens from manual error in maintaining data library catalogs.

Data in a file or database could be modified in error, losing the original value of the data. This could happen through an undetected bug in a program, or it could happen through erroneous input to a computer program.

The data in files and databases could be misused by giving or selling it to others outside the company. Proprietary data could be provided to a competitor. Customer, supplier, or employee lists could be provided to mail order houses.

There have been a number of cases of computer fraud. A classic example is the programmer who modified a program which posted interest against savings accounts. The fractional portion of the accrued interest, less than one cent, was added to his own account. The books balanced. Nobody noticed the miniscule loss of income to the individual accounts. The programmer's account accumulated an average of half a cent per account per update period. The frequency of such computer fraud is unknown, because companies are embarrassed to report it or to prosecute the thief.

## Risks to Programs

The risks associated with computer programs are enumerated in *Figure 14.3*. Programs could be lost the same way that files and databases could be lost. The medium on which the program is stored could be lost or damaged, or the medium could be used to store other data, overwriting the program.

1. Loss—Physically Misplaced
2. Loss—Damage to the Medium
3. Damage—Untested Change
4. Misuse—Copies to Others
5. Misuse—Unauthorized Access

***Figure 14.3.*** Program risks

Another risk is that the program could be damaged logically through implementation of a program change without adequate testing. This is a particularly insidious danger, since it might be a long time before the damage is discovered. And, of course, a damaged program could result in damaged files and databases.

Programs could be misused by giving or selling them to others, outside the company. Programs with proprietary logic could be provided to a competitor.

In the case of the example of savings account fraud, it was the program which was modified to accomplish the illegal changes to data records.

Data is accessed from files through the use of programs. The programs could be used by unauthorized personnel to access data to which they have no right. Management generally takes great care to avoid disclosure of personnel and payroll data. Proportionately less attention is paid to the security of other types of data.

## Risks to Computer Equipment

The risks associated with computer equipment are presented in *Figure 14.4*.

Like all other assets, computer equipment is subject to physical damage or destruction. It is also subject to theft, especially the smaller, personal computer type of equipment. Although personal computer equipment can be readily replaced, loss of a large computer can be traumatic. A significant portion of the functions of the business can be brought to an abrupt halt.

The use of computer equipment could be effectively lost if the electric power to operate the equipment is lost.

1. Loss—Physical Destruction
2. Loss—Theft
3. Loss—Loss of Power
4. Damage—Damage to Environment
5. Damage—Physical Abuse
6. Misuse—Unauthorized Use

***Figure 14.4.*** Computer equipment risks

For larger computers, the loss of air conditioning or the loss of a chilled water supply could also make the equipment inoperative.

An angry employee could purposely damage computer equipment. An inattentive or careless employee could damage computer equipment by accident. Radical fluctuations in the power supply could damage sensitive electronic components.

Computer equipment could be used by unauthorized personnel, or it could be put to unauthorized use by authorized personnel. Fraud is an unauthorized use. Keeping bowling scores or football pools on the company computer could well be unauthorized use of the equipment.

## Risks to System Documentation

The risks associated with system documentation are shown in *Figure 14.5*. Documentation is usually in manual form. In recent years, some documentation has been stored in mechanical form. It is accessed from computer terminals by users and programmers.

1. Loss—Physically Misplaced
2. Damage—Physical Damage
3. Damage—Deterioration
4. Misuse—Copies to Others

***Figure 14.5.*** System documentation risks

Where documentation is maintained in mechanical form, it is subject to the same risks as files and databases. Where it is used as printed material, it is subject to the same risks as computer equipment—physical loss, damage, and deterioration.

In either printed or mechanical form, documentation can be misused by being given or sold to competitors.

## Asset Security

The security of vital assets can be maintained in a variety of ways. Of course, the best way to secure an asset is to reduce the likelihood of the asset being lost, damaged, or misused. But, since no security measure can be foolproof, it is best to make provisions for what to do if the asset is lost, damaged, or misused.

## Exercise 14.3

What do you think could be done to secure data-related assets? Certainly different measures could be taken for physical assets such as computer equipment, and logical assets such as files and databases.

## Possible Security Measures

One good thing about electronic data is that it can be readily copied. If a copy is available, the loss of the original is nothing more than an inconvenience. The same is true of damaged electronic data—if the damage is recognized. There is little that can be done if the asset has been misused.

## Security of Files and Databases

Protection from physical loss or damage of files and databases can be ensured by providing a secure environment. This means an environment protected from fire and acts of God. It means locks and limited access to the areas where the storage media are kept. It also means good library catalog and handling disciplines (*Figure 14.6*).

1. Prevent—Secure Environment
2. Prevent—Secure Access
3. Prevent—Test Disciplines
4. Recover—Backup Databases
5. Recover—Backup Transactions

***Figure 14.6.*** File and database security

If there are good program test disciplines, the vital data can be protected from being damaged by programs.

Although prevention is the best protection, it is not foolproof. Provision must be made for recovery when data has been lost. And it will be lost.

Good file maintenance disciplines include regular backup of files and databases. After the update of a file, a copy is made and stored in a remote location. If the original file is lost, the copy is retrieved and recopied to make a new master file. Processing then begins as if nothing had happened.

If bad input data or a program bug have damaged the data in a database, it might be necessary to repeat the processing. To prepare for this eventuality, backup copies are made of transaction files just as they are for master files. Several generations of such files are kept in a remote site. The number of generations of backup is determined by the frequency of processing and by the expected time lag before the likely discovery of errors in the databases.

## Security of Programs

A program stored on a magnetic medium is a file just like a data file. For that reason, any security measures appropriate to a file are also appropriate to a program (*Figure 14.7*).

1. Prevent—Secure Environment
2. Prevent—Secure Access
3. Prevent—Test Disciplines
4. Recover—Backup Copies

***Figure 14.7.*** Program security

A secure environment provides a significant degree of protection against the loss of programs from accidental mishandling or from natural disaster.

Restricted access to the programs provides protection against intentional damage or misuse of the programs by those who normally don't need to work with them. However, it doesn't provide protection against misuse by those who are authorized to access the programs. It is like a bank vault which protects your valuables from the public at large, but doesn't protect them against the keeper of the vault.

Good test disciplines protect programs from accidental bugs. This in turn protects files and databases.

Nonetheless, programs will be lost, and bugs will occur. People do make mistakes. Since programs are really files, they should be backed up through several generations of old copies. Thus, in the advent of a problem, a backup copy of a program can be retrieved. It is like making a new copy of a photo from the negative.

## Security of Computer Equipment

The best way to protect computer equipment from loss, damage, or misuse is to have a secure environment (*Figure 14.8*). Locked doors and security screening of those admitted behind the doors are basic precautions. This restricts physical contact with the equipment to those whose work requires such contact.

1. Prevent—Secure Environment
2. Prevent—Secure Access
3. Prevent—Backup Power
4. Prevent—Fire Protection
5. Recover—Backup Facility

***Figure 14.8.*** Computer equipment security

A backup electric power source is an expensive, but effective, means of maintaining availability of the equipment when its power source is lost. Fire detection equipment and a fire retardant system, such as carbon dioxide gas, are also effective protections.

If, however, the computer equipment is lost to use, some sort of backup facility is necessary to ensure continued processing capability. The off-site backup of files, databases, and programs serves this end well, since these materials are already available to the backup site.

For small equipment such as personal computers and minicomputers, it is relatively simple to maintain and use backup equipment.

For maxicomputers, the concept of a backup site is difficult. It is extremely expensive to maintain duplicate equipment. It is also difficult to use the equipment of some other company, since most large computers are uniquely configured to a specific company's needs.

## Security of System Documentation

System documentation usually exists in paper form. It is rather simple to secure it from unauthorized or careless handling by keeping it in a secure storage location when not in use. But, even with this protection, it deteriorates with use (*Figure 14.9*).

1. Prevent—Secure Storage
2. Recover—Backup Copies

***Figure 14.9.*** System documentation security

With today's paper copying facilities, it is rather easy to set aside a master copy from which to replace lost documentation.

Much current documentation is being prepared on word processing equipment. In this case, the backup copy is simply stored on a number of diskettes.

## Security from Misuse

The best way to deal with potential misuse of assets is to prevent it. Although any asset can be replaced, sometimes easily, there is no way to recover from assets given to a competitor. You still have the asset from your backup system, but the competitor also has the asset and the advantage of knowing proprietary information about your business.

If any of the data-related assets of the business are used for fraudulent purposes, the resources are still present, and are possibly intact at the end of the criminal act. If the programs or data have been modified, they can possibly be restored. The determining factor is the length of time from their change until the fraud is discovered. There is a limit to the amount of time that backup copies are retained.

The lost money from the fraud is probably gone forever. The repair to the data-related assets can do nothing to recover from the loss of other assets.

## Exercise 14.4

Do you think that the installation of security mechanisms could result in inconvenience? Of course it can. Keeping jewelry in a bank vault creates the need to go to the bank to obtain the jewelry when you want to wear it. So, what are some of the inconveniences which you can visualize to be the result of security measures for data-related assets?

## Inconveniences from Security Measures

It takes time and money to make and store backup copies of files, databases, transactions, programs, and system documentation.

Employees must carry keys, or badges, or other identification to obtain access to physically secured areas where equipment is located.

It takes time and money to maintain duplicate equipment resources, especially if they must be tested periodically to see that they are available.

The protection of data and programs from unauthorized users requires logical security measures invoked by employee identification numbers and passwords. Once an employee has access to the computer, he has logical access to all data and programs, unless each separate file is protected by some sort of logical security. This is complex and expensive to maintain.

## Exercise 14.5

Put yourself in the shoes of different people within the business, and ask yourself what your opinion might be of the need for security and the inconvenience from security measures. There are different attitudes in those who feel ownership responsibility for the assets, those who actually use the assets, and those who observe from the sidelines.

## Security Perspectives

The different viewpoints on security are listed in *Figure 14.10.*Users definitely want their resources protected from damage, loss, or misuse. The typical user is more sensitive to this with electronically-stored data than with paper-stored data. The reason is that the user cannot see the asset, and must trust the data processor.

The user doesn't want unauthorized people to see data about the performance of his/her operating unit. There might be data which could embarrass the user. But, at the same time, users want to have easy access to their own data. They don't want security measures to cause them any significant inconvenience or expense.

The systems staff, like the user, chafe at inconveniences caused by security measures. They dislike the complexity which security measures add to their work. After all, it is the systems staff who must set up and administer the

| USER |
|---|
| 1. Protection from Misuse<br>2. Dislike of Controls |
| **SYSTEMS STAFF** |
| 1. Avoidance of Complexity<br>2. Unrestricted Access |
| **AUDITOR** |
| 1. Asset Protection<br>2. Avoidance of Lawsuit |
| **MANAGEMENT** |
| 1. Distrust of the Unseen<br>2. Fraud and Espionage |
| **COMPUTER OPERATIONS** |
| 1. Avoidance of Needless Work<br>2. Avoidance of Criticism<br>3. Avoidance of Rework |
| **PRESS** |
| 1. News—Sensation |

***Figure 14.10.*** Security perspectives

security measures. They also want unrestricted access to programs and data. They need this so that they can respond quickly to fix bugs and repair damaged data files.

The auditor feels directly responsible for the protection of the assets of the business, but must also rely upon the systems staff to set up and maintain that security. The auditor is in a position of having to trust someone else in an area of complex technology where he or she doesn't have in-depth knowledge.

In large multinational companies, the auditor is subject to another significant pressure. A federal law called the "Foreign Corrupt Practices Act" threatens him or her with fines and possible imprisonment if the data assets of the company are jeopardized.

Although top management of the business generally doesn't directly use the data resources, they have some of the same worries and concerns as the users do about the unseen data and the complex technology. Top management also have a concern about the potential for fraud and espionage. Management can never be sure that some of the proprietary data about the business has not been given to competitors.

The people who operate the computer equipment find the security measures to be complications to the normal operation of the business. They are the ones who must make backups, save them, and retrieve and replace outdated backup files. They don't ever want to be criticized for being the cause of the loss of critical resources. And they dislike the pressures which are present any time a program or processing error requires them to recover data and redo processing.

The press and other communications media seem to love the dangers which necessitate security measures. Any story about fraud, industrial espionage, or loss or assets makes good copy.

## Balancing Risk and Security Expense

Security measures are like life and health insurance, or insurance on a house or automobile. The idea is to avoid a catastrophic loss, or at least to be in a position to recover from a catastrophic loss. It is a balancing act. The amount of insurance should be more if the danger is greater. Unfortunately, it is not an easy matter to determine the degree of risk of loss of assets from any specific cause.

Experience seems to indicate that the greatest risk to data-related assets comes from inadvertent acts and not from premeditated acts. Programs are changed in error. Files are misplaced or are overwritten in error. For these reasons, the provision of backup and recovery mechanisms appears to be mandatory.

The degree of protection required against premeditated acts is far less clear. It is something only the top management of the company can determine. How worried are they? How much are they willing to spend for peace of mind?

## Summary

The provision of good data security measures is expensive. The implementation of security procedures interferes with the user's free access to data. For these reasons, there is a tendency to shortcut security.

*Security* is the protection of vital assets from loss, damage, or misuse. In recent years, management has come to recognize that data about the business is a vital asset. The security of that asset is of significant concern, since traditional security procedures aren't always appropriate for mechanized data.

The data-related *assets* of the business are data files and databases, programs, computer equipment, and systems documentation. These assets are exposed to physical damage or loss. The electronically-stored assets are subject to erroneous change and to loss by reuse of the storage medium, resulting in writing new data over the vital data. All assets are subject to theft, fraud, or unauthorized distribution to competitors.

The security of vital assets can be maintained in a variety of ways. The best way to secure an asset is to reduce the likelihood of the asset being lost, damaged, or misused. Since no security measure can be foolproof, it is best to make provisions for what to do if the asset is lost, damaged, or misused.

The most common security measures are backup and recovery routines to replace inadvertent loss of electronically-stored assets. There is no good way to recover from fraud or the distribution of proprietary data to competitors.

Different people have different perspectives on security. The people who use the assets chafe at any inconvenience caused by security measures. The people who feel responsibility for the assets seek a greater degree of protection from loss.

Security measures are like insurance on a house or automobile. The idea is to avoid a catastrophic loss, or at least to be in a position to recover from a catastrophic loss. It is a balancing act. The amount of insurance should be more if the danger is greater.

# 15

# *Case: Production Material*

## Introduction

The maintaining of records of materials inventories is a far more complex task than most people realize. Many companies conduct annual physical inventory counts. They do this to correct their records for errors in reporting and for undetected loss of material (stock shrinkage is a euphemism for theft). Some people contend that as many errors are put into the records by a physical inventory count as are removed. The purpose of this chapter is to demonstrate the difficulty of counting, and to illustrate the myriad opportunities for material to enter and leave inventory.

## Exercise 15.1

How would you go about the task of counting a pile of production parts? Consider a pile of several hundred parts. What do you think are accurate and speedy ways of counting the material? Consider several alternatives.

## Counting Techniques

Most people can't count reliably. The more intelligent the person, the more likely that he or she will make an error in counting a large number of objects. The reason is that counting is a dull, repetitive exercise. The mind begins to wander. If the counting is done in a distracting environment, such as in a factory, the likelihood of a counting error is increased.

If the objects can be stacked, they can be piled up in regular stacks of a given number, usually five or ten. This is a more reliable technique than counting them individually, as in one, two, three, etc.

If the objects are of a reasonably consistent weight, they can be counted by scale. This technique is of limited accuracy if the weight of individual parts varies more than a very small amount compared to the weight of the average part. The technique is useful if an approximate count is adequate.

One of the best techniques is to place the parts in a container which is designed to hold a given limited number. It is a sort of fixture for holding and transporting the parts. The Japanese have gone to great lengths to design such containers for their parts. The typical quantity in a container, or in one layer of material in a container, is five. This provides a significant discipline to the counting of the parts.

## Materials Flow

The flow of production materials through a manufacturing facility is not as simple and straightforward as most people tend to think. *Figure 15.1* is a flowchart of typical material movement.

## Order Material

Material is ordered by the Purchasing department. This is the point at which the entry of materials is triggered. In a typical build-to-stock company, the materials are ordered in monthly quantities.

The purchase order states that the materials are to arrive about ten days before the first day of the month in which they are needed. Finished parts are to arrive ten days before the first day of the month in which they are to be assembled into final product. Rough materials are to arrive ten days before the first day of the month in which they are to be machined into finished parts. These manufactured parts are to be completed by the first day of the following month. They are to be assembled into the final product during that following month.

## Receive Material

When the material arrives at the plant, receiving clerks check it in. They pull a copy of the purchase order from a file cabinet as reference data. They verify that the right part or parts are in the package. They do not verify that the correct quantity of material has been received.

Wrong material is returned to the supplier.

Instructions are retrieved from another file for disposition of the material. If it is from a supplier of questionable quality, a specific quantity of the material is diverted to the Quality Control department for inspection.

The received quantity and the date are marked on the copy of the purchase order to make it a receiving report. The material is recorded as received even if a portion of it is sent to Quality Control. The material is moved to the appropriate locations in tubs on which move tags are attached. The move tags identify the part number, the quantity, and the destination of the contents.

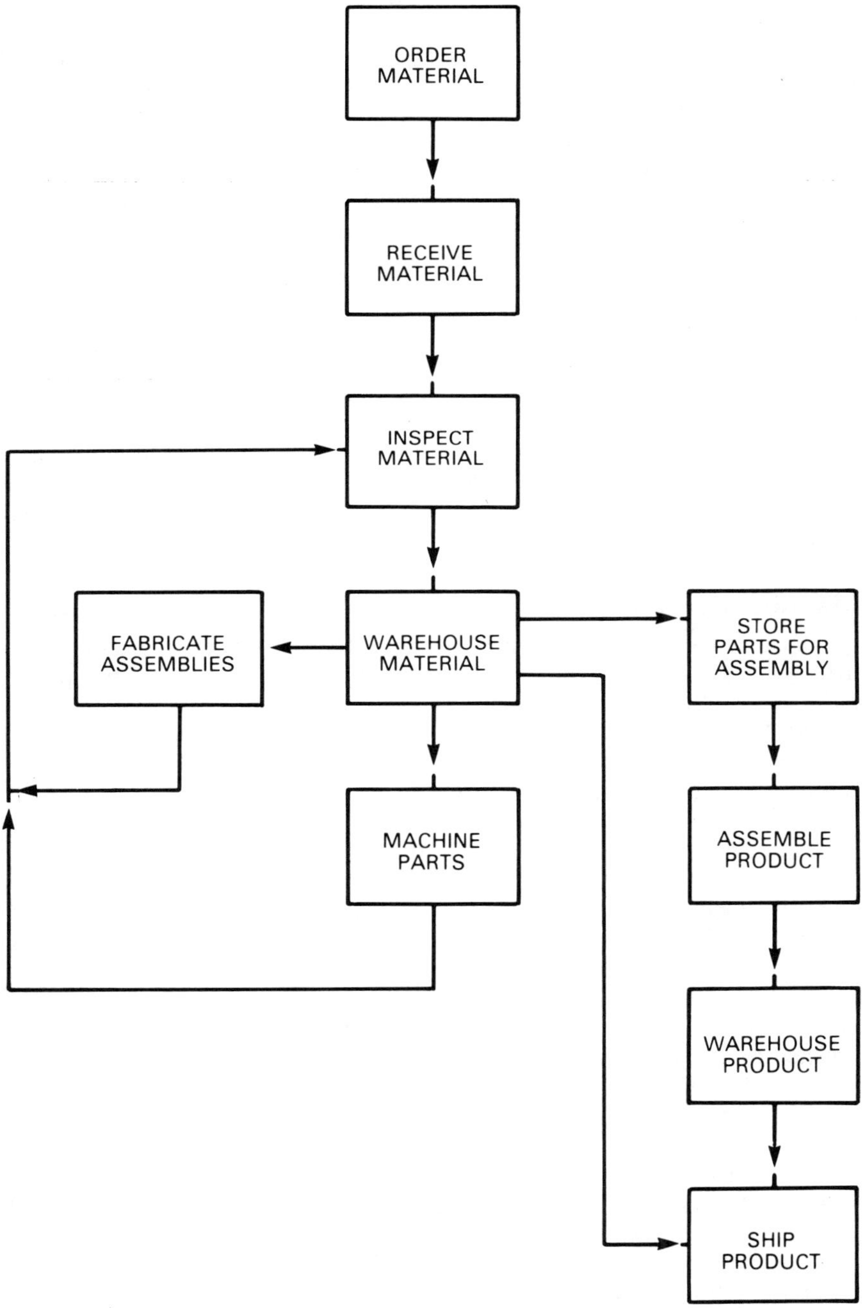


***Figure 15.1.*** Materials flow

## Inspect Material

Quality Control inspects material by rules appropriate to the quality performance history of the supplier. Any rejected materials are reported so that replacements can be ordered. The same is done for any materials lost by a destructive testing process. Accepted, intact materials are forwarded to the warehouse function under the control of a move tag.

If a load is rejected in the inspection process after some of it has been moved to the warehouse, it is ordered to be pulled from stock and returned to the supplier. The deduction of material from inventory is reported by the warehouse.

## Warehouse Parts

The total inventory record of each part is updated daily from the reports of such acceptance or rejection of material. The total inventory includes all materials in the plant, no matter where they are stored.

No material is actually stored in a warehouse. No material is stored in a secure or fenced area. The whole plant is considered to be a warehouse. The total inventory record does not indicate where the material is stored. In local storage areas, the control of material is done through manual records of the location of loads.

## Machine Parts

The foreman of a machine line orders the needed quantity of rough material based upon the quantity authorized by the work order. The order is placed by phone.

The Material Distribution department retrieves the ordered material by use of manual location records. They send the requisitioned material to the foreman under the control of a move tag.

The rough material remains in the total inventory record. It remains until the foreman reports the completion of the first operation on the work order. Then the material is subtracted from the rough material count. An equivalent quantity of material is posted to the total inventory record as being in-process under the identification number of the finished part. This posting is performed daily.

The foreman reports the production of finished parts each day. These are posted against the total inventory record daily, increasing the count of finished parts, and decreasing the count of in-process parts.

The foreman writes scrap tickets each day as materials are spoiled in the production process. The total inventory record is then updated each day to deduct the material from the appropriate record—rough, in-process, or finished inventory.

When the total batch of rough material has been transformed into finished parts or scrap, the work order is closed out. A clerk compares the count of material delivered to the count of finished parts and the count of scrap. Discrepancies are resolved. The total inventory record is adjusted the same day. Finished parts are moved to the warehouse function under the control of move tags.

## Fabricate Assemblies

The management approach to the subassembly areas is very similar to that of the machine lines. The quantity of subassemblies is authorized by a work order.

The foreman of a subassembly line orders the needed quantity of component parts based upon the quantity of the subassembly authorized by the work order. The material order is placed by phone.

The Material Distribution department retrieves the ordered material by use of manual location records. They send the requisitioned material to the foreman under the control of a move tag.

The component parts remain in the total inventory record, even after the subassemblies have been completed. This is quite a different practice from the management of rough material inventories.

The foreman reports the production of finished subassemblies each day. These are posted against the total inventory record daily, increasing the count of finished subassemblies, but not decreasing the count of finished parts.

The foreman writes scrap tickets each day as materials are spoiled in the production process. The total inventory record is then updated each day to deduct the scrapped component parts from inventory.

When the total batch of subassemblies has been completed, the work order is closed out. A clerk compares the count of material delivered to the count of finished subassemblies and the count of scrap. Discrepancies are resolved. The total inventory record is adjusted the same day. Finished subassemblies are moved to the warehouse function under the control of move tickets.

The component parts are not removed from inventory until they are assembled into final products or shipped as components of options on final products. The subassemblies are booked into inventory not as real materials, but as things on which labor has been expended and costs accrued. In effect, these inventory records are a cost accounting device, not a material control device.

## Store Parts for Assembly

Component parts and subassemblies are ordered for the bins along the assembly line. This was described in the line stock function in Chapter 9. The materials are logged out of the manual inventory records from the place where they have been stored. They are not logged into the assembly storage records, since there are no such records. They are still considered as a part of the total plant inventory records.

## Assemble Product

Components from the bins are assembled into final products on the assembly line. A limited number of options are also assembled into final products from the bin materials along the assembly line. Other options are installed on final products from materials marshalled into assembly bays.

If materials are damaged or in any way scrapped in the assembly process, they are not reported as lost inventory.

The quantity of completed final products is reported daily.

At the end of the month, the piece part and subassembly inventory records are updated to reflect the quantity consumed in final product. Both subassembly counts and the counts of the components of the subassemblies are updated. But, the inventory records of assembled options are not updated upon the *assembly* of product. They are updated upon the *shipment* of product. Those components of options which are on unshipped final product are still maintained on the total inventory record as components.

## Warehouse Product

The completed final products are logged into a finished product inventory record. They remain in that record until shipped.

## Ship Product

Product is reported as shipped on the same day it is shipped. The finished product inventory record is updated daily.

At the end of the month, the subassembly and component part inventories are finally updated to reflect the materials which have been assembled into options on final product.

Both options (as kits) and component parts are shipped to the field as replacement parts. The component parts are deducted from total inventory the day they are shipped. The components of the options are deducted from total inventory at the end of the month of shipment.

---

## Exercise 15.2

Mark the flowchart in *Figure 15.1* to show the points at which material can enter the physical inventory of the plant. Place an "I" (input) by each function box where you feel this takes place. Remember that there are different kinds of inventory.

---

## Material Entry Points

The points at which material enters inventory are shown in *Figure 15.2*. Purchased materials, both rough and finished, enter at the point where material is received. Finished manufactured parts enter as an output of the manufacture parts function. Finished subassemblies enter as an output of the fabricate assemblies function. Finished final products enter as an output of the assemble product function.

---

## Exercise 15.3

Mark the flowchart in *Figure 15.1* to show the points at which material can leave the physical inventory of the plant. Place an "E" (exit) by each function box where you feel this takes place. Remember that there are different kinds of inventory.

---

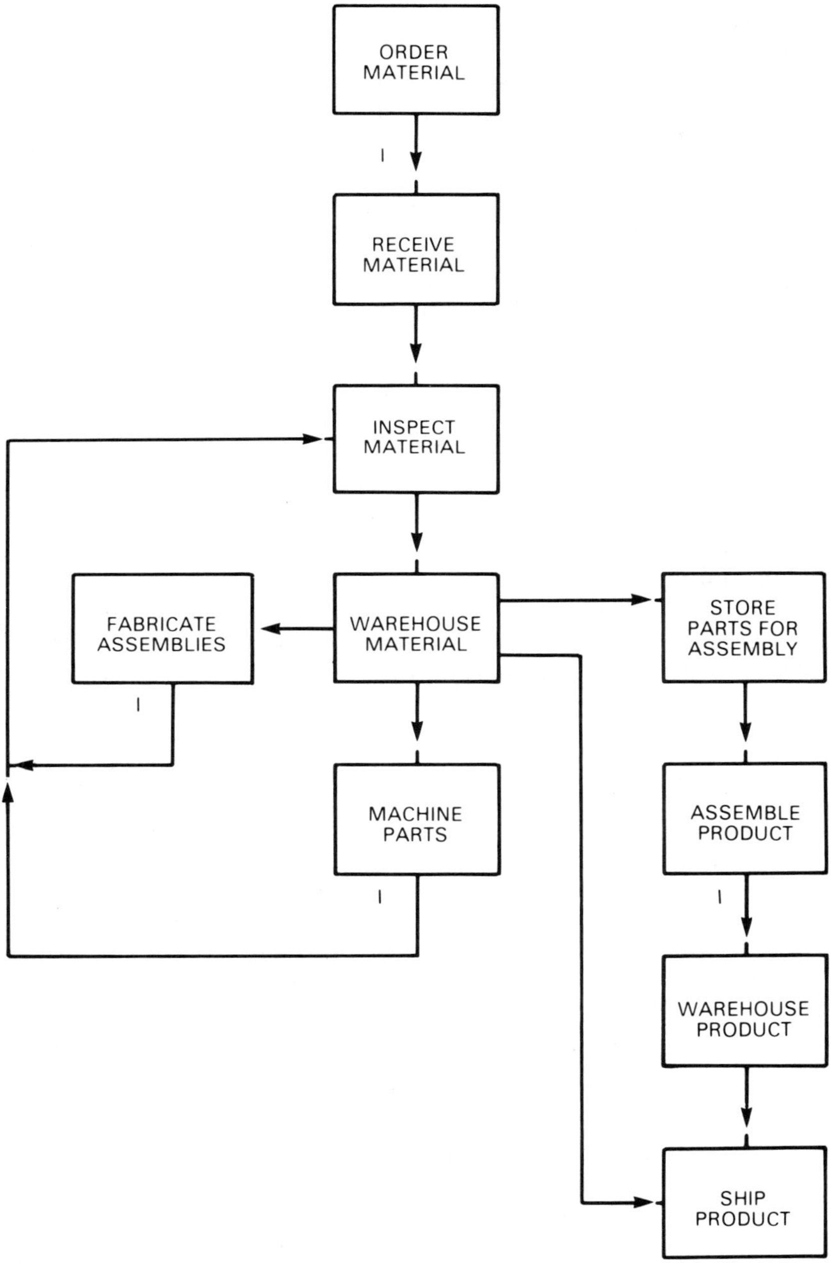


***Figure 15.2.*** Material entry points

## Material Exit Points

The points at which material leaves inventory are marked in *Figure 15.3*. Finished and rough materials leave inventory (actually they never enter) when they are rejected in the receive material function. These materials also leave inventory (they have been logged in by receiving) when they are rejected in the inspect material function.

Rough materials leave inventory in the machine parts function when they are converted into finished parts. The in-process materials are logged in and out of inventory as the material progresses through this function.

Finished parts and a small variety of rough materials leave inventory when they are fabricated into subassemblies. They leave inventory as physical materials from storage locations, but are maintained in the total inventory record as if they are available.

Finished parts and subassemblies leave inventory when they are assembled into final product. Again, the inventory record is not always updated to reflect the actual status of the physical inventory.

Final products, finished parts, and options leave inventory in the ship product function.

---

## Exercise 15.4

These are not the only places where materials can leave inventory. Mark *Figure 15.1* with an "L" (loss) at the places where material can leave inventory as lost—scrapped, stolen, or actually misplaced.

---

## Material Losses

As you can see in *Figure 15.4*, material can be lost at any point. Normally, the loss is from scrap. The materials inventory system described here is obviously deficient in the reporting of scrap.

Material can readily be lost by being misplaced. The whole factory is considered as a warehouse. Unless the manual records are rigidly disciplined, materials can be set in an out of the way place and forgotten.

Material can be stolen anywhere. Such theft would be difficult to recognize, since the records are not precise at any point in time. The smaller the item, and the higher its value, the more likely it is to be stolen—the more likely there is to be "stock shrinkage."

---

## Exercise 15.5

Now mark *Figure 15.1* with an "M" (manual) at the places where manual record-keeping errors can cause inventory records to be inconsistent with actual physical material availability.

---

## Manual Record Errors

The points at which manual reports are made of inventory transactions are the points where manual reporting errors can be made (*Figure 15.5*). They are also the same points where material can be lost.

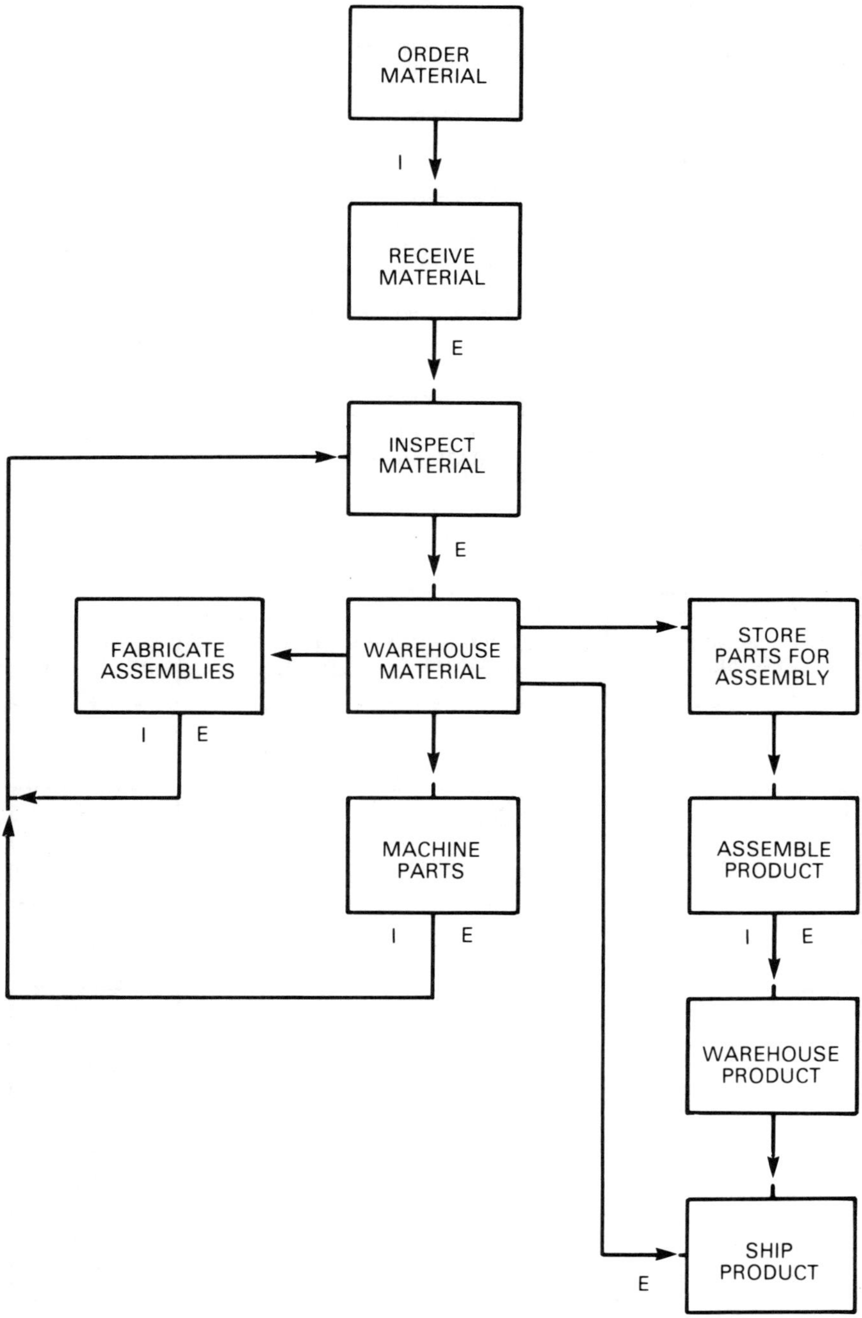


***Figure 15.3.*** Material exit points

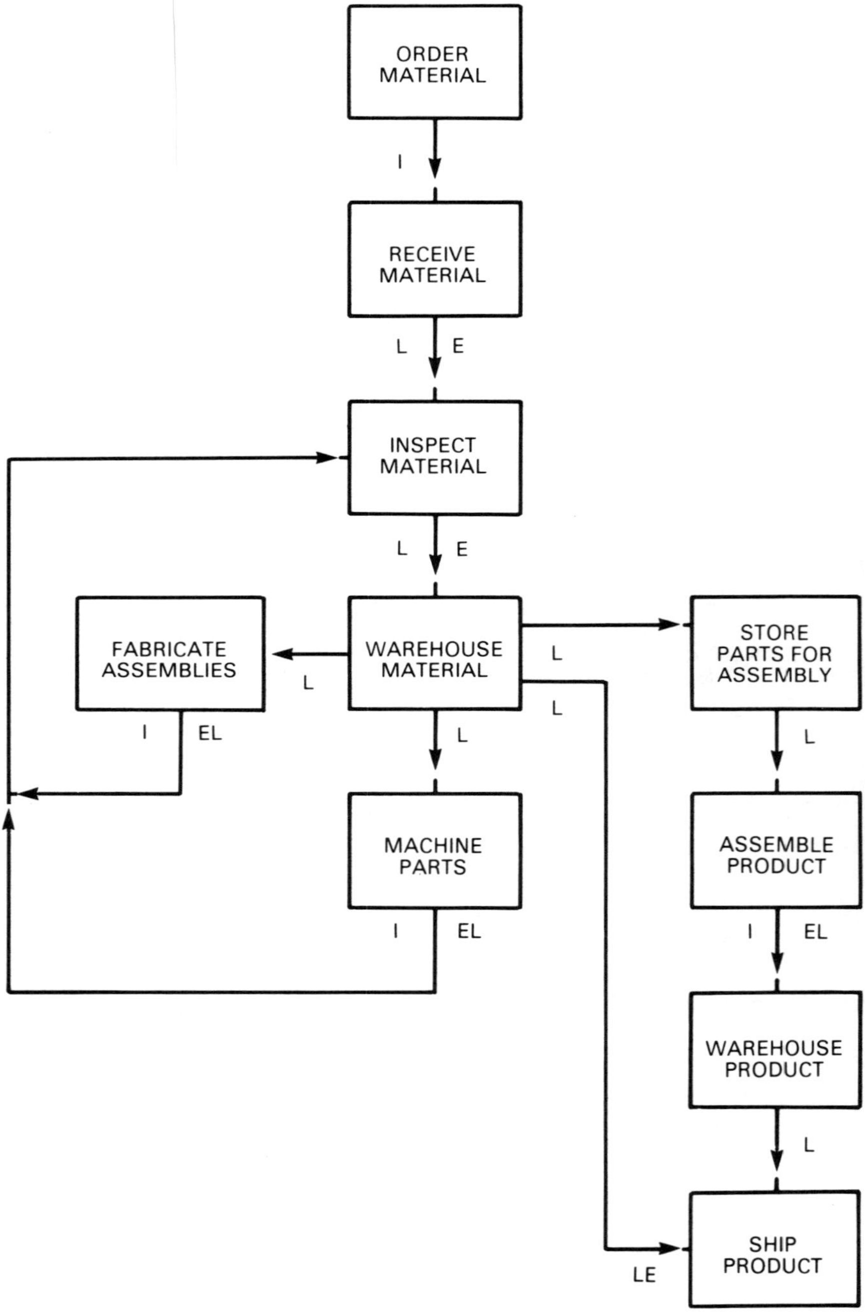


***Figure 15.4.*** Material loss points

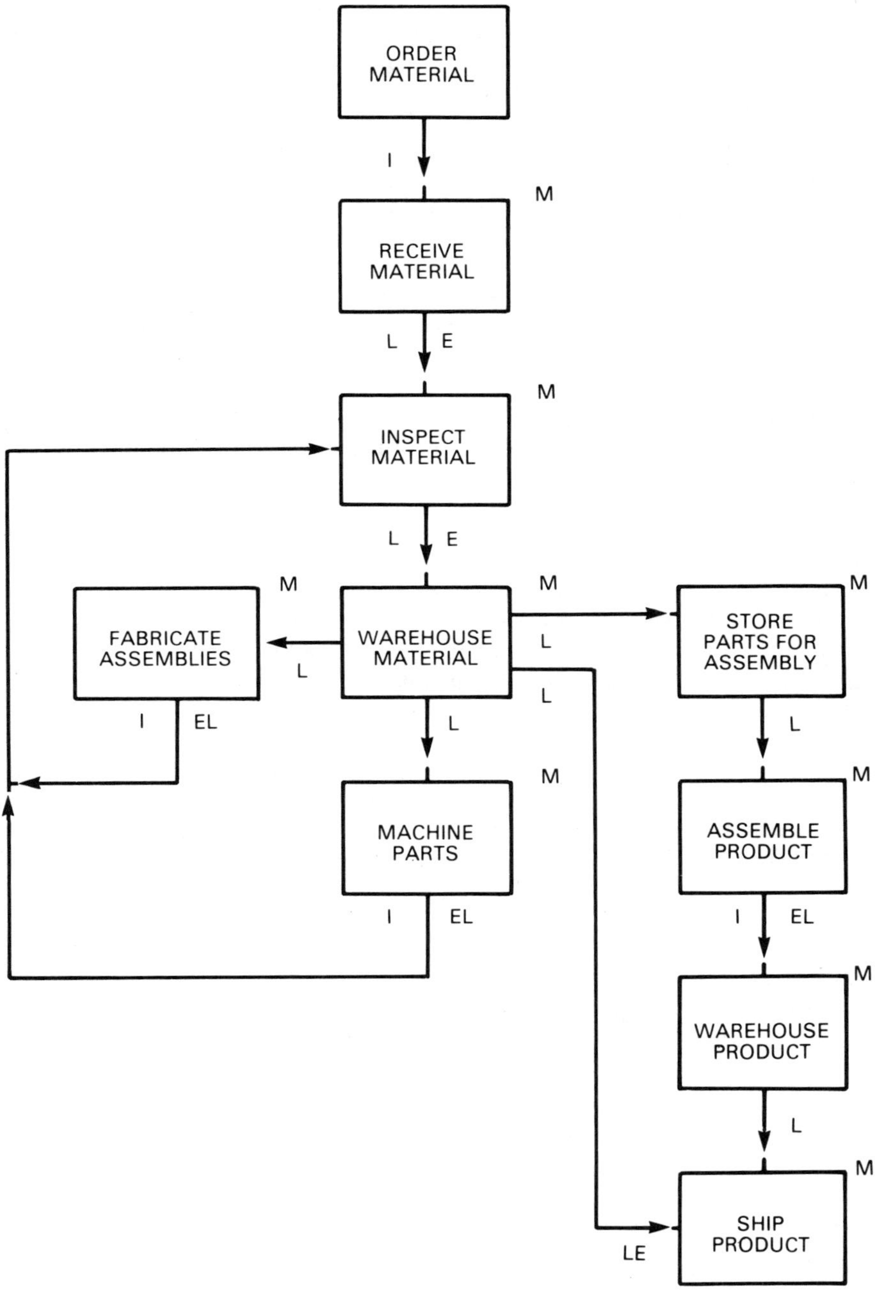


***Figure 15.5.*** Opportunities for manual record errors

When one looks at *Figure 15.5* without dimensions of the volume of material and data flow, it seems a wonder that inventory records reflect reality at all.

One standard way of accommodating for the error has been a regular material test count program. In some companies it takes the form of an annual physical inventory. In other companies it takes the form of a year-round statistical test count program. In such a program, more time and attention are paid to those materials which have the highest value.

---

## Exercise 15.6

Some problems have been identified or hinted at in the text. Other problems are yet to be identified. Make a list of problems which you can identify in the inventory management system described in this chapter.

---

**Problem 1.** The receiving function does not provide an accurate starting count of materials. The inventory record begins with an opportunity for error.

**Problem 2.** There is an automatic inventory record error due to the lack of consistency and discipline in the reporting of scrap and lost material. This occurs in the assembly area.

**Problem 3.** There is a lack of information as to the true status and availability of parts which have been assembled into subassemblies. The same problem exists with parts which have been assembled into options on final products. The material might be installed in a product, but the inventory record suggests that it is still available for use in the assembly of more product.

**Problem 4.** The monthly reporting of consumption of materials in the assembly of final product leaves the inventory record incomplete the rest of the month. This causes an error equivalent to the one described in Problem 3.

**Problem 5.** There is a lack of physical material security. This could lead to theft and misuse of materials. This is especially true with small and expensive materials.

---

## Exercise 15.7

What possible solutions can you suggest to reduce or eliminate these problems?

---

***Solution 1.*** Where practical, material could be received in packages of preset quantities. The best way to ensure the accuracy of the count is to construct the package like a fixture.

An egg carton ensures that more than 12 eggs are not present. A quick glance is sufficient to determine if any of the slots are empty, meaning there are less than 12 eggs.

If such a disciplined container is impractical, materials must be counted. At least, they should be counted until the accuracy of the supplier is demonstrated.

***Solution 2.*** Disciplines and incentives could be put in place to motivate the reporting of scrap and lost materials. As was demonstrated in Chapter 9, people do as they are measured.

***Solution 3.*** The rules of the inventory record-keeping system could be changed to calculate the current inventory position of all materials. This would probably need to be done daily to provide records reliable enough to be used to control the acquisition and distribution of materials.

***Solution 4.*** Product could be broken down so that inventories of parts and subassemblies could be updated each day. The deduction of materials in subassemblies and options should be done just as it is for the components of final products. After all, a component which is assembled into a subassembly or option is unlikely to be available for other use.

***Solution 5.*** A disciplined warehousing function could be established, behind a fence if necessary. A physically secure storage area is especially appropriate for materials subject to theft.

The just-in-time (JIT) concept for procurement and production of materials would significantly reduce the magnitude of the inventory management and record-keeping problem. There would certainly be a smaller volume of material to track.

---

### Exercise 15.8

Who owns the inventory? Who is accountable for it? Who can affect it?

---

## Responsibility for Inventory

Many different parts of the organization can affect inventory. This begins with the person who forecasts sales. It moves to the one who sets the master production schedule; it passes through Material Planning and Purchasing, through Material Distribution, Manufacturing, Assembly, and ends with Shipping.

All should be accountable for the accuracy of the data they provide and for the discipline with which the physical materials are handled.

The company owns the inventory, but since people do as they are measured, it is possible to motivate better disciplines by assigning selective inventory ownership. If Sales owns finished inventory and is measured by it, excess finished stock can be reduced. If Assembly owns bin inventory and is measured by it, scrap is more likely to be reported. In many companies, the assignment of accountability for inventory is vague or nonexistent.

---

### Exercise 15.9

Can or should there be a difference between the rules for maintaining physical inventory records and the rules for maintaining accounting records of the value of inventory?

---

## Departmental Inventory Records

The rules for maintaining inventory records should be based on sound materials management principles. The rules of accounting for materials should be based upon sound accounting principles. If one takes precedence over the other, both will suffer. For example, if accounting practices take precedence (as they did in this case), then materials records become unreliable and cause an equivalent unreliability in the accounting records.

## Exercise 15.10

Can inventory management problems be reduced by adopting a just-in-time materials management philosophy?

### Just-in-Time

Just-in-time means less materials in storage and less materials in process. This simplifies the counting and control problems. If carried to the extreme, however, it can result in materials shortages due to failures by the supplier or failures in the production process. Like all new philosophies, just-in-time should be approached with prudence.

### JIT Depends on Assembly Systems

The systems for procurement and production of materials depend upon several factors. They depend upon the variety of products, the variety of product options, and assembly practices.

In the home appliance and electric hand tool examples in Chapter 9, the assembly of final products is a batch process. This suggests that the production of assembly components could also be a batch process, or it could be a process which operates at a steady rate, with delivery of materials to the assembly line in batches which are convenient. The planning and purchase of materials for a batch process is straightforward, since the scheduled quantity of assembly is known in advance.

The manufacture of backplanes is also a reliable system for materials planning and procurement. The components are limited in number. The variation in the assembly process is in the location of the wires. There is not much variation in the quantity of material used. Where there is variation, it is in low-cost components, such as the wire assemblies.

The Japanese auto factory is set up for a stable rate of production, even though a mix of products is assembled on the assembly line. Each model is assembled at a stable rate. The assembly sequence is a repeating sequence such as: model A, then B, then B, then C, then ABBC, ABBC, etc.

If there are many options and if the material lead time exceeds the promised response to a customer order, then the production process is complex. Material must be provided in advance against a market forecast.

### JIT Depends on Manufacturing Systems

For many people, JIT gives the image of one at a time manufacturing of parts immediately before they are needed in the assembly process. But many parts are best made in batches, even if there is no economic impact from process setup time. Consider an eight-cylinder engine. There is no sense in making and delivering cylinders one at a time. They are needed by the assembly process eight at a time.

Even if a process can be cost effective at a unit of one manufacture, the material delivery and removal mechanisms might not be cost effective at unit of one levels. It is often cost effective to have the supplier deliver materials in quantity. Can you imagine a truck driving up to the plant to drop off a single steering wheel?

Consider a simple case of a supplying cell which produces parts for a using cell, which assembles the parts into subassemblies. Three units of production are involved (*Figure 15.6*). The supplying cell has a lot size which is convenient or cost effective for the parts it produces. The using cell has its own convenient lot size. The material transfer device, the delivery mechanism, also has its own convenient lot size.

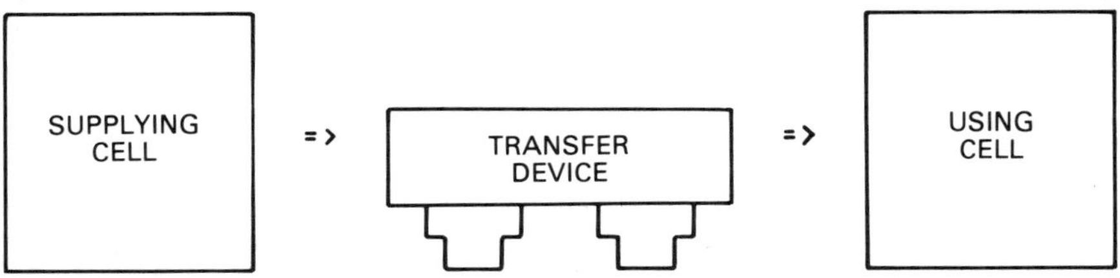


***Figure 15.6.*** Material handling components

It is an exceptional condition when each of the three units of production has the same lot size. It is even more exceptional when the lot size is one piece. When the lot sizes are different, material must be stored somewhere. Several examples will illustrate the point.

1. The supplying cell makes 10 parts at a time. The using cell makes 40 subassemblies at a time. The transfer device can carry 20 parts. The supplying cell must therefore have output storage space for 20 units. In fact, it might as well make parts in lots of 20 units. The assembly cell must have input storage of 40 units.
2. The supplying cell makes 40 parts at a time. The using cell makes 10 subassemblies at a time. The transfer device can carry 20 parts. The supplying cell must have output storage for a minimum of 10 and a maximum of 40 units. The assembly cell must have input storage space for at least 10 parts, and could have space for 40 parts. If it doesn't have space for 40 parts, the supplying cell cannot make more parts until the undelivered 30 parts have been moved elsewhere. If both the supplying cell and the assembly cell have space for at least 20 parts, then the transfer device can carry full loads.

Where it can be managed, the manufacture, delivery, and assembly of units of one are preferable. In a way, the storage rack in the Japanese auto factory accomplishes that purpose. It provides a modest surge tank, which provides some degree of scheduling flexibility to the supplying cell. It also buffers against temporary interruptions in production.

## JIT Impact on Record Keeping

It should be obvious that to the extent a factory approaches unit of one production, it also eliminates in-process inventory. There is no need to maintain records of the quantity of material in-process since it is a small, rather stable quantity.

The only reporting needed for material consumption is the reporting of final product assembly and the reporting of scrap. The verification of inventory records through test count routines is quite simple, since the quantity of material is small, and it is not stored in a variety of locations.

How should material be received or checked into the factory? Should each lot be recorded as received? Or should it be presumed that the material has arrived, since the assembly schedule has been met? There is a significant opportunity here for an additional simplification of record keeping if supplier relations are good.

## Summary

It is very difficult to pinpoint responsibility for inventory, since many people in different departments can affect it, but Material Handling seems to have the most physical contact with production inventories.

It is difficult for people to count accurately. This is especially true where there are distractions. Periodic test counts are appropriate, especially for small and expensive items. The count of materials as received and stored can be enhanced if the materials are packaged in preset quantities.

Assigning specific accountability for various inventories can help to ensure disciplined material management and accurate reporting.

It is a mistake to let accounting rules dictate the rules by which materials are managed. These rules should be established for the purpose of minimizing and controlling the physical inventories. The better this is done, the more accurate the accounting can be.

A just-in-time philosophy for management of materials reduces the amount of reporting which is necessary, since smaller quantities of materials are procured, and in-process inventories are minimal.

The degree of complexity of information systems in a JIT environment depends directly upon manufacturing, materials, and assembly strategies. The simpler the strategies are, the simpler the information systems are, and the less need there is for the use of the computer.

# 16

# *Input Disciplines*

## Introduction

The processing of any information system, mechanical or manual, is dependent upon the quality of the data to be processed. One of the oldest and tritest sayings in the computer field is: "GIGO—garbage in, garbage out." The purpose of this chapter is to give users an enhanced awareness of their responsibility for the input to information systems, and of their responsibility during system definition to establish the degree of computer controlled data editing and checking which should be performed.

## Keypunch and Batch Data Entry

In the early days of the use of computers in business, the Data Processing department maintained a keypunch section where input data was converted from documents to punched cards for input to the computer. The user prepared input transactions by filling out forms. These forms were sent to the keypunch section daily. There they were keypunched and key verified for input to the computer. The user established a count of the documents. The keypunch section verified that the resulting count of cards was equivalent.

In the 1960s the Data Processing department began to force the data entry or keypunch function back to the user organization. Later, development of key to disk devices and of on-line terminal access to computers made this transfer of responsibility easier.

## Exercise 16.1

What are the relative advantages and disadvantages in this move of the data entry function from the Data Processing department to the user organization?

## Data Entry Location

As in any other change in a business practice, the result is a mixture of advantages and disadvantages. The more significant results of moving data entry to the user listed are in *Figure 16.1*:

| |
|---|
| + User Sense of Responsibility |
| + More Reasonable Expectations |
| + Easier Grief Resolution |
| + Reduced Document Verification |
| - Impact of Work Load Surges |
| - Increased Local Budget |

***Figure 16.1.*** Impact of local data entry

+ It gave the user a greater sense of responsibility for the quality of the input data. It was no longer possible to blame people in another organization for any deficiencies in the input.
+ The user became more reasonable in his or her expectation of acceptable accuracy and timeliness of the data input function. When work is done for you by another organization, it is difficult to understand the occasional failures and the impediments to quality work. When the work is being done in your own area by your own people, you are more aware of difficulties, and are correspondingly more tolerant of lapses in performance.
+ It simplified the resolution of grief, since the person doing the data input function was familiar with the business purpose of the input data. In addition, the input clerk had ready access to the person who originated the input data. Points of ambiguity could be clarified quickly.
+ Direct input of data to the computer proved to be a most significant advantage to the user organization. It provided a mechanism for immediate verification of the accuracy of the input data, and for immediate correction of grief. This improved the reliability of the processing of the data. It also made possible a significant reduction in the cost of data entry.
- Surges in the work load were more difficult to accommodate. The keypunch section in Data Processing had a rather large staff which could absorb work load fluctuations. In the individual user depart-

ments, the data input staff was smaller in number. Therefore, it was less able to flex with changes in the work load.

The user departments tended to resist the transfer of function at first. It increased their budgets without giving them any perceived increase in output or performance. Besides, the work had been done for them for so long, they felt that it was a defined responsibility of Data Processing.

## Edit—A Definition

The immediate verification of the accuracy of input data is called an *edit* process. It is a process which verifies the accuracy and syntax of a computer record or of an input transaction.

---

## Exercise 16.2

When data is entered into a computer it is possible to edit a single field of the transaction at a time. It is also possible to edit the whole transaction to verify the contents of the individual fields in context with one another. What types of field and transaction validation do you perceive as being possible?

---

## Field Edits

A field of data can be edited as a whole, and it can be edited in parts. Some of the principle options are listed in *Figure 16.2.*

1. Alphabetic or Numeric Data
2. Placement of Decimal Point
3. Reasonability Range of Number
4. Specific Values of Codes

***Figure 16.2.*** Field edits

Individual positions within the field can be checked to see if they are alphabetic, numeric, or a special character. As an example, consider a part number in the form of ANNNNN, an alphabetic character followed by five digits. In the part number field of a transaction, the edit process could check that the first character is a letter, and that the next five characters are numbers.

The placement of a decimal point in a number could be checked. For example, in a field representing an amount of money, the decimal point could be verified as being present in the third position from the right.

A numeric field could be edited to verify that it contains a number within given limits of reasonability. For example, a labor report for an employee would be unreasonable if it stated that the employee had worked 200 hours the previous week.

A field representing a code of some sort, such as "M" or "F" to represent the sex of an employee, could be edited to see that it only contained one of the allowed values.

In all of these examples, the edit process acts as a sort of filter to detect the most obvious errors. There is no way that the edit process can guarantee the accuracy of the data. Even in such a simple case as the sex code, the contents of a field can pass the edit and still be inaccurate.

## Transaction Edits

A transaction can, of course, be edited field by field, but it can also be edited by comparing the values of different fields. This is an edit in context, an edit of syntax. Refer to *Figure 16.3*.

1. Value Within a Specific Field
2. Dependent Values in Fields
3. Presence of a Master Record
4. Ability to Update the Master

***Figure 16.3.*** Transaction edits

An edit can verify the presence or absence of a value in a specific field. For example, consider the name of an employee as three successive fields. If the family name is not present, there is definitely an error. An error message should be displayed. The first name should be present, or there is a likelihood of an error. This might cause the display of a warning message. The middle initial could be absent, since many people have no middle name. No warning message would be appropriate.

The presence of data in one field can dictate the presence or absence of data in another field. As an example, consider a transaction representing an attendance report by an employee. If the number of hours reported for a day is zero, the reason field should contain a value, usually a code of some sort, stating that the employee was on vacation or ill.

Each transaction contains data about some sort of event, such as a report of attendance, or a report of receipt of material. The transaction contains data about some thing: an employee, a component part of the product. The thing, employee, or part, is identified by an identification code—an employee number or a part number. The computer can check the master record on a file or database to verify that such an employee or part is on file.

If the computer verifies that a master record actually exists for the subject item of the transaction record, it can do further editing by attempting to update the master record. It can see if the employee is on active duty. It can see if the received material was actually ordered. If the transaction represents the shipment of a quantity of material, the computer can verify that the reported quantity shipped is not greater than the quantity in inventory.

## Degrees of Transaction Editing

From the above discussion, it might be apparent that there are three degrees of thoroughness in editing transactions (*Figure 16.4*). The amount of editing actually performed for a specific type of transaction depends upon the user's decision on where to balance the expense of editing against the value of accuracy in the transaction. Value of accuracy in a transaction might be better stated as avoidance of the expense of correcting grief after processing has been completed.

1. Batch Transaction Edits
2. On-line Transaction Edits
3. Edits Against a Database

***Figure 16.4.*** Degree of transaction edit

## Batch Transaction Edits

The batch editing of transactions consists of examining each transaction as a stand-alone record, with no reference to the presence or absence of a master file record. It also is limited to indirect reporting of the resulting grief and warning messages. There is no on-line response to the person doing the input. This is the type of editing which was done for keypunched transactions. The characteristics of this type of edit are listed in *Figure 16.5.*

1. Editing Only Within the Transaction
2. Delayed Grief Correction
3. Master File Currency not Critical
4. Regular File Backup Required
5. Batch Controls Advisable

***Figure 16.5.*** Batch transaction editing

Only limited editing, field edit and syntax edit within the individual transaction, are possible.

The correction of grief is delayed until the whole set of transactions has been processed and a grief report has been printed. This is usually an overnight process. The user submits the transactions on one day, and then corrects the grief the next day.

Presuming that the correction of grief is reliable, the master file is always one or two days out-of-date with the events which generated the transactions. A shipment of material was received on Monday. The transaction was edited

Monday night. If the transaction was correct, the master file was updated and available on Tuesday. If the transaction was in error, a correcting transaction was submitted for editing and processing on Tuesday night. Presuming that no new error had been created, the master file would be up-to-date (with Monday's activity) on Wednesday morning. For this type of editing to be acceptable, the currency of the master file must not be a significant requirement.

Each time the master file is updated, a copy of it must be made as a backup. The file of transactions is also retained in a secure place. If the master file is damaged, the backup copy can be retrieved, and the batch of transactions can be reprocessed.

Because a volume of transactions is entered into a transaction file from a volume of source documents, it is easy to overlook a few documents or to create duplicate transactions. This is particularly true if the work is spread among a number of data entry clerks. For this reason it is prudent to establish batch totals of the number of source documents. These totals can be verified manually against the number of mechanized transactions which are developed in the data entry process.

## On-Line Transaction Edits

The on-line editing of transactions includes all of the editing capability of batch edits. It also offers the capability of verifying the presence of the appropriate master file record (*Figure 16.6*). The transactions can be batched, or they can be processed individually as soon as each transaction is entered into a terminal.

1. Edit for Master Record Presence
2. Immediate Grief Correction
3. Master File Currency Not Critical
4. Regular File Backup Required
5. Batch Controls Advisable

***Figure 16.6.*** On-line transaction editing

If the transactions are edited as they are entered, grief can be identified and corrected immediately. This, of course, speeds processing and reduces the possibility of added errors during grief correction.

In this type of editing, even though the master file is read to validate the transaction, the transaction itself is not processed to update the master record. The currency of the data in the master file is not of great concern. In this case, the master file is updated overnight, after all of the day's transactions have been accumulated and edited. The master file is up-to-date the first thing in the morning after a day's business.

As with batch editing of transactions, the updating of the master file is done in a batch process. Each time the master file is updated, a copy of it must be made as a backup. The file of transactions is also retained in a secure place. If the master file is damaged, the backup copy can be retrieved, and the batch of transactions can be reprocessed.

Batch controls of input transactions are advisable if the transactions are batched before being submitted for editing. The reasoning is the same as for batch editing.

## Transaction Edit Against a Database

The most complete transaction edit technique is to validate the transaction against the contents of the database. This is much more thorough than just verifying the presence of a master record (*Figure 16.7*). The edit is a full edit, because it verifies that the contents of the transaction are consistent with the contents of the database. As an example, an inventory transaction cannot remove from inventory a greater quantity of material than the master record says is present. It cannot put into inventory more material than has been ordered.

1. Full Editing Capability
2. Immediate Grief Correction
3. Immediate Database Update
4. Regular File Backup Required
5. No Batch Controls

***Figure 16.7.*** Transaction edits against a database

As in the previous case, transaction grief can be corrected on the spot.

This type of edit is possible where there is not a lot of contention for access to the database for other purposes. This type of edit is necessary where the database must be up to the minute with the flow of work in the business. In this case, the transaction is not only edited, but the master file is updated at the same time.

Generally, each transaction is processed as it occurs. There is no batch updating of the master file. It would be impractical to make a backup copy of the master file with each individual update. It would also be foolhardy to never back up the master file. The normal backup process consists of a daily or weekly backup of the master file and a daily or weekly logging of the transactions which have been processed against the master file.

Because the transactions are not batched, batch controls are inappropriate. Since the day's business is processed as it occurs, there is little possibility of lost transactions or of redundant entry of transactions.

## Exercise 16.3

Can you identify specific examples of mechanized information systems where each of the three types of edit is appropriate?

## Batch Edit Example

The processing of a payroll is by nature a batch process. The mailing of checks and the reporting of taxes are tasks which are done periodically. For this reason, batch editing of transactions can be quite appropriate.

## On-Line Edit Example

The processing of customer invoices can readily be done as a batch process at the end of a day, but the editing of the order transactions is best done on-line. The computer can verify that the customer is represented on the master file. It might also verify that the customer's credit rating is good.

## Database Edit Example

Any inventory transaction has the possibility of requiring the database to be accurate to the moment of the transaction. This is particularly true in businesses where the inventory is kept to a minimum. In this case, the editing is done as a part of the master record update process. In effect, if the transaction is processed without problem, it must have been a valid transaction.

## User Responsibility

The user has the responsibility for the entry of transactions and for the correction of grief. In fact, even when the transactions were entered by a keypunch staff within the Data Processing department, it was the user who had the responsibility to record the original transaction on paper and the responsibility to correct grief.

The data processor must advise the user on techniques and costs of the various types of editing. It is the user who has the responsibility to determine the degree of editing which is to be implemented in a new mechanized system. This is done in the definition phase.

## Summary

The move of data entry responsibility to the user area gives the user greater control over the accuracy of input data. It also gives the user a greater sense of responsibility for the quality of the input data.

The advent of the technical capability of on-line processing makes it possible to edit transactions more completely. It also makes it possible for grief to be reported immediately upon entry of a transaction. The resulting immediate correction of grief brought data entry economy and improved the reliability of mechanized systems.

The immediate verification of the accuracy of input data is called an *edit* process. It is a process which verifies the accuracy and syntax of a computer record or of an input transaction.

There are three degrees of editing input data. The simplest and most limited is *batch editing*. A more thorough edit is an *on-line edit* which verifies the presence of the appropriate master record in the database. The most thorough edit is a *complete edit* of the transaction against the contents of the database.

The user not only has the responsibility to enter the transactions, but he or she also has the responsibility to determine the degree of editing required.

# 17

# *Bills of Material*

## Introduction

The bill of material (B/M) is one of the most important and useful documents in a manufacturing facility. As was illustrated in an earlier chapter, there are practical reasons for different functions within the organization to have different bills of material. The purpose of this chapter is to explore in more detail why there are different bills. The intent is to develop an awareness that there must be multiple bills—but that there must be only one system of bill of material control.

## Bill of Material

A *bill of material* is a structured, level-by-level listing of the components of a product, including part number, part name, quantity used, and a linkage from each level of the assembly to subassemblies and components (*Figure 17.1*). Note that the product can contain a number of levels of subassemblies which are components of higher level subassemblies or of the top level assembly. The linkage between levels of assembly and their components is illustrated by the physical arrangement of the product structure in the figure.

---

## Exercise 17.1

1. What is the part number of the top level assembly in the clock in *Figure 17.1*?
2. Is B1 an assembly?

**Exercise 17.1** (*Continued*)

3. Is B1 a subassembly?
4. Is B1 a component of A1?
5. Is E1 an assembly?
6. Is E1 a subassembly?
7. Is E1 a component? Of what?

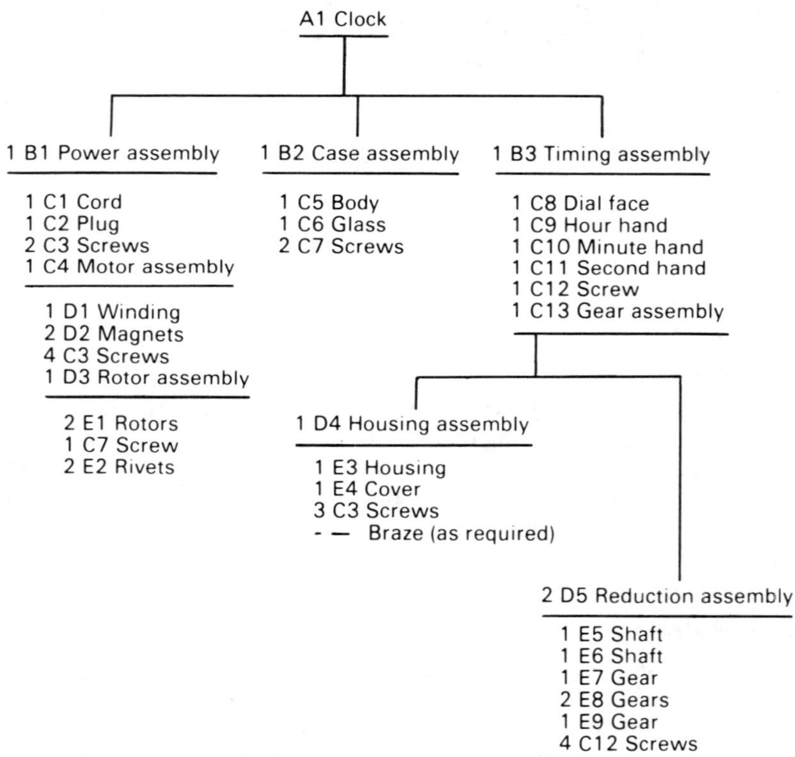


***Figure 17.1.*** Bill of material

## Material List

A *material list* is a simple listing of the components of a product, without any intermediate levels of assembly. A cake recipe is a simple material list accompanied by mixing and preparation instructions. A comparison of the contents of a bill of material and a material list is made in *Figure 17.2*. A material list of an assembly is sometimes called the *consist* of the assembly.

| BILL OF MATERIAL |
|---|
| Part Number<br>Part Name<br>Quantity used in the next higher assembly or subassembly<br>Linkage from each level of assembly to the components |
| **MATERIAL LIST** |
| Part Number<br>Part Name<br>Quantity used in the product—total product |

***Figure 17.2.*** Bill of material and material list comparison

## Types of Bills of Material

There are several other types of bills of material which are in common use in various functional areas of a manufacturing facility.

A *quick deck* is a summary of all quantities of each component which is used in a complete product. It is a material list of the total product without any reference to intermediate levels of subassembly. In some inventory management operations, the quick deck is the device for swift calculation of material requirements.

Consider a product which has two subassemblies. In one subassembly the component Cl is used in a quantity of four. In the other subassembly component Cl is used in a quantity of two. In a quick deck of the product, there would be a quantity of six of component C1. For a schedule to manufacture 10 of the product, 60 units of Cl would be required (10 x 6).

A *where used* (W/ U) is an upside-down bill of material. It lists all of the next level assemblies and subassemblies in which a component or subassembly is used, including quantities of the component in each next level. A next level assembly is one which contains the component directly, not one which contains the component indirectly through a subassembly. A where used list is sometimes called a *guzinta* since the component *goes into* the assemblies on the list.

A *top level where used* is a list of all of the products (top level assemblies) in which a component or subassembly is used.

*Figure 17.3* is a summary of the types of bills.

## Exercise 17.2

Refer to the clock bill of material in *Figure 17.1*.

1. What is the consist of D4?

2. What is the next level usage of E5?

3. What is the top level usage of C12?

**Exercise 17.2** *(Continued)*

4. What is the quantity of C12 used in D5?
5. What is the quantity of C12 used in B3?

---

**Bill of Material:** A structured list of material of a total product.
**Material List:** A single level bill of material of a product or of an assembly.
**Quick Deck:** A summarized material list of a total product.
**Where Used:** A list of all of the next level usage of a component.
**Top Level Where Used:** A list of all of the products on which a component is used.

***Figure 17.3.*** Bill of material definitions

## Uses of Bills of Material

The Design Engineering department is the original source of the bill of material. This is the department in which the product is originally defined. The following list illustrates how different departments use the different types of bills of material to suit their own needs.

**Design Engineering.**

*Bill of material*—To describe the product for other departments.

*Top level W/U*—To determine all usages of a part which is being considered for change.

*Where used*—To determine the portion of a product which is affected by a reported failure of a specific component.

**Materials Planning.**

*Quick deck*—To calculate the quantity of components required to build a scheduled quantity of product.

*Bill of material*—To prepare and maintain a quick deck as Design Engineering changes the product.

**Production Engineering.**

*Bill of material*—To plan the method of manufacturing the product.

**Assembly.**

*Material list*—To assemble a portion of a product.

**Accounting.**

*Material list*—To calculate the material cost of a product.

*Bill of material*—To calculate the total cost of a product, including assembly labor.

## Differing Bill of Material Contents

Different departments have reason to need different contents within their local views of the bill of material of a single product. The reason for this is that they perform different functions relative to the product.

Consider the bill of material which might exist for a bicycle. The Design Engineering department would tend to describe the major subassemblies of a bicycle as the front wheel assembly, the rear wheel assembly, the frame assembly, and the power train assembly. The bicycle would never be built in terms of such subassemblies.

As an example, the rear sprocket, part of Design Engineering's power train, would be physically assembled as part of the rear wheel assembly. The pedals and front sprocket would be physically assembled as part of the frame assembly. Finally, the chain (the only remaining part of the power train assembly) would be the last component installed on the bicycle, after the wheel assemblies were installed.

The following list illustrates some of the more obvious departmental differences.

- Design Engineering finds it most convenient to describe product in terms of bills which are organized by function—a bill for the engine of a vehicle, a bill for the transmission, a bill for the throttle control. The bills contain all components of these portions of the product. They even contain components of some purchased subassemblies for which the Design Engineering department maintains design control.
- Assembly finds it most convenient to use material lists which represent the sequence in which the components are physically assembled. For example, the power train of a bicycle is never assembled as a whole. It is assembled in bits and pieces as part of the rear wheel and as part of the frame. Assembly is not interested in the material list of a purchased subassembly. Sometimes the subassembly of components results in a collection of parts which has no convenient counterpart in the Design Engineering bill—thus causing the need for a new part number to identify the subassembly which only exists for a short period of time during the assembly process.
- Materials Planning needs a bill of material which reflects the physical subassembly process. This is particularly important if the lead time of subassembly is long enough to affect the procurement time of components. The bills of material do not need to include all components of a product. They only need to include those which are purchased or internally manufactured. Sometimes, Design Engineering doesn't know the exact quantity of an item, as in braze on the clock or in the number of shims on a shaft. Then, Materials Planning must estimate a quantity per assembly in order to calculate requirements. Materials Planning might convert the bill of material into a quick deck to perform the calculation.
- Accounting needs the same bill of material as Materials Planning. However, if Materials Planning used a quick deck, it would not serve the needs of Accounting to calculate the cost of producing subassemblies.
- Sales needs a material list which includes the options which can be ordered with the product. In a way, these are not part of the product if

they are add-ons. However, if at least one of the alternative options is required as a built-in option, then it certainly is a part of the product. An example in automobiles is the convention of representing a manual transmission as a part of the standard product, and an automatic transmission as an option.

## Exercise 17.3

Ask yourself if there is need for a master bill of material. If you think there is, then consider why you think the master bill of material is needed. Next, try to identify which bill must be the master—and the reason why.

## Master Bill of Material

Obviously there must be a master bill of material of the product. If each department defined the product as it wished, the business would operate no more effectively than an anarchy.

Design Engineering has the responsibility to design the product. The other departments have varying responsibilities for producing the product and for providing it to the customer—the product as designed by Design Engineering.

Since the design of the product controls all aspects of procurement, assembly, and sale, the Design Engineering bill of material must logically be the master bill.

### A Single Bill of Material?

Although the idea of a single bill of material within a company seems to hold the promise of efficiency of communication among departments, the fact is that a single bill of material is very often unworkable. Design Engineering would have to structure the master bill of material in the fashion in which the product was to be produced, even though engineers think about the product functionally. Every time that the Assembly department found a new and better way to sequence the subassemblies of the product, the Design Engineering department would have to change its bill of material—even though the final product would not have changed in the least.

### A Single Bill of Material System

The information system challenge is to provide a single master bill of material and a mechanism whereby each functional area can view the common product structure to suit its own needs. In addition, a control must be in place to ensure that these departmental views are consistent with the original Engineering intent.

The answer is to have a single bill of material control system. There might be different images on paper and even in computer records, but the different records are under a single logical control system for consistency.

By the guidelines discussed earlier, this is a natural application of the computer. There is a frequent need for calculation; many records are to be used at a single time; there is a need for great accuracy; and there is the possibility of significant complexity of logic.

*Figure 17.4* suggests how the records might be organized in a master bill of material system. The indicator "top" describes the A1 clock as a final, top level product.

The B1 power assembly is physically assembled as part of the B2 case assembly, even though Design Engineering views it as a separate assembly. For this reason, B1 is flagged in the Assembly department and Accounting department records as part of B2. In the same way, C1 and C2 are assembled as part of C4.

| PRODUCT | DESIGN ENG. | ASSEMBLY | MATL. PLAN. | ACCTG. | SALES |
|---|---|---|---|---|---|
| A1 Clock | top | top | top | top | top |
| B1 Power assembly | 1 | 1-B2 | 1 np | 1-B2 | ns |
| C1 Cord | 1 | 1-C4 | 1 | 1-C4 | ns |
| C2 Plug | 1 | 1-C4 | 1 | 1-C4 | ns |
| C3 Screws | 2 | 2 | 2 | 2 | ns |
| C4 Motor assembly | 1 | 1-B2 | 1np | 1-B2 | ns |
| D1 Winding | 1 | na | ip | ip | ns |
| D2 Magnets | 2 | na | ip | ip | ns |
| C3 Screws | 4 | na | ip | ip | ns |
| D3 Rotor assembly | 1 | na | ip | ip | ns |
| E1 Rotors | 2 | na | ip | ip | ns |
| C7 Screw | 1 | na | ip | ip | ns |
| E2 Rivets | 2 | na | ip | ip | ns |
| B2 Case assembly | 1 | 1 | 1np | 1 | ns |
| C5 Body | 1 | 1 | 1 | 1 | ns |
| C6 Glass | 1 | 1 | 1 | 1 | ns |
| C7 Screws | 2 | 2 | 2 | 2 | ns |
| B3 Timing assembly | 1 | 1-B2 | 1 np | 1-B2 | ns |
| C9 Hour hand | 1 | 1 | 1 | 1 | ns |
| C10 Minute hand | 1 | 1 | 1 | 1 | ns |
| C11 Second hand | 1 | 1 | 1 | 1 | ns |
| C12 Screw | 1 | 1 | 1 | 1 | ns |
| C13 Gear assembly | 1 | 1 | 1 np | 1 | ns |
| D4 Housing ass. | 1 | 1 | 1 np | 1 | ns |
| E3 Housing | 1 | 1 | 1 | 1 | ns |
| E4 Cover | 1 | 1 | 1 | 1 | ns |
| C3 Screws | 3 | 3 | 3 | 3 | ns |
| Braze | ? | ? | 2gm | 2gm | ns |
| D5 Reduct. ass. | 2 | 2 | 2 | 2 | ns |
| E5 Shaft | 1 | na | ip | ip | ns |
| E6 Shaft | 1 | na | ip | ip | ns |
| E7 Gear | 1 | na | ip | ip | ns |
| E8 Gears | 2 | na | ip | ip | ns |
| E9 Gear | 1 | na | ip | ip | ns |
| C12 Screws | 4 | na | ip | ip | ns |
| **Option** | | | | | |
| C8 dial face | so | so | 50% | so | so |
| K1 Dial face | op | op | 30% | op | op |
| K2 Dial face | op | op | 20% | op | op |

***Figure 17.4.*** Master bill of material records

None of the components of the clock are sold as final products, so they are flagged in the Sales department record as "ns," meaning "not sold."

The C4 motor assembly is purchased as a complete unit from an outside supplier. Although Design Engineering is interested in the consist of the assembly, Materials Planning and Accounting have no interest in it and have flagged the components as "ip" meaning that they are included as a part of a purchased assembly. The Assembly department records the components as "na," meaning "not assembled."

The braze is used in an indeterminate amount, varying with the dimensional tolerances of the parts and variation in the brazing process. In order to provide adequate quantities, Materials Planning has estimated that 2 grams ("gm") of braze will be used per average assembly.

The C8 dial face is a standard option, "so." This means that C8 will be provided on any clock on which the customer has not specified an alternative dial face. Past sales records suggest that 50% of clocks will be sold in this configuration. Options K1 and K2 are sold in 30% and 20% of the orders.

Note that in the master bill of material record, each subassembly has a part number, even if it is not used by all functional areas. This enhances communication among departments.

> **LAW**
>
> **You Can't Control What Isn't Named.**
>
> The inventory of an assembly of material cannot be managed unless there is a part number by which the assembly is identified.

The thrust of this law is that the inventory of an assembly of material cannot be managed unless there is a part number by which the assembly is identified.

The Assembly department builds the product up through subassemblies. No other department is really concerned with how the assembly process is done. But on occasion, the Assembly department builds up a supply of subassemblies in advance for various reasons. For example, they might want to provide an inventory buffer to support continued production while the subassembly area is being rearranged. In this case, the Material Distribution department would need to store the subassemblies and return them upon demand. The presence of a part number to identify the subassembly greatly enhances the ability of the two departments to communicate without ambiguity.

There is a corollary example which illustrates the importance of this law. It occurs when a single option can be sold on several different final products or can be sold as a final product itself. An example would be a dashboard clock which is an option on two different automobile models and is also sold to dealers as a parts sales item which can be dealer-installed. The hardware for installing the clock is most likely different between the automobile models. Different cover panels must be removed from the several models to make an opening for the clock. The clock as a parts sales item will need to include the hardware to allow it to be installed in whatever model the customer has.

*Figure 17.5* illustrates the relationship of the several varieties of options. Note that the cover panel itself must also be an option—although nominally a part of the standard model. Each variation of the clock must have a unique part number in order for it to be planned, produced, assembled, and distributed without ambiguity.

| | LUXURY SEDAN | COMPACT SEDAN | PARTS SALES |
|---|---|---|---|
| **CLOCK** | **C1** | **C2** | **C3** |
| Case assembly | 1 D1 | 1 D2 | 1 D1 |
| Dial face | 1 E1 | 1 E2 | 1 E1 |
| Power assembly | 1 F1 | 1 F1 | 1 F1 |
| Timing assembly | 1 G1 | 1 G1 | 1 G1 |
| Screws | 4 H1 | | 4 H1 |
| Screws | | 4 H2 | 4 H2 |
| **COVER** | **L1** | **L2** | |
| Cover | 1 M1 | 1 M2 | |
| Clips | 4 N1 | 2 N2 | |

***Figure 17.5.*** Varieties of an option

Note that the luxury sedan in *Figure 17.5* contains either C1 or L1 depending upon whether or not the customer orders a clock. The compact sedan contains either C2 or L2. If C3 is installed at a dealer's shop, then either the equivalent of L1 or L2 is removed from the car, and either H2 or H1 screws are discarded from the C3 kit.

> **LAW**
>
> **People Don't Know Their Neighbors**
>
> People often perform their functions in ignorance of how their performance affects neighboring functions.

The thrust of this law is that people often carry out their jobs without being aware of how their performance can affect neighboring functions.

An ongoing communications confusion within manufacturing enterprises is a demonstration of this law. People fall into the habit of performing their function as best they can to satisfy the performance measures applied to them. Relatively few people seem to exhibit concern about how the results of their work affect peers in other departments. The major exception to this rule occurs when a person is measured by the quality of service provided to a neighboring organization, as measured by that organization.

## CIM Impact on Bills of Material

In a just-in-time environment there is no room for error in the provisioning of production materials. Correspondingly, the bill of material which drives material procurement and production cannot have errors.

Normally, material will be provided based upon the assembly schedule for final product. The subassembly of modules must be completed and the modules must be delivered to the assembly line just before the assembly process begins. Thus, the subassembly process must begin with some lead time in advance of the start of the assembly process.

For the same reasons, the manufacture of piece parts must begin with some lead time in advance of the start of the subassembly process.

The rough material for manufacture must be ordered from the supplier with some lead time in advance of the start of the manufacturing process.

The bill of material needed to direct this activity to a precise schedule is an integrated bill of material which is structured to represent the sequence of activities in assembly and subassembly steps. It shows the lead time for each processing step and the quantity of each item required at that step.

The best way to ensure accuracy in this bill of material is to place it in a bill of material control system under the control of the Design Engineering bill of material. Such an integrated bill of material control system is consistent with the integration of data called for by the concepts of CIM.

## Summary

The *bill of material* is the vehicle by which the structure of a product is communicated throughout the manufacturing organization. The bill of material is recorded in five variations, depending upon the business purpose to be served (*bill of material, material list, quick deck, where used,* and *top level where used*).

Different departments maintain bills of material which are customized to the needs of the department, often omitting items included in bills in other departments, and containing items missing from the bills in the other departments. Because of the need to establish reliable communications among departments, it is mandatory to maintain a single bill of material control system by which all departmental views of the bill are kept synchronized to the master bill of material from Design Engineering.

**LAW—You Can't Control What Isn't Named.** The inventory of an assembly of material cannot be managed unless there is a part number by which the assembly is identified.

**LAW—People Don't Know Their Neighbors.** People often perform their functions in ignorance of how their performance affects neighboring functions.

Just-in-time manufacturing requires a single bill of material control system with a manufacturing view of the sequence and lead time of procurement, manufacture, and assembly.

# 18

# *Coding and Classification*

## Introduction

A law described in Chapter 17 says, "You can't control what isn't named." All assets of an organization have a name. Sometimes, even often, the name is abbreviated or supplemented by some sort of a code for convenience. In fact, no record, physical or logical, is stored or retrieved except through the use of a code. Until the 1970s there was no body of research work on principles for good and durable code structures. The advent of computer files and databases triggered a study of code disciplines.

Most managers are unaware of their dependency on good codes. The purpose of this chapter is to give the reader an appreciation of the importance of good coding systems. The manager will need to help in the development and improvement of codes as the business changes. He or she will have to be involved either as a user or as a data processor.

## Exercise 18.1

Can you define what is meant by the word *code*? It is used in a number of contexts in industry. Look in the dictionary. It contains a variety of definitions.

## Code—A Working Definition

For practical purposes, a *code* is simply defined as a brief label used as a substitute for a thing or for the name of a thing.

## Uses of Codes

Codes are used for a variety of purposes. The most common purposes are illustrated in *Figure 18.1*.

A code is used to identify a thing as uniquely different from any other thing. "Benjamin Franklin" is a code which is used to distinguish a famous historical figure from other people. "LAX" is a code which is used to distinguish the Los Angeles airport from other airports. "A" is a code distinguishing a particular vowel sound from other sounds. ".-" is a code which is used in simple telegraph communications to distinguish the letter "A" from other letters.

1. To Identify a Thing as Unique
2. To Classify a Thing as Part of a Group
3. To Abbreviate the Label of a Thing
4. To Encrypt a Message

***Figure 18.1.*** Uses of codes

A code is used to classify a thing as belonging to a set of things with similar characteristics. "Franklin" is a code which classifies a number of people as belonging to the same family (not as precise a classification as other possible examples). "American" is a code identifying the country of origin of millions of people. "M" is a code which classifies approximately half of the human race as being male.

A code can be used to abbreviate the label of a thing. "JFK" is a code which is widely recognized as an abbreviation for the name of a former president. "IL" is a post office code which is an abbreviation for the name of the state of Illinois. "TGIF" is a widely recognized code which is often expressed by workers on a Friday. Shorthand is a system in which simple codes are used by a stenographer to abbreviate syllables and whole words.

The set of instructions in a computer program is called *code*. The instructions are usually not an abbreviation, but are in a language which people can readily understand and manipulate. A compiler program within the computer translates the people-oriented code into a highly symbolic code which is used internally to drive the computer.

A code can be used to encrypt a message. The encryption can be used to speed the transfer of the message. In this application the code is a sort of abbreviation. The encryption can also be used to secure the meaning of the message from unauthorized people. The cryptogram in the daily newspaper is an example of encryption.

In the remainder of this chapter the emphasis will be on the first two uses of codes—to identify things and to classify things.

## Exercise 18.2

Write down examples of identification and classification codes. Think of codes such as airport codes, state codes, etc. List them. To the right of the name of each code, write an "I" or a "C" to identify each as an identification code or a classification code. Some codes are both. Leave more room to the right. Later you will be writing example values, and other ideas about the codes.

## Examples of Codes

*Figure 18.2* is a set of examples of identification and classification codes. There is probably a significant overlap between your list and this figure.

| CODE | IC |
|---|---|
| 1. Phone Number | I |
| 2. College Course Number | IC |
| 3. Part Number | I |
| 4. Social Security Number | I |
| 5. Sex | C |
| 6. Machine Tool Number | I |
| 7. Machine Class Code | C |
| 8. Product Serial Number | I |
| 9. State Abbreviation | I |
| 10. ZIP Code | I |
| 11. Expanded ZIP Code | I |
| 12. Airport Code | I |
| 13. Tire Code | IC |
| 14. Account Code | IC |
| 15. Computer Model Code | IC |
| 16. Dealer Code | I |

***Figure 18.2.*** Examples of codes

In idealistic terms, all classification codes are identification codes, since they identify a class of things with similar characteristics. But many classification codes are used primarily to label things as belonging to a class, and are not often used to discuss the class itself. An example is "M" or "F" for male or female. The labels "male" and "female" are used instead of the code when talking about the class itself.

The use of some specific codes for both classification and identification will become clearer when example code values are discussed.

## Exercise 18.3

What are some of the advantages and disadvantages in using codes? Look at your list and visualize how the different codes have impacted you.

As an example, consider the ZIP code (did you overlook it?). Its purpose is to help the U.S. Post Office to expedite the sorting and delivery of mail, but the post office uses the code as literally as a computer would. If you write the wrong ZIP code, the letter is returned to you. This is a delivery delay and a loss of the investment in postage. But, if you fail to write the ZIP code, the letter will be delivered.

## Relative Advantages of Codes

*Figure 18.3* is a summary of advantages and disadvantages from the use of codes.

+ Reduces Time to Read and Write
+ Reduces Opportunity for Error
+ Simplifies File Maintenance
- Awkward to Look Up Values
- Record Label Change

***Figure 18.3.*** Relative advantages of codes

The use of a code simplifies the writing of information or the entry of information at a keyboard. It makes reports shorter and allows for more columns of meaningful information on a report.

The use of a short code reduces the error potential in transcribing information from one medium to another. The less characters one has to write, the less opportunity for error, such as transposition of numbers. This has been demonstrated with long identification codes, such as some companies' long part numbers.

The use of codes reduces the time and error in maintaining files of information. A good example is the patient files in a medical office. A common technique is to affix a color code to the spine of the file. The code represents the first two letters of the patient's last name. It is easy to find files once the code has been committed to memory. It is even simpler to insert folders into the proper place on the shelf. The color contrast quickly signals any folder which is out of place.

Codes do have some compensating disadvantages. If a code has a great number of values, the translation of the code must be looked up in a catalog. This is time-consuming and error-prone. An example might be the Dewey decimal system for library books. It is convenient for the librarian who works with it every day. It is not so simple for the casual reader who searches for a book once in a while.

Once a code has been assigned to an item, records about the item tend to be stored and retrieved by the use of the code. This is evidence that the use of a code is a significant convenience. However, there is a resulting inconvenience if the code is changed. Then, all of the records, physical and logical, must be changed. An example is the last name of a woman who marries and then takes her husband's family name. Personnel and medical records for her must be changed.

## Exercise 18.4

Now expand your list of identification and classification codes. Write down an example of one or two specific values for each code. An example is "M" for the code signifying sex. Another is the value "IL" for the state code.

## Examples of Code Values

The list of codes in *Figure 18.2* has been expanded in *Figure 18.4* to include examples. It is obvious from looking at the list that there seems to be a wide variety of code conventions and disciplines. The thinking you did in Exercise 18.3 should have made you aware that some of the coding conventions cause problems for you. There are definite guidelines and rules for establishing codes to make them as convenient as possible. These will be explored later in this chapter.

| CODE | IC | EXAMPLE |
|---|---|---|
| 1. Phone Number | I | (309) 675-1293 |
| 2. College Course Number | IC | IE409A |
| 3. Part Number | I | 3B4506 |
| 4. Social Security Number | I | 328-48-2975 |
| 5. Sex | C | M or F |
| 6. Machine Tool Number | I | M29476 |
| 7. Machine Class Code | C | D12R |
| 8. Product Serial Number | I | 12D18394 |
| 9. State Abbreviation | I | ME, MO, MI |
| 10. ZIP Code | I | 61614 |
| 11. Expanded ZIP Code | I | 61614-3186 |
| 12. Airport Code | I | ORD, PIA, LAX |
| 13. Tire Code | IC | TT 676 15 BW |
| 14. Account Code | IC | 12-47-65-38 |
| 15. Computer Model Code | IC | IBM-XT |
| 16. Dealer Code | I | C231 |

***Figure 18.4.*** Examples of code values

## Types of Codes

There are a number of different types of codes. The variety is not as limited as *Figure 18.1* might seem to suggest. An analysis of the types of codes will provide more insight into the variety of coding conventions exhibited in *Figure 18.4* and in your own list. These following examples are from the list in *Figure 18.4*.

Nonsignificant identifiers are codes which identify, but do not classify. Sometimes these codes are assigned in various office locations. An example is the part number in a company with a number of product design locations. This requires the use of a central computer control of the assignment of part numbers or the assignment of blocks of numbers to the various design locations. The first approach is expensive. The second approach is inexpensive, but gives an accidental meaning to the part number. Examples of such codes are part number (sometimes), and social security number.

Abbreviations are truncations of names, such as people's names. This is convenient, but can be confusing. There are many people with the same initials. The airport code and the sex code are examples of abbreviations.

Symbolic codes are codes which carry a readily interpretable meaning. An example is the tire code. "TT" stands for tractor tire. "676 15" stands for the dimensions or size of the tire. "BW" indicates that the tire is a blackwall.

Hierarchical codes are segmented codes where the meaning of each succeeding portion depends upon the value of its predecessor. Examples include account codes, part classification codes, the Dewey decimal system, and the binomial system of scientific nomenclature.

Polycodes are codes of characteristics of an item. The item may be classified by a string of one to many code values, each describing a feature of the item. Such codes are coming into use to describe features of parts. The purpose is to aid in the selection of appropriate production processes.

## The Need for Good Codes

Since codes are convenient, they are the primary device by which records are stored and retrieved. This is true about both manual records and computer records. There is hardly a record which is not managed through a code of some sort.

It is important that the logical structure of a code be established carefully. If it is not, the code will have a limited life expectancy. Then a significant expense will be incurred to change all records. This is particularly expensive in computer programs, which are difficult to change. It is especially difficult if logical decisions within the programs are based upon specific code values.

It is also important to exercise good discipline in the assignment of specific values of a code to specific items. Two items could be given the same code value in error. An item could be given an ambiguous code value. In the code value "12O87" the O is a capital letter, not the value zero. It should be apparent that the choice of "O" could cause significant misunderstanding.

## Rules for Good Coding

There are a number of sound rules or guidelines which have been developed in recent years to guide the development of codes (*Figure 18.5*). Some of the rules guide the structuring of codes. Others guide the assignment of code values. Unfortunately, some of the rules contradict one another. The design of a code requires compromise between conflicting principles. It is no different from the need to compromise between comfort and fuel economy in the design of an auto.

1. Uniqueness
2. Expandablility
3. Conciseness
4. Convenience
5. Versatility
6. Sortability
7. Stability
8. Meaningfulness
9. Comprehensibility

***Figure 18.5.*** Coding rules

## Rule 1—Uniqueness

There should be a one-to-one correspondence between a value of a code and the item which the code represents. If there are several items identified by a single code, it is ambiguous and cannot be used to manage information about any of the items. If there are several values of the code for a single item, it will be impossible to tell which value to use when storing or retrieving data about the item.

## Rule 2—Expandability

A code should have the capacity to handle growth in the population of items to be identified or classified. The logical capacity of the code should be at least ten times the number of items originally envisioned as belonging to the population.

Consider as an example a numeric code to identify the units of local government which are authorized to vote in a national political convention. A two digit number could handle 98 units of government if the values "00" and "99" are eliminated. (The uses of these boundary values will be discussed later.) This capacity would seem to be adequate, since there are only 50 states, but what about the District of Columbia, Puerto Rico, and the Virgin Islands? Who is to say that there will never be more than 98 units of government?

One reasonable alternative would be to use a three digit number. This would give a capacity of 998, omitting boundary values. Another alternative would be to use two alphabetic characters. This would give a capacity of 674, omitting boundary values. The current state code could be extended for this purpose.

If all of the values of a code are assigned, there is the virtual certainty the need will develop to assign a code value to one more item. Then the code structure will have to be redone. New values will have to be assigned. And worst of all, existing records, and possibly computer programs, will have to be changed to reflect the new code structure and new code values.

## Rule 3—Conciseness

The fewer the characters in a code, the better. If a code is concise, the risk of error in manual transcription is minimized. Time is saved when writing a value of the code. Space is saved in printed reports and on terminal screens. The values of the code can be more readily remembered.

But, this rule conflicts with the previous rule. A balance must be struck. This is a part of the compromise process. In the example of local governments, the apparently logical compromise would be to use the two letter state code which already exists.

## Rule 4—Convenience

The code should be structured so that it is easily understood and applied. A concise code has this characteristic by default. A longer code, such as a phone number, does not.

The structure of the phone number as written establishes a significant amount of convenience. If you were to call the Chicago information operator from long distance, you might have difficulty in reading and dialing 3125551212. You find it much more convenient to deal with the number represented as (312) 555-1212. The structure of the representation breaks the number into manageable pieces for both the eye and the memory.

People can remember only a relatively small number of code values. For this reason, every attempt should be made to avoid the need to look up values in a code book. Did you ever try to mail a package through UPS without knowing the ZIP code? Of course, this concern is a natural conflict with the rule on expandability. Sometimes it can be accommodated by structuring the assignment of values. The regional assignment of ZIP codes is of assistance. It at least tells you if the code you just looked up is in the right ball park. You should be able to tell Aurora, Colorado from Aurora, Illinois.

## Rule 5—Versatility

The code should be readily adaptable to new conditions. This need occurs most often for classification codes. As the environment changes, unexpected sets of items must be classified.

A good example is a business which begins to diversify its product line. New products must be classified into new model families. It would be expensive and confusing to restructure the old model code. Many manual and computer records would have to be changed. The logic in many computer programs would have to be changed. And probably most traumatic, people would have to forget the meaning of the old code values and learn new ones.

The types of codes which are most subject to the need for expansion are hierarchical codes, such as a chart of accounts or a commodity code. To maintain versatility, the rule of expandability should be honored for each of the segments within a hierarchical code.

## Rule 6—Sortability

The code should be readily sortable. It should be simple for a computer to sort. This requires that the sort considers the code value as a single field of data. The sorting process is significantly complicated and lengthened if a code must be sorted on segments of the code value. The sort sequence should be obvious to the person reading a report or a catalog. Otherwise, it is difficult to locate specific values.

One key to sortability is to avoid intermixing alphabetic and numeric values within a single position of the code. A numeric value offers 10 unique meanings for a single code position. An alphabetic value offers 26 unique meanings (considering the alphabet used by the English language). A mixed alphanumeric value offers 36 unique meanings. This can be expanded even farther by using special characters such as %, #, @, and &. The expansion possibilities are tempting as an answer to the principle of expandability, but the sort sequence has now become a nightmare for the reader. What comes first: 0, A, $, or #?

## Rule 7—Stability

The classification of items should be based upon enduring characteristics if at all possible. If not, then the code values must be changed as the characteristics of the item change. Then it becomes necessary to change database records about the item.

Classification of people by enduring characteristics is nearly impossible. Women marry and take their husband's family name. People go to court to change their name to something they like better. Some people even change their sex. Employees change from full-time to part-time.

So, what is to be done? The problem can be reduced somewhat by careful selection of the coding rules. The problem is also not so serious for classification codes as it is for identification codes. It is the identification code which is most often used to store and access records. It is the classification code which is most often used to direct logical choices within a computer program.

## Rule 8—Meaningfulness

A code should be readily interpreted by the reader, if possible. This is the reason so many mnemonic codes are developed, such as the state code.

These codes should leave little margin for misinterpretation. They can do this if the rules for code assignment are apparent.

Consider the state code. What does "MI" stand for? Is it Mississippi, or Missouri, or Michigan, or Minnesota? Most people will know that it refers to

Michigan. But not all people will know that. When in doubt, a person tends to invent a value for the code based upon perceived rules. The most consistent "rule" in the state code is that it consists of the first two characters of the state name. But the rule isn't consistent. The code for Missouri is "MO."

## Rule 9—Comprehensibility

The code should be readily comprehensible. That is, it should be readily understood when code values are communicated from one person to another either by writing or by speaking. There are obvious pitfalls which should be avoided.

If both alphabetic and numeric values can appear within a code, then care should be taken when writing the letters I, O, S, and Z; and the digits 1, 0, 5, and 2. When written carelessly, I and 1 resemble one another. The same is true about O and 0, S and 5, Z and 2. A common approach is to avoid assigning the alphabetic characters I, O, S, and Z.

When written carelessly, the letters V, U, and J can be confused with one another. These should be avoided unless the code is a mnemonic one in which the value of the whole code provides a hint as to the value of individual characters.

When spoken, the letters B, D, and V can sound alike. This is particularly true within an international business where people speak with various accents. The letters W and V can also be confused when spoken by someone whose native language is not English.

Finally, M and N can sound like one another when spoken.

The military has long avoided confusion by applying words as codes by which to express the letters of the alphabet. They use such conventions as "alpha" for "A" and "bravo" for "B."

## Code Rule Conflicts

As you can see, there are many conflicts among the rules. Each makes sense by itself, but each seems to drive the structure of a code into a different direction from one or more of the other rules. There is no way around this problem except careful code design and intelligent compromise. A proposed new code should be tested against all of the rules, with weak points highlighted. Then, if an alternative code structure is attempted, it too should be tested in the same way. The final choice for a new code structure should be the one which causes the least possible pain.

---

## Exercise 18.5

Review your list of codes and the list in *Figure 18.4* to identify exceptional strengths and weaknesses.

---

## Appraisal of Example Codes

An assessment of the primary strength and weakness of each of the example codes will help to clarify the rules. This is not an absolute assessment. After all, the judgement is subjective, just as it is for a gymnastics contest.

The *phone number* is an excellent example of a convenient code. The segmentation of the number into three parts facilitates reading and remembering. But, the code is not concise. It is ten digits long. Fortunately, for memory purposes, most telephone calls involve only the last seven digits.

The *college course number* is meaningful, since the first two characters are mnemonics for the department which is offering the course. In this case the department is Industrial Engineering. The three digit number also carries a meaning. The first digit in the example tells that the course is a fourth-year course. But, the code is not expandable, since it can accommodate only 100 courses for each college year. This might seem adequate, but it is not, since historic records are kept of past courses.

This example of a *part number* is concise, especially when compared to the tire code, but the part number is difficult to sort and file. This is because it has an alphabetic character imbedded within it. If the alphabetic character were the first character, the sorting problem would be reduced. If it were the last character, the sorting problem could be reduced further.

The *social security number* is even more convenient than the telephone number. Read the number and notice that you tend to fall into a rhythm while reciting the digits. 328, pause, 48, pause, 2975. Like the telephone number, it is not concise. It does, however have about ten times the needed capacity.

The *sex code* is certainly meaningful. "M" stands for "male," and "F" for "female." It is also concise and really has no deficiencies. It even sorts females ahead of males.

The *machine tool number* is sortable, since the alphabetic character is at the beginning of the code. But it is not very expandable, since the "M" position can only identify 26 different types of machines.

The *machine class code* has the same characteristics as the machine tool number. The example represents a radial drill of a specific size. The advent of numerically controlled machine tools, and then machining centers, stretched the capacity of the alphabetic symbolism beyond limit.

The first three characters of the *product serial number* tell the type of product. The last five digits tell that this is the 18394th such unit of product assembled. The code is convenient and meaningful, but it is not concise, nor is it readily expandable.

The *state code* is meaningful as discussed earlier, but some of the values can be misinterpreted. It also exhibits deficiency relative to the rule about meaningful codes.

The *ZIP code* is concise. It is also meaningful, since the first few digits tell the general geographic area of the country. But, it was not very expandable, since new requirements forced the addition of a four-digit suffix.

The *expanded ZIP code* provides a unique value for each local post office or major post office box, but the code is no longer concise. It takes a large directory to aid people in looking up the ZIP code for a location.

The *airport code* is quite concise at three characters. It is also meaningful in that the characters are mnemonic. But, since there are so many airports, the meaning is not always obvious. An example is ORD for the O'Hare airport in Chicago, because it is built on the site of an old orchard.

The *tire code* is very meaningful, as discussed earlier, but its expandability is severely limited by the imbedded conventions for the size and type of tire.

The *computer model code* is obviously meaningful, but it is not at all sortable. It is, of course, questionable whether there is a need to sort it.

The *dealer code* indicates the number (meaningless) of a dealer in sales area "C" or "Central." It is meaningful because of the prefix, but it is not stable. The territory can always be divided into new sales areas. This would require recoding the dealers and changing dealer database records.

## Mixing Identification and Classification

It is almost always a mistake to use a single code for two purposes, identification and classification, at the same time. It is tempting to do so, because the value of the code conveys more to a reader if it also describes key characteristics of the item it represents. Such a code is really an identification code, but it contains meaning.

Examples are shown in *Figure 18.4*. They are the part number, the machine number, the product serial number, and the tire code.

Two problems tend to occur when meaning is built into an identification code. The first problem is that the expandability is severely limited. There is also an almost irresistible temptation to use the meaning within the logic of computer programs.

Codes with limited expandability tend to require change. This makes it necessary to change computer program logic and database record content. It is a significant price to pay for a visual convenience. It is better to use both an identification code to identify an item, and a classification code which can be stored in records about the item to add visual information.

## Boundary Values

In a computer, the first and last possible values of a code are convenient. They can be used as indicators to start or end a list of items. An example would be the values "AA" and "ZZ" to begin and end a list of codes composed of two alphabetic characters. Another example would be the values "00" and "99" to delimit a list of two-digit code values. These values or blank spaces can be used in a record to indicate that no meaningful value has yet been established for an item. Because of the convenience of boundary values in computer programs, they should not be assigned as meaningful values, but should be held in reserve.

## Dates are also Codes

Dates are codes to represent specific days in the flow of time. They also require some special disciplines.

## Exercise 18.6

How would a citizen of the United States write the date for the fourth day of the month of July in the year 1986? How would someone from Europe write it? How would a soldier in the U.S. Army write it? How is a date best represented in a computer? See how well you can answer these questions. The answers should reveal something.

## Date Disciplines

Of course, the answers are the same, but they are expressed in a variety of formats.

The U.S. citizen writes 7/4/1986 or 7/4/86 or July 4, 1986. The European writes 4/7/1986 or 4/7/86 or 4 July 1986. The soldier writes 4JUL86. In the first two examples, it is unclear whether the date is the fourth day of July or the seventh day of April, unless it is obvious who wrote the information. At any rate, there are a variety of ways of expressing a single piece of information.

How do you talk to a computer? The computer is literal. It must know what format you intend to use, and then you must stick to that format. The military format is unambiguous. Or is it? Is the date 1986 or 1886 or 2086? It is safer to write the full four-digit year. The end of the century is coming.

The primary task done with dates within a computer is a comparison of them to determine a span of time or to sequence a series of records chronologically. To do this with any of the above representations, the computer has to pull the date into pieces. It is not represented in a hierarchical format. The sort sequence must be by year, then by month, then by day. So, the best way to represent a date within a computer is 19860704. This way two dates can be compared and sequenced as whole numbers eight digits long. It is a significant processing economy.

## Check Digits

A *check digit* is a unique form of code to ensure accurate transcription of information from one form to another. Consider an employee identification code of five digits. If there is an error in writing the number, the wrong person might be paid. To protect against this, the number can be written as a six-digit number. The sixth and final digit is the check digit.

There are a number of mathematical rules whereby a check digit can be calculated from the original five digits, as in twice the first digit plus three times the second digit, etc. The units portion of the result is the check digit. Thus, when an employee identification number is entered into a computer, the computer program follows the prescribed mathematical routine to validate the check digit as entered. If the calculated value of the check digit and the entered value don't agree, there was an error in the writing or entry of the number. This might have been a transposition of two of the digits. The check digit concept can identify more than 99% of substitution or transposition errors.

## Group Technology—A New Concept?

Group technology is not a new concept, but a new name for a refinement of an old concept. Group technology is a label applied to the gathering of like items so that they can be treated in a like manner. Its immediate application is to aid in the design of new product and in the design of cost-effective production processes for new products.

This has been done for years. It began about the time that the assembly line came into use. A factory was laid out into commodity lines where parts of equivalent geometry were produced. There were spur gear lines, ring gear lines, housing lines, and tube assembly lines. A single processing engineer did all of the process design for a single commodity line. If Design Engineering released a new ring gear, the drawing was sent to the processor of the ring gear line. This, in a simple fashion, was an application of group technology.

The processor kept examples of production routings for different parts in his desk drawer. He would leaf through these to find one which would best serve as an example for the new part. As staff turnover occurred at the processor desks, and as product technology changed, example production routings did not fit as well as they originally did. Processes changed. It was unusual for old parts to be reprocessed after the changes in processing technology. As a result, the concepts of group technology were applied only in a general fashion.

The manual technique for applying group technology left holes. Today, group technology depends upon disciplined classification and coding techniques to fill those holes.

## CIM Depends upon Group Technology

The advent of cellular manufacturing reduces the economic advantage once experienced by gathering similar parts into commodity lines. The exceptional flexibility of cells and machining centers allows equipment to be dedicated to the production of parts directed toward a single subassembly process. But similar parts still require similar processes.

It is not as easy as one might think to identify parts which require similar processing. It is easy to identify ring gears as similar to one another. But the name of a part can be deceptive. A shim can be similar to a disk, to a washer, or to a spacer.

A close analysis of similar parts led to the identification of a number of parts features which require similar processes. This includes features such as holes, keyways, and milled pockets.

Computer aided process planning (CAPP) uses these similar parts features as a guide to the development of production processes for new parts. This is done in two ways. A generative process planning system selects a series of processing steps based upon the features to be produced. These features are identified by code values in a database. A variant process planning system selects a production routing for a similar part and then modifies it to produce the specific features of the new part.

In computer assisted engineering (CAE), the parts are encoded to identify similar shapes, sizes, and functions. This assists in the selection of parts for new designs. The encoding of similar parts reduces the volume of new parts and allows the wider use of existing parts.

## Group Technology Depends upon Classification and Coding

Parts are encoded based upon similar shapes, sizes, and function. Features on parts are encoded based upon similar characteristics, such as surface finish, diameter, and hardness. Production machines are encoded based upon similar capabilities, such as horsepower, capacity, and accuracy. Tools are encoded based upon similar characteristics, such as diameter, length, and ideal speed and feed. Materials, cells, and inspection tools may be encoded, in addition to fixtures and holding device components.

These code values are used, usually by computers, to identify similar parts and to match production processes to part features. The development of code structures and the assignment of code values require a joint effort by Engineering, Manufacturing, and Materials people. Often a person in one department encodes an item for the benefit of someone in another department. This is another indication that computer integrated manufacturing is an integration of systems.

The codes are used to design new parts, to develop production processes, to make cost comparisons, and to prepare parts catalogs.

## Group Technology Coding Systems

The two most common types of codes used in group technology are the hierarchical code and the polycode. Sometimes they are combined into a composite code.

Two examples of common coding systems are the Brisch system and the MICLASS system. Both tend to mix the characteristics of hierarchical codes and polycodes.

The Brisch system tends to be more of a hierarchical code wherein the meaning of one element of the code depends upon the value of the neighboring value to the left (*Figure 18.6*).

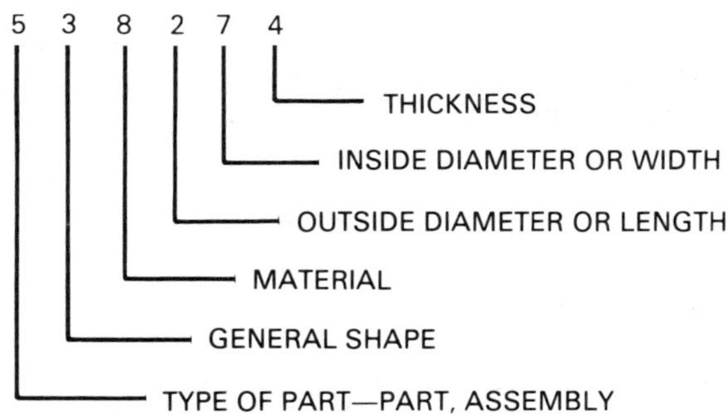


***Figure 18.6.*** Brisch code example

An example of the MICLASS system is shown in *Figure 18.7*. Both of these systems require the use of a computer to aid in the encoding of items. The computer also maintains a database of encoded items. These are used to print catalogs and to aid in mechanized planning and control systems such as CAPP.

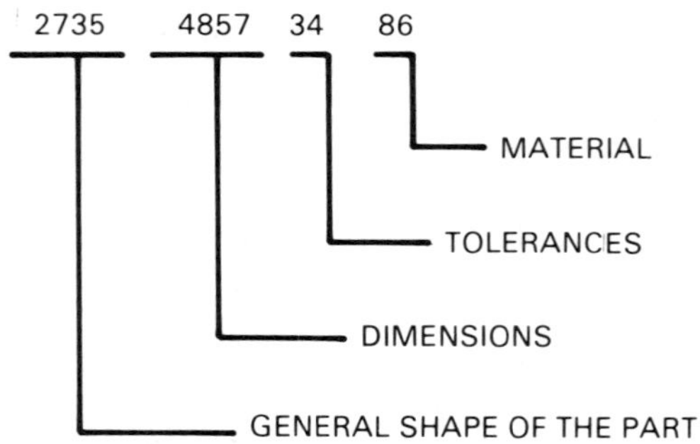


***Figure 18.7.*** MICLASS code example

## Summary

A *code* is a brief label used as a substitute for a thing or for the name of a thing. An *identification code* is used to identify a thing as uniquely different from any other thing. A *classification code* is used to classify a thing as belonging to a set of things with similar characteristics.

The use of a code simplifies the writing of information, or the entry of information at a keyboard. It makes reports shorter and allows for more columns of meaningful information on a report.

Since codes are convenient, they are the primary device by which records are stored and retrieved. This is true about both manual records and computer records. There is hardly a record which is not managed through a code of some sort.

It is important that the logical structure of a code be established carefully. If it is not, the code will have a limited life expectancy and a significant expense will be incurred to change all records. This is particularly expensive in computer programs, which are difficult to change. It is especially difficult if logical decisions within the programs are based upon specific code values.

There are a number of rules or guidelines for the development of sound codes. Codes should be unique, expandable, concise, convenient, versatile, sortable, stable, meaningful, and comprehensible.

Two problems tend to occur when meaning is built into an identification code. Its expandability is severely limited. And, there is also an almost irresistible temptation to use the meaning within the logic of computer programs.

*Dates* are codes to represent specific days in the flow of time. They also require some special disciplines.

A *check digit* is a unique form of code to ensure accurate transcription of information from one form to another.

*Group technology* depends on accurate classification and coding systems. This requires departments to encode items for the use of other departments. This is another indication that computer integrated manufacturing is an integration of the systems in a manufacturing enterprise.

# 19

# Summary

## Introduction

It should be of value to take a few moments to review the concepts which have been presented in this book. There are a variety of topics, but all relate to a central theme.

## Major Concepts Explored

As a reminder, here are some of the major concepts which were explored in the text:

- A comparison of a computer and a system, and their proper relationship to one another.
- A variety of industrial cases to illustrate systems principles. In the process you gained some practical experience in systems analysis.
- A comparison of the concepts of build-to-stock and build-to-order. You observed the significant operating systems differences which exist between the two approaches to the manufacturing process.
- The relative responsibilities of users and of systems and of data processing personnel for the development and operation of systems, manual or mechanized.
- A series of specific disciplines for the development of information systems. These included the team development concept, the method of defining a new system, the method of testing a new system, and a method of maintaining project control over the development.

- A series of specific disciplines for the operation of a mechanized system. These included data input disciplines, security measures for data-related assets, and classification and coding disciplines.
- A novel, but promising technique, functional analysis, for analyzing and improving the information systems by which a business operates.

## Laws

A number of "natural" laws were discussed in the text. They are observations of likely human behavior relative to information systems. For your convenience, they are listed here:

| | |
|---|---|
| Chapter 2 | LAW—Use it or lose it. |
| Chapter 5 | LAW—Data accuracy is in proportion to its visibility. |
| | LAW—Data is in the eye of the beholder. |
| Chapter 6 | LAW—Data is only as accurate as its use requires. |
| | LAW—Manual data transcription is error prone. |
| | LAW—Mechanically available data generates new uses. |
| Chapter 9 | LAW—We do as we are measured. |
| | LAW—A system which can be manipulated will be. |
| Chapter 17 | LAW—You can't control what isn't named. |
| | LAW—People don't know their neighbors. |

## CIM is Systems, Not Technology

Much recent literature advertises technological advances in computer graphics, computer control of machinery, etc. But CIM is not just the application of technology. By definition, it is the application of the computer to manufacturing systems. These are integrated procedures aimed at improved methods of design, production, and distribution of product.

CIM, properly implemented, is the integration of manufacturing procedures; aided, where appropriate, by computer technology.

## Summary

A computer is a tool which can on occasion be of great assistance in operating a system. A system is a group of things which work together through common procedures to accomplish a purpose. It is really the procedures which represent the system of the organization.

Systems don't function well unless they are carefully thought out. They must take into consideration the interdependences of the various units within the organization. Specific rules of operation and measures of performance should be developed for the individual operating units to ensure cooperation with the system.

There are three important measures of performance of an operating department. An internal measure is the cost per unit of output of the product for which the department is responsible. One external measure is the quality of the product as perceived by the user. The other is the timeliness of delivery of the product to the user.

The product of an organization is the reason for the existence of the organization. The product might be a physical thing, such as a component part of an assembly or, it might be a service such as sweeping the floor, or it might be information, such as a projection of future sales.

The systems/procedures are based upon specific strategies of the organization aimed at accomplishing its assigned mission. The mission is simply to deliver the product.

Often a systems problem can be resolved by a change in operating rules. The problem is often a result of applying the wrong measures to an operating department, motivating it to deliver the wrong product. A systems problem can often be the result of inadequate or outdated strategies. Only after these possibilities have been explored is it practical to look to the application of a computer to improve the operation of the system. Otherwise, there is the danger of using the computer as a band-aid to cover up poor business practices.

# Appendix A

# *Answers to Selected Exercises*

### Exercise 2.3

1. Input - student class requests
   Process - assignment of students to classes
   Output - student class schedules and class rosters
   Procedure - class size limits
   Reference data - students already enrolled in each class
2. Input - food and air
   Process - motion, action, thinking
   Output - waste products
   Procedure - conversion of food and air into energy
   Reference data - temperature, pulse, etc.
3. Input - sick people
   Process - curing
   Output - well people and, unfortunately, corpses
   Procedure - rigid rules for medication and surgery
   Reference data - patient life signs, dosage charts
4. Input - ink
   Process - transfer of ink to paper
   Output - writing
   Procedure - flow of ink through the nib
   Reference data - pressure of pen on paper

### Exercise 3.2

Master Data = Planning
Status = Operating (direct)
Control = Operating (direct)
Trigger = Operating (remote)
Feedback = Measuring (immediate)
Analysis = Measuring (for long-term planning)

## Exercise 3.3

The trigger system would probably not have to be mechanized, because it has a relatively small amount of data. But it might be mechanized.

The master system would probably need to be mechanized, since it is used heavily by the control system during its operation. It would need to be processed at least weekly to update the master file.

The status system is similar to the master system.

The feedback system would possibly need to be mechanized due to the high volume of transactions. It would need to feed data to the status system at least weekly.

The analysis system is not used directly by the control system, so the determination of whether or not it needs to be mechanized is a separate decision. It certainly would not be processed as frequently as the control system under normal circumstances.

## Exercise 5.3

The sequential storage media are:

Punched Cards
Paper Tape
Magnetic Tape
Magnetic Strip

## Exercise 5.5

The random storage media are:

Fixed Disk
Mass Storage
Laser Disk
Floppy Disk
Memory Chips

## Exercise 6.10

1. There is a 6% error possibility for each of three fields of data—part number, quantity, and bin location. The possibility of a record being correct in all three is .94 x .94 x .94 or 83%. Therefore the probability of the correct record for either bin is 83%, and the probability of the record being correct for the total inventory of the part is .83 x .83 or 69%.
2. There is a 6% probability that you will write down the wrong part number for the part, thus causing not only an error for that part, but an error for the part whose number you recorded by accident.

## Exercise 8.3

Accounting, possibly
Assembly
Data Processing
Field Service
Manufacturing
Master Schedule
Material Handling
Material Planning and Purchasing
Order Entry, possibly
Shipping, possibly

## Exercise 11.2

1. 1, 5
2. 6, 9
3. 5, 6, 7

## Exercise 11.3

1. 15/16 = 94%
2. Possibly four or more days, since estimation of the percent of completion in *Figure 11.4* wasn't accurate. It took four actual days to complete two days of the original estimate.
3. Possibly only five days or less, since the estimate in *Figure 11.4* seemed to be reasonably accurate.
4. Probably about six days, since the estimates have been reasonably accurate.

## Exercise 17.1

1. A1.
2. Yes. It contains four components.
3. Yes. It goes into A1.
4. Yes.
5. No. E1 contains no components.
6. No. Although E1 is a component of a higher level, D3, it contains no components.
7. E1 is a component of D3.

## Exercise 17.2

1. The consist of D4 is 1 of E3, 1 of E4, 3 of C3, and some amount of braze.
2. The next level usage of E5 is D5.
3. The top level usage of C12 is A1.
4. 4.
5. 9 (1 + 2 x 4).

## Exercise 18.6

1. 7/4/1986 or 7/4/86 or July 4, 1986
2. 4/7/1986 or 4/7/86 or 4 July 1986
3. 4JUL86
4. 19860704

# Appendix B

## *Department Descriptions*

### Accounting

The Accounting department manages the books of the enterprise, keeps tax records, manages budgets, calculates costs, pays bills, and receives monies from customers. This department might also set product prices.

### Assembly

The Assembly department completes the assembly of the final product. This department might assemble subassemblies and might package the final product. Assembly might also be responsible for inspecting final product.

### Data Processing

The Data Processing department develops or procures computer software to serve business functions. It helps line managers to define their system and information needs, and the necessary solution to those needs. It procures computer related equipment and operates it to process data for the enterprise. This department might control the procurement of personal computers and related equipment operated by other departments.

### Design Engineering

The Design Engineering department is responsible for designing the product so that it can be procured or produced. It is responsible for maintaining existing product by making necessary changes for cost reduction, reliability, or safety reasons.

### Field Service

The Field Service department is responsible for maintaining the product in the hands of the customer. This might involve providing a supply of spare parts. It might involve providing repair tools and facilities, training repair staff, and tracking chronic product failures until the causing problem is resolved.

## Manufacturing

The Manufacturing department is responsible for producing the component parts which are assembled into final product. This department might be responsible for subassembly of portions of the product to be delivered to final assembly. It might also be responsible for inspecting completed parts and subassemblies.

## Marketing

The Marketing Department is responsible for determining what products should be added to or deleted from the product line, or what major changes should be made in existing products to serve the marketplace. This department sets the specifications for new product to be designed. It also might be responsible for setting prices.

## Master Schedule

The Master Schedule department is responsible for setting the rate of production of final products and for keeping finished product inventories in balance with demand.

## Material Distribution

See Material Handling.

## Material Handling

The Material Handling department is responsible for receiving material from suppliers, for storing received material, completed parts, subassemblies and final products. It is in charge of delivering the materials to the point of need. This department might be responsible for maintaining inventory record counts.

## Material Planning and Purchasing

The Material Planning and Purchasing department is responsible for determining the quantities of production and indirect materials to be procured and produced to meet master schedule and spare parts needs as projected. This department selects suppliers, places orders, and tracks supplier performance. It might also maintain inventory records.

## Order Entry

The Order Entry department is responsible for prioritizing customer orders for completion, either from the assembly process or from finished product inventory. It might be responsible for verifying that a customer order describes a complete product with valid options.

## Production Engineering

The Production Engineering department is responsible for the design, procurement and installation of all equipment in the facility for production, assembly, material handling, and office functions. This department might set the standards for manufacturing and for assembly rates of production.

## Quality Control

The Quality Control department is responsible for ensuring that the product, and field support of the product, meet predefined quality and reliability standards. This might be done by inspecting and auditing production and field service operations. It might be achieved by certifying the processes and leaving inspection to those who make the product.

## Sales

The Sales department is responsible for the merchandising of final product, and possibly spare parts. It is responsible for advertising, and for calling on distributors and/or customers. This department might be responsible for setting prices. It could also verify that a customer order describes a complete product with valid options.

## Shipping

The Shipping department is in charge of arranging transportation and loading of material to be shipped—final product and spare parts to customers, returns to suppliers. This department might be responsible for inventories marked for shipment and might include and/or attach labels, shipping documents, user manuals, and tools.

# Appendix C

# *Functional Analysis*

## Introduction

Functional analysis is a novel systems planning technique developed by the author over a period of years as an outgrowth of the college level course on which this text is based. The technique was developed as an aid to the students in completing a systems analysis case project about a small business. The students responded so well to the technique that it was piloted in the business world. To-date its use has been limited, but has been quite successful. For this reason the technique is included for your consideration. A teaching guide which supplements this text recommends that the teacher include a case study project in the course work, using this technique to aid in handling the project.

## Business Systems Planning

For some years, IBM has been conducting Business Systems Planning (BSP) workshops for client companies with reasonable success. A first step in such a workshop is to define corporate strategies. The next step is to determine critical success factors. The third step is to define systems (computer systems) needs. To the author, this approach has always seemed to have two basic deficiencies.

The first deficiency is that it makes quantum jumps in the thought processes from strategies to success factors to computer systems. Corporate strategies are not always clearly defined. If they are defined, they are not always consistent. It is not always apparent what success factors apply to specific corporate strategies, nor is it always apparent what systems are needed to accomplish a success factor. It is tempting to define new systems needs as computer systems.

The second deficiency is that BSP, like most systems planning techniques, seldom involves adequate participation from line management, and seldom involves enough different functional areas within the company.

## Desires vs. Conflicts

When people plan improvements in the systems by which they manage, they usually try to extend the systems they already have. The result is that systems become ever more complex with only marginal improvement.

When management seeks to improve systems, the focus is usually on a rather narrow aspect of the business, a single department or even a subfunction within a department. Expanding the area of focus to multiple functional areas is seen as an unnecessary complication. As a result, any improvement is narrow and is likely to have some negative impact on neighboring departments. Indeed, many managers are quite ignorant of the impact of their day to day work on other departments.

Functional analysis provides an organized methodology for planning improved systems for a number of related departments at the same time without undue complication. By doing this, envisioned systems improvements are tested for potential impact on multiple departments. The technique provides a way to identify and resolve conflict between departments. It ends the narrow suboptimizing which has been done in the past.

## Class Project

As previously stated, the use of functional analysis is recommended to support a class project. The students who participate in such a project are in for a significant amount of work, but they gain a significant benefit. The project expands their comprehension of the theory of information systems, and also their comprehension of how a business functions. They learn a valuable analysis technique which they might see fit to use in their own business career. They learn that teamwork is essential to the success of a business—something which the Japanese have been demonstrating for several decades. Finally, they become more aware of the need to take heed of the impact their actions have on others.

## Analytical Steps

Functional analysis takes place in a series of logical steps. These are listed in *Figure C.1.* Some of these steps may be taken in parallel. The dependencies are delineated in *Figure C.2.*

1. Business Description
2. Business Mission
3. Measures of Business Performance
4. Business Goal
5. Department Mission
6. Measures of Department Performance
7. Department Subfunctions
8. Business Strategies
9. Department Strategies
10. Organizational Conflicts
11. Information Flowchart
12. Subfunction Description
13. Rules to Resolve Conflicts
14. Computer System Requirements

***Figure C.1.*** Functional analysis steps

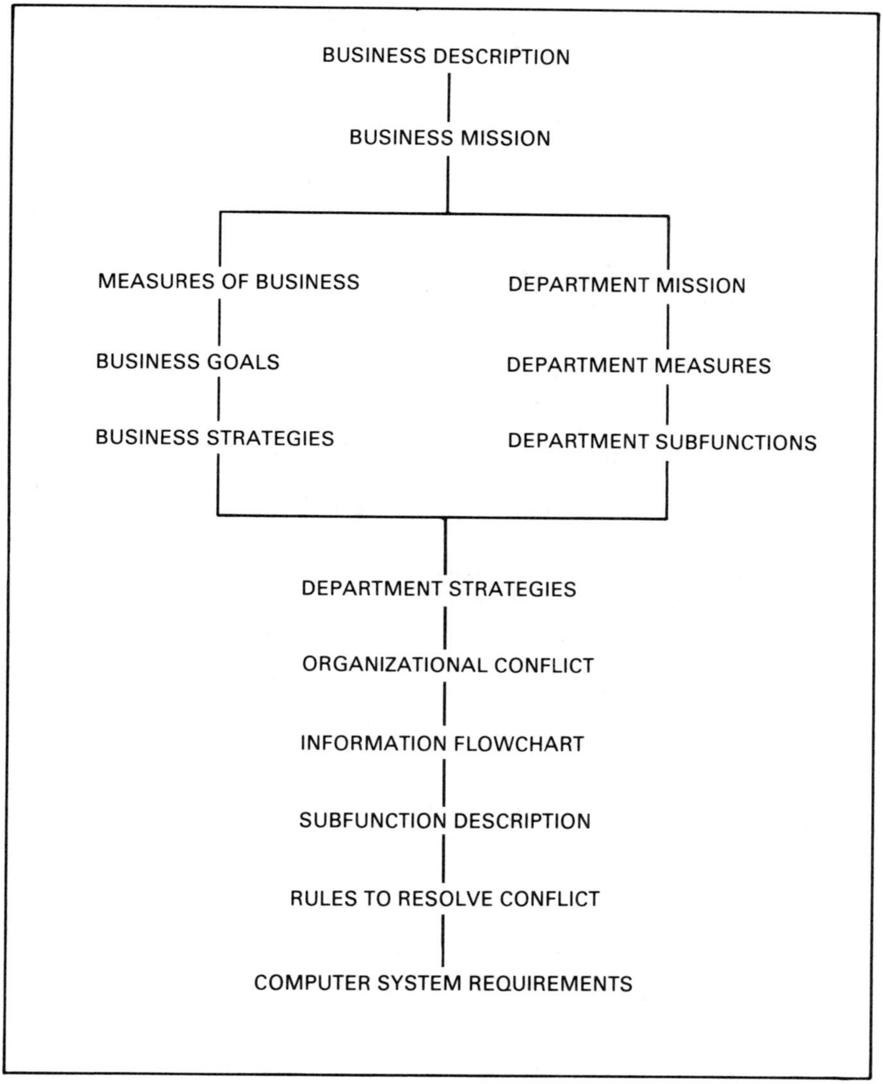


***Figure C.2.*** Sequence of steps

The first step is for the department representatives as a group to describe the business in a reasonably succinct fashion. An example of such a description is presented in *Figure C.3*.

HYDROCLEAN CASE

Description of Company
* $200 million annual sales
* Manufacturer of washers and driers
* Located in Midwest
* Markets products to department store chains

Description of Product
* Three models of each
* Four color schemes for each—baked on
* Retailer's label glued on when requested

Physical Facility
* Two assembly lines, each capable of handling both products
* Warehouse for storage of finished product
* 40-hour work week
* Manufacture of frames, drums and finish panels
* Purchase of hardware, motors and electronic controls
* Subassembly of control panels and heating units

Product Change
* Major change each model year
* Only safety or emergency change within model year
* Part number change if a changed part is not interchangeable with the old part
* Change part number of an assembly if a changed component changes the fitup or performance of the assembly as a whole

Scheduling
* Product is built to stock
* Product is sold from the warehouse

***Figure C.3.*** Business description

The second step is for the department representatives as a group to define in a simple statement the mission of the business. A mission is the product or service which the business is responsible to provide to the customer. *Figure C.4* is an example.

The mission of the company is to market company-built gardening equipment for the family home market.

***Figure C.4*** Business mission

The third step is for the department representatives as a group to define three measures of the performance of the company's mission. The measures are to be in terms of cost per unit of product or service, the quality of the product or service, and the timeliness with which the product or service is provided. An example is shown in *Figure C.5*.

1. Profit, as a percent of sales
2. Sales volume, as a percent of the total market
3. Lost sales from lack of finished product inventory, as a percent of total sales

***Figure C.5.*** Measures of business performance

The fourth step is for the department representatives as a group to develop a goal of the business for each of the business measurement statements. A *goal* is defined as a statement of a specific measure of mission accomplishment to be achieved. *Figure C.6* is an example.

1. 8% profit as a percent of sales in 1987
2. 30% of the total market by the end of 1988
3. Less than 2% lost sales in 1987

***Figure C.6.*** Business goals

The fifth step is for the representative of each involved department to define in a simple statement the mission of his or her department. A mission is the product or service which that department is responsible to provide for the enterprise (*Figure C.7*).

The mission of the Design Engineering department is to provide production drawings representing the product to be manufactured.

***Figure C.7.*** Department mission (Design Engineering)

The sixth step is for each department representative to define three measures of the performance of the department's mission. The measures are to be in terms of cost per unit of product or service, the quality of the product or service, and the timeliness with which the product or service is provided (*Figure C.8*).

1. The cost to design the average new product
2. The cost in the first year of production to resolve design deficiencies
3. Percentage of product designs delivered within one month of the scheduled target date

***Figure C.8.*** Measures of department performance (Design Engineering)

The seventh step is for each department representative to identify from three to six subfunctions which his or her department performs (*Figure C.9*).

1. Select Source
2. Define Process
3. Order Tooling
4. Track Jobs
5. Checkout Process

***Figure C.9.*** Department subfunctions (Production Engineering)

The eighth step is for the representatives of the departments as a group to develop statements of strategy for the business as a whole. *Strategy* is defined as a statement of a principle of operational behavior or judgement which serves as a guide for day-to-day decisions, so that the measures of accomplishment of mission will be acceptable (*Figure C.10*).

1. Produce only those components which are not standard catalog items of suppliers.
2. Produce items which have winter season demand, to stabilize labor requirements.
3. Market product only through chain stores.
4. Market product under chain store label if required.

***Figure C.10.*** Business strategies

The ninth step is for the representatives of the departments as individuals to develop statements of strategy for their individual departments. An example is shown in *Figure C.11*.

1. Maintain at least two sources of supply for every item.
2. Certify suppliers for quality and timeliness to avoid need for receiving area checkout.
3. Guarantee suppliers annual business volume if order quantities can be set only a week in advance.

***Figure C.11.*** Department strategies (Purchasing)

The tenth step is for the department representatives separately and together to develop statements of conflict between their organizations. These conflicts arise naturally out of different missions, different strategies, and different measurements of mission accomplishment. The causes of the conflict should be identified (*Figure C.12*).

| | |
|---|---|
| OF: | Order Entry |
| WITH: | Assembly |
| OVER: | Assembly Schedule |
| CAUSE: | For ease of assembly, Assembly department will want to sequence some customer orders in such a way that they will be produced later than the customer promise date from Order Entry department. |
| SOL'N: | The two departments will set parameters governing the mix of product which can be effectively managed on the assembly line in a given day. Order Entry must seek agreement of Assembly if there is a need to exceed the limits on a given day. |

***Figure C.12.*** Organizational conflicts

The eleventh step is for the department representatives to develop a chart of the information and material flow between their subfunctions and those of the other departments. *Figure C.13* is an example.

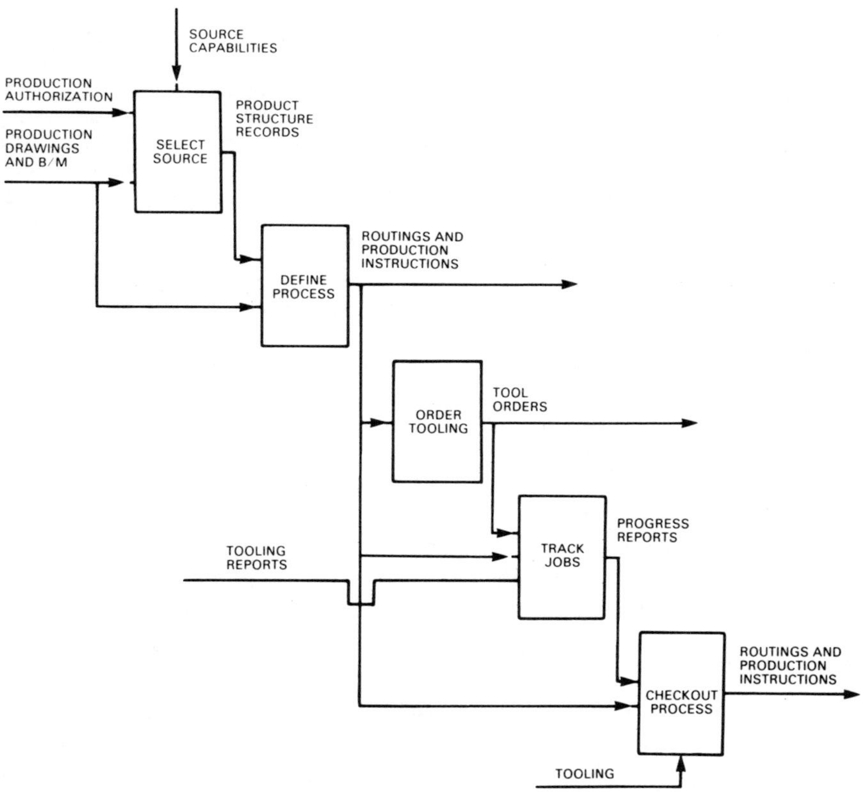


***Figure C.13.*** Information flowchart

The twelfth step is for the department representatives to develop a description of each of the subfunctions within their respective departments (*Figure C.14*).

| | |
|---|---|
| Function: | Establish a date and authority to begin production and sale of a new product. |
| Trigger: | Scheduled review of readiness of a new product for production. |
| Response: | Decision reached during meeting, or another review scheduled. |
| Horizon: | Decision three months before first production date. |
| Input: | PP04—Product specifications.<br>DE04—New product evaluation. |
| Control: | AC03—Cost targets. |
| Output: | MS03—Production authorization. |

***Figure C.14.*** Subfunction description (Authorize Production)

The thirteenth step is for the department representatives to work out among themselves ways of resolving the interdepartmental conflicts. As they discuss these challenges, they could find themselves forced to change any of the materials developed in the preceding steps. After all, most of the preceding work was typical suboptimization from a departmental point of view. The results of the necessary compromises are recorded in the subfunction descriptions as rules. A *rule* is defined as a specific guideline for day-to-day decisions to ensure conformance to strategies. *Figure C.15* is an example.

| | |
|---|---|
| Function: | Establish a date and authority to begin production and sale of a new product. |
| Trigger: | Scheduled review of readiness of a new product for production. |
| Response: | Decision reached during meeting, or another review scheduled. |
| Horizon: | Decision three months before first production date. |
| Input: | PP04—Product specifications.<br>DE04—New product evaluation. |
| Control: | AC03—Cost targets. |
| Output: | MS03—Production authorization. |
| Rules: | 1. Authorization for production cannot be given if performance and cost targets are not met.<br>2. Joint judgement is reached on quality risks.<br>3. If the product doesn't conform to standards, authorization will be withheld. |

***Figure C.15.*** Rules to resolve conflicts (Authorize Production)

The fourteenth step is for the departmental representatives as a group to determine which of the systems represented by subfunctions require the support of computer processing (*Figure C.16*).

| | |
|---|---|
| Title: | Maintenance of the total bill of material. |
| Purpose: | To maintain an accurate and timely bill of material to enhance the precision of material requirements planning. |
| Reasons: | 1. High volume of calculation. |
| | 2. Complexity of calculation. |
| | 3. High accuracy requirements. |

***Figure C.16.*** Computer system requirements

Although this planning process is lengthy in number of steps, it is more effective than alternative techniques which take fewer, larger steps and leave many opportunities for unidentified and unresolved conflict and inefficiency.

The concept of statements of strategy is usually a cause of much debate and misunderstanding. For this reason, two other definitions are appropriate to avoid confusion.

*Objective.* A specific milestone or a specific capability to be put in place by a specific time in order to enable accomplishment of a goal, corporate or departmental.

*Plan.* An intended course of action aimed at accomplishing a goal.

Note that goals, objectives, and plans are transitory, whereas missions, measures, strategies, and rules tend to be enduring. Functional analysis is aimed at developing enduring systems. For this reason, the development of objectives and plans is not a part of the functional analysis process, but is left to the normal budgeting process. The results of a functional analysis provide an excellent basis for developing objectives and plans.

## Summary

Functional analysis is a practical and effective technique for systems analysis. In the process of defining compatible departmental systems, the various departments are forced to rethink the business as a whole. This is logical, since the business is a system with departmental subsystems.

# Glossary of Terms

## A

**ACCESS.** The act of making logical contact with a database record for the purpose of reading or updating it.

**ARTIFICIAL INTELLIGENCE.** The use of a computer to emulate the operation of human perception and reasoning, most often restricted to the implementation of "expert systems" to make diagnoses based upon varied input describing a situation of concern.

**ASSEMBLY LINE.** A slowly moving conveyor on which products are assembled from materials stored in bins along the conveyor.

**ASSEMBLY ROUTING.** Instructions and time standards for the assembly of a product on an assembly line.

**ATTACHMENT.** A product option, usually one which can be added conveniently after the product has been assembled on an assembly line.

**ATTRIBUTE.** A fact or characteristic about an entity.

## B

**BILL OF MATERIAL.** A structured, level by level listing of the components of a product.

**BIN TAG.** A tag fastened to the front of a bin of material to identify the material and to tell the quantity of it used on each model of product.

**BUG.** An error condition in a computer program or in a mechanized information system.

**BUILD-TO-ORDER.** A manufacturing/assembly strategy whereby the units of final product are built complete to customer order, and are not built unless there is a customer order in hand.

**BUILD-TO-STOCK.** A manufacturing/assembly strategy whereby the units of final product are built in anticipation of customer order to maintain an inventory from which units are retrieved and modified as necessary to fill a customer order.

**BURDEN.** The work load on a machine or on a machine operator.

## C

**CAD/CAM.** Computer Aided Design/Computer Aided Manufacturing, the use of the computer to aid in the integration of product design, process design, and production management.

**CAE.** Computer Aided Engineering, the use of the computer to aid in the design of product.

**CAPP.** Computer Aided Process Planning, the use of the computer to develop process plans.

**CHECK DIGIT.** A mathematically produced digit at the end of a code, used to verify that the digits in the code have not been recorded in error.

**CIM.** Computer Integrated Manufacturing, the use of the computer to improve the operation of a manufacturing enterprise in a systematic way.

**CLASSIFICATION CODE.** A code which describes an entity as belonging to a group of related entities by means of some common characteristic.

**CODE.** A brief label used as a substitute for the name or a description of a thing.

**COMMITMENT.** The act of dedicating the necessary resources to the completion of a project.

**COMPUTER.** An electronic device for processing data.

## D

**DATABASE.** An organized collection of logically related data about a single type of entity, intended as a common reference source for multiple purposes.

**DECISION SUPPORT SYSTEM.** A set of computer hardware and software with appropriate communications to provide a manager or staff person with personalized computing capabilities by which to gather and analyze data.

**DELIVERABLE.** A completed product of a development phase of an information system.

**DIRECT MATERIALS.** Materials which are assembled into product.

**DURABLE TOOL.** A fixture or holding device to aid in the production of a part or assembly.

## E

**EDIT.** A computerized verification that the contents of a transaction are without error according to predefined rules.

**EFFECTIVITY.** The date on which a product change or a manufacturing change is instituted in the factory.

**ENGINEERING DRAWING.** A graphic drawing with written specifications describing the dimensions and physical properties of a portion of a product, a part, or an assembly.

**ENGINEERING NOTICE.** A summary of the bill of material, the effective date, and other key data about an engineering drawing.

**ENTITY.** A thing about which data is maintained.

## F

**FIELD.** A logical space where a piece of data is to be stored, similar to a space on a form.

**FILE.** A set of records which is organized in a specific sequence by the use of an identifier or controlling key.

**FIXTURE.** A holding device to secure a part on a machine to ensure accuracy in producing the finished dimensions.

**FREEZE PERIOD.** A period of time in which an order for procurement or manufacture of material, or assembly of product, cannot normally be changed due to material lead times.

**FUNCTIONAL ANALYSIS.** A step-by-step technique for developing improved, integrated strategies and systems for a business or for a portion of a business.

## G

**GOAL.** A statement of a specific measure of mission accomplishment to be achieved.

**GRIEF.** Erroneous or missing data in a database or data file.

**GT.** Group Technology, the gathering of parts, assemblies, and processes into families or groups with fundamental similarities.

## H

**HARDWARE.** The physical components of a computer.

**HIERARCHICAL DATABASE.** An arrangement of records in a logical structure of dependencies.

## I

**IDENTIFICATION CODE.** A code which uniquely labels an entity to distinguish it from all other like entities.

**INDIRECT MATERIALS.** Materials which are not assembled into product, but which are needed to operate the business—paper, cleaning supplies, etc.

**INFORMATION SYSTEMS.** Organized procedures and disciplines for providing the flow of information required to manage the functions of an enterprise.

**ISSUED WORK ORDER.** A work order which has been sent to the factory to authorize production of a batch of parts.

## J

**JAD.** Joint Application Development, a technique for refining the definition of specifications for a computer system.

**JIT.** Just-In-Time, a strategy for production materials management which brings the material from the source of supply to the point of use no less frequently than daily, based upon the quantity of material required for scheduled production.

## K

**KEY.** A code which provides an identification of the contents of a record about an entity.

## L

**LEAD TIME.** The length of time from when material is ordered until the time when it can normally be expected to be delivered.

**LINE CHECKER.** A person who examines assembly line bins to verify the quantity of materials and to determine replenishment quantities.

**LINE LOAD.** The process of distributing assembly tasks among assemblers for work efficiency.

**LINE STOCK.** The process of ordering the material required to replenish the materials in assembly bins.

## M

**MASTER SCHEDULE.** A plan and authorization for the assembly of a specific quantity of each model of final product for a number of time periods into the future.

**MATERIAL LIST.** A simple listing of the components of a product without any intermediate levels of assembly.

**MEASURE.** A yardstick by which the performance of a mission is measured.

**MISSION.** The product or service which a department is responsible to provide for the enterprise.

**MODULE.** A portion of a mechanized information system which can be operated before the completion of the whole system.

**MRP.** Material Requirements Planning, the use of the computer to track and replenish production material inventories.

## O

**OBJECTIVE.** A specific milestone or a specific capability to be put into place by a specific time to enable accomplishment of a goal.

**OPEN WORK ORDER.** A work order which has been released to the factory, but has not yet been completed.

**OPERATING SYSTEM.** Programs provided by the manufacturer of a computer to tell the computer how to perform its basic functions, such as how to "read" the input from a terminal.

**OPERATION.** A step of production of a part in which the part is processed over one of a series of machines or work stations.

**OPTION.** A feature of a final product which is offered in place of another feature.

**OPTION SCHEDULE.** A master schedule for the procurement and/or production of specific quantities of product options for a number of time periods into the future.

## P

**PERFORMANCE.** A measure of the effectivity of a man or a machine, measuring productivity as a percent of the time standard set on the work order.

**PERISHABLE TOOL.** A cutting tool which is subject to wearing out in the production of a part.

**PHASE.** A stage of development of some portion of the deliverables for a mechanized information system.

**PLAN.** An intended course of action aimed at accomplishing a goal.

**PRODUCTION MATERIALS.** Parts and assemblies which are assembled together to form a final product.

**PRODUCTION ROUTING.** A description of the series of steps required to produce a part or a subassembly over a series of machine tools or work stations.

**PROGRAM.** A series of instructions which direct a computer to perform a specific task.

**PURCHASED FINISHED.** Production materials which are purchased from suppliers as completed parts with no additional labor required other than assembly into final product.

## Q

**QUERY.** The process of asking an ad hoc question about specific entities in a database.

**QUICK DECK.** A summary of all quantities of each component which is used in a complete product.

## R

**RANDOM ACCESS.** Access to a single record without the need to read preceding records.

**RECONFIGURATION.** The process of deleting unordered options and adding ordered options to make a unit of stock product conform to the requirements of a customer order.

**RELATIONAL DATABASE.** A database which is structured to look like a series of simple files, each accessed through its own series of keys.

**RISK.** The probability that a new mechanized information system might in some manner fail to meet expectations.

**ROUTING.** Another name for production routing.

**RULES.** Specific guidelines for day-to-day decisions to ensure conformance to strategies.

## S

**SEQUENTIAL ACCESS.** Access to records in a file or database starting with the first record and proceeding record by record in the order in which the records are stored.

**SETUP.** The labor required to install durable and perishable tooling on a machine to enable it to produce a specific part.

**SHORT LIST.** A list of the production materials which are in short supply or are in danger of being in short supply to support the assembly of product.

**SOFTWARE.** Another name for the programs which direct the operation of a computer, often used as a label for the operating system provided by the manufacturer of the computer.

**STOCK ORDER.** An order for a unit of final product with a selection of commonly ordered options as a hedge against future customer orders.

**STOCK PRODUCT.** A unit of final product with a selection of commonly ordered options.

**STOCK STATUS.** The quantity of production material in inventory and on order.

**STRATEGY.** A statement of a principle of operational behavior or judgement which serves as a guide for day-to-day decisions, so that the measures of accomplishment of mission will be acceptable.

**SYSTEM.** An organized procedure for performing a function, a collection of components working together to accomplish a common purpose.

## W

**WALK-THROUGH.** An exercise in testing the specifications or design of a portion of a system to ensure that they are satisfactory, usually conducted as a simulation of the operation of the system.

**WHERE USED.** An upside down bill of material showing the higher level assemblies in which a part is used.

**WORK ORDER.** The authorization to produce a given quantity of a production part or subassembly by a specific date.

**WORK TICKET.** A document which lists the tasks and the standard times for assembly of a portion of a product.

## Z

**ZONE.** An area of an assembly line within which are located specific assembly tools, and within which specific assembly tasks are to be performed.

# Index

## A



## B



## C

## D

## N



## O



## P

## Q



## R

## U



## V



## W